Captive Arizona, 1851–1900

Captive Arizona
1851–1900

VICTORIA SMITH

University of Nebraska Press
Lincoln & London

Library of Congress Cataloging-in-
Publication Data

Smith, Victoria, 1953–
Captive Arizona, 1851–1900 / Victoria
Smith.
     p. cm.
Includes bibliographical references
and index.
ISBN 978-0-8032-1090-5 (cloth: alk. paper)
1. Arizona—Race relations—History—19th
century. 2. Arizona—History, Military—
19th century. 3. Captivity—Arizona—
History—19th century. 4. Indian captivities—Arizona—History—19th century.
5. Frontier and pioneer life—Arizona.
6. Indians of North America—Arizona—
History—19th century. 7. Mexicans—
Arizona—History—19th century.
8. Whites—Arizona—History—19th century.
9. Imperialism—Social aspects—Southwest,
New—History—19th century. 10. Anti-
imperialist movements—Southwest, New—
History—19th century. I. Title.
F820.A1S65 2009
305.8009791′09034—dc22
2009009853

Set in Trump Mediaeval by Bob Reitz.

For my grandchildren, my precious:
Jesse, Justin, Charlotte, Georgie, Hailey,
Leo, Annabelle, Artemisa, Adam, Ali,
Elias, Noellie Rose, and Amber Lee

CONTENTS

ILLUSTRATIONS

ACKNOWLEDGMENTS

Numerous people helped guide this book, or in some other manner made significant contributions both tangible and intangible during the years of its creation. Most of these were listed at length in my dissertation, *White Eyes, Red Heart, Blue Coat: The Life and Times of Mickey Free.* For the sake of space, I will simply add to that list here.

My gratitude to Mr. Al Bates of Prescott, who shared his files on Bessie Brooks; to Doug Hamilton, who shared my interest in the Penningtons, and made sure the geography was covered to his satisfaction; to Jim Turner, who shares my interest in Arizona's "back-row" characters; to my former student Efran Carmona, who found Olive Oatman as interesting as I did; to Dave Goodman, for the law; to Ben Rader, ever helpful; to anthropologist Robert Kilts, for the excellent map; and to my efficient graduate research assistant, Dave Everson, the best. My editors—Elisabeth Chretien, Ann Baker, Colleen Clark, Gary Dunham, and Matt Bokovoy—deserve much of the credit, as do the anonymous reviewers who demanded the book be what it has become. The University of Nebraska Research Council, the University of Nebraska James Rawley Foundation, the University of Nebraska Harold and Esther Edgerton Fellowship, the University of Nebraska History Department, the University of Nebraska Ethnic

Studies Institute, and the University of Nebraska Native American Studies Program, as well as the Arizona Historical Society, provided much appreciated funding for research travel. The staffs of the many libraries, archives, and museums consulted here have always been efficient, helpful, and very, very patient. The librarians, archivists, and staff of the Arizona Historical Society in Tucson deserve special mention here: Debra Shelton, Kim Frantz, Dave Tachenberg, Debbie Newman, Robert Orser, Crystal Burke, and Mary Flynn. My apologies to those I may have overlooked.

Writers and especially historians—human time machines, ever conscious of two worlds—have a way of sucking the air out of any room occupied by loved ones unfortunate enough to get caught in their mental vortex. Scrambling to interact with the everyday world when needed, so as not to alienate those we care for, we then turn sharply back to the thought at hand, before it runs away. No matter—if it was truly valuable, it would return again when the time was right, just like family and friends. I have driven a number of people to distraction over the years as they waited for my long-talked-about book. They deserve acknowledgement here.

Roger, Trudy, Leo, Lisa, Daniel, Nate—no one waited longer; Carlos, who traveled ten thousand miles with me through Indian country; my siblings, Terry and John; my parents, John and Sheila—for my Cherokee/British heritage, and for a love of Arizona, history, travel, and books, many books.

To all those who howled with me under countless *Yoeme* moons: Ax and Olga, Faith and Jack, Jesse and

Chiqui, John and Yolanda, Josie and JP, Liz and Leon, Rene and Amanda, Sonja and George, Stormy and George, Gangkey, Freddie, Rudy, Cisco, Chris, and Pedro—your companionship made all the difference. May the coyotes always sing us to sleep.

INTRODUCTION

This book examines captivity in territorial Arizona in order to further the academic understanding of U.S. imperialism and Native American anti-imperialism in the American West.

Captivity in Arizona between the time of the Treaty of Guadalupe Hidalgo of 1848 and the attainment of statehood in 1912 was endemic, occurring in a kaleidoscope of configurations: intertribal captivity, Mexican captivity of Native Americans, white captivity of both indigenous and Mexican people, and indigenous captivity of whites and Mexicans. While whites and Mexicans fought a long war of attrition against the native peoples of Arizona, and natives fought a losing defensive war against the imperialists, all practiced captivity as an aspect of war.

Captivity systems were racially and culturally distinct in Arizona, but certain features of captivity as a tactic of war, whether offensive or defensive, were ubiquitous. Externally, captivity depleted one's enemies' human resources and punished one's enemies emotionally. Internally, captivity was fueled by a need to enslave or adopt captives to augment labor forces (including domestics and combatants), to use in ceremonial sacrifice, to sell or barter as slaves, to sell or barter in exchange for imprisoned or enslaved community members, or to expand marriage pools. Alternately, captives also functioned as a source of "orphans" for those wishing to adopt children. Subliminally, the successful absorption of a captive into a host society signified that the captor's culture was preferable to the captive's natal society. At the biological level, captivity diversified the captor's gene pool, and, in the case of indigenous people, augmented tribal populations undergoing the stress of war, decreased natural production, and unnaturally increased mortality.

As an objective exercise, captivity was an effective technique of war. As a subjective experience, however, captivity was a personal ordeal, a difficult, trying, painful experience that tested the fortitude of the captured. Moreover, captivity not only posed a physical threat but confronted the territory with a complex of accompanying social challenges as well. Generally speaking, captivity multiplied the fear, mistrust, and hatred that underlay the region during the territorial era.

The captivity lens refracts historical light away from many of the usual characters associated with Arizona history—usually Native American, Mexican American, and, of course, white males—and onto the women, children, elderly, and disabled among these peoples, turning over new academic ground with a sharp stick. As becomes evident, pervasive captivity in Arizona Territory tied competing societies together with bonds that chafed the frontier's social fabric. The study of captivity in Arizona exposes the soft underbelly of territorial history, laying bare the vital organs of race, class, and gender that fueled particularly violent and protracted decades of warfare in the region between 1848 and 1912. Moreover, captivity led not only to revised perceptions of racial and cultural identities but also to revised conceptions of self; it was on this ability to reconceptualize themselves that captives learned to survive.

Captivity has fallen under academic scrutiny ever since psychologist William Ackernecht published "White Indians" in 1944. Ackernecht asserted that whites captured by Indians found unity of thought and social cohesion in, as well as intense attachment to, their adopted indigenous families through a process of indigenous-initiated education and incorporation into native social organization. This proved, he believed, that in their "downfall and persecution this culture still retained values which could make it worthwhile even for white people to stay within its orbit." The study of "the assimilation of white persons captured by Indians" was advanced in 1973 with the publication of J. Norman Heard's *White into Red*. Using captivity narratives from the seventeenth through nineteenth centuries, Heard examined the reasons why some nonindigenous captives preferred death to assimilation while others became "white Indians." This early exploration of racial construction in relation to captivity credited indigenous processes of adoption and intermarriage with their captives' willingness to acculturate.[1]

James Axtell contrasted the high rate of successful acculturation of captives by indigenous societies with the low rate of indigenous conversion to Christianity in "The White Indians of Colonial America" in 1975. Like Heard, he was interested in the "educational processes" that converted white captives into "white Indians" so successfully and frequently. The indigenous system of adoption and full incorporation into tribal rights played a major role in the acculturation of captive children, Axtell learned, while intermarriage and children provided compelling reasons for older white captives to remain with their captors. Axtell found other factors that convinced white captives to stay: "a strong sense of community, abundant love, and uncommon integrity," as well as "social equality, mobility, adventure . . . [, and] freedom."[2]

A volume edited by Alden Vaughn and Edward Clark in 1981, *Puritans among the Indians,* focused on the redemption of white captives. It constructed a system of captivity types, but it lacked the focus that gender-based inquiry would later bring to the topic. In 1985 James Axtell published a full-length comparative study of the effectiveness of French, British, and Native American acculturation processes entitled *The Invasion Within.* As Heard had earlier, Axtell perceived intermarried whites not as civilizing agents, but as subverters of white social paradigms.

In 1993 June Namias used the methodologies of feminist theory to deconstruct captivity narratives in *White Captives.* Her analysis differentiated the captivity experience by gender and identified "captive types" based on their responses to their captivity. Most recently, James Brooks's *Captives and Cousins* examined the social spaces where captivity knit New Mexicans together in the territorial era. *Captive Arizona,* in contrast, examines the social spaces where captivity frayed the fabric of social relations in Arizona across racial lines. Though white captives have an academic historiography, the same historiography exposes a scarcity of academic work on indigenous people captured by whites. *Captive Arizona* helps fill this void.

Arizona historians and Indian Studies scholars will note the absence of Yavapai captives Carlos Montezuma and Mike Burns from this work. Captured by U.S. Army troops months apart in 1872, the boys were ultimately sent east for educations, returning to their tribe only later in life. Montezuma, who in the interim earned a medical degree and developed a successful practice, returned to Arizona to help the Yavapais negotiate the realities of twentieth-century reservation life. After receiving an education at Indian boarding schools in the East, Mike Burns also returned to the Yavapais, often working in tandem with Carlos Montezuma. Most important, he wrote a lengthy, detailed history of the Arizona Territory from the perspective of Arizona's indigenous people.[3]

Academics have begun scrutinizing the lives of both these former captives. Peter Iverson compiled a biography of Montezuma in 1982, focusing on his substantial contributions to Native American tribal persistence in the early twentieth century. Susan Rockwell has edited Mike Burns's lengthy territorial history/autobiography. With the assurance that academic interest in these two captives will continue, the present work turns instead to Montezuma and Burns's contemporary, young Yavapai captive Bessie Burns—captured by whites in 1869—who makes her academic debut here. Like her counterparts, Bessie would challenge whites' legal construction in Arizona. Admittedly, though, the absence of Montezuma and Burns creates an underrepresentation of captive indigenous males in this book. It is left to future historians to examine these men's pivotal roles within the context of *Captive Arizona*. The present work makes no direct substantial contribution to their biographies, other than to alert historians interested in the life of Mike Burns that he was enrolled at Haskell Indian School in the latter half of the 1880s, a fact only recently come to light.[4]

Military historians will question the omission of Merejildo Grijalva from a study in Arizona captivity. An Opata Indian of Sonora captured by the Chiricahua Apaches in childhood, Grijalva eventually became Cochise's personal slave. Escaping with the help of white civilians in the late 1850s, he went on to become the territory's prototype captive turned army scout and guide. Chiricahua historian Ed Sweeney's 1992 biography *Merejildo Grijalva: Apache Captive, Army Scout* "captures" the basic facts of the scout's life for a future, expanded, postmodern examination of this pivotal captive. With Grijalva's retirement from frontline action in the 1870s, the vacancy posed by his departure from the army created an opening for the rise of a less historically understood captive/scout, Mickey Free, on whom this work chooses to focus in Grijalva's stead.

One final work contributes to scholars' understanding of captivity in Arizona Territory. Brian McGinty's *The Oatman Massacre*, published in 2005, conducts an academic discussion on Arizona's most well-known captive, Olive Oatman. Among other issues, McGinty addresses those concerning Oatman's Mormon roots; deconstructs the many published editions of Oatman biographer Royal

Stratton's *Captivity of the Oatman Girls*; clarifies specifics surrounding Olive's original captors, the Yavapais, and her subsequent captors, the Mohaves; and reminds historians of the Mohave perspective on Olive's captivity. McGinty also raises the legitimate issues of men who chose to marry former captives—a theme *Captive Arizona* continues—and of the Mojaves' fear of reprisal from whites. The present work expands upon McGinty's conclusions, discussed further.

Captive Arizona's cultural boundaries are delineated by its geography. In the northern reaches of mountainous central Arizona, from Hell Canyon and the old Beale trail into Chino Valley north of the Prescott region, lived the Yavapais, a band of the Yavapai tribe proper, and to their southwest, the Tolkepayas, a southern Yavapai band. In between lay Fort Whipple and Prescott, the first town established by U.S. citizens in Arizona Territory or, more correctly, in Yavapai territory. South of the Yavapais, the Pima and Maricopa tribes farmed along the Gila River, and west of the Yavapais, stretched for miles along the Colorado River near modern Needles, California, lived the Mohaves. South of the Mohaves lay the land of the Quechans, or Yuma tribe proper, and below the Quechans the Cocomaricopas and the Sea of Cortez, where Seri, Tohono O'odham, and Yaqui Indians would one day mingle with Mexicans in the seaside village of Puerto Peñasco.

Linked by a common language and origin belief, but riddled with rivalries and shifting alliances, the Yuman tribes give way to the Mexicans and indigenous people of Sonora before the boundary of *Captive Arizona* turns again to the Santa Cruz River valley and Tucson. Occupied by the indigenous Tohono O'odhams, the "Desert People," in the late 1600s, Spaniards and the presidios of Tubac—and further north, Tucson—had dispossessed them by 1776, and reduction of the local O'odhams to the San Xavier Del Bac Mission soon followed. The O'odhams watched as Mexicans then took possession of Tucson from the Spaniards in 1821. From the Mexican community at Tucson—which increasingly saw its population and social infrastructure eclipsed by emigrating whites—*Captive Arizona* stretches southeast to the presidio at Santa Cruz, Sonora, where Spanish, Mexican, and indigenous peoples converged into a singular community that would later seed the presidios at Tubac and Tucson.

From Tucson and Santa Cruz, Sonora, *Captive Arizona* encompasses the pine and hardwood–studded mountains of the Chiricahua Apache band, the Chokonens, which ranged from the Graham Mountains and San Pedro River valley of southeastern Arizona south to the Nednai Chiricahuas in the Sierra Madres of Mexico. From the Chokonens, the cultural boundary of *Captive Arizona* extends eastward to the Chiricahua Apaches of western New Mexico, and Chihuahua, generally known as the Chihennes, or Warm Springs Apaches.

Finally, the cultural boundary of *Captive Arizona* turns west, where it enters east-central Arizona and the territory of the Western Apaches. Cousins and rivals of the Chiricahuas, although they sometimes intermarried, the Western Apaches spoke a distinct dialect of Athapascan; they organized themselves around matrilineal clans, which the Chiricahua social organization lacked, and around influential clan chiefs, which the Chiricahuas discarded in favor of leadership based on heredity and ascription. The tribes of northern Arizona, colonized by whites—especially Mormons—are sufficiently different in geography, history, and culture from those of central and southern Arizona to warrant their own regional study of captivity.

Regardless of historic cultural traditions, Native Americans, whites, and Mexican Americans taken captive during the territorial period were usually children and very young women, while captors were invariably men. The Yavapais, Mohaves, Tohono O'odhams, Yaquis, Chiricahuas, and Western Apaches examined in this work had conducted systems of captivity, assimilation, and slave trades prior to the arrival of Europeans. With the intrusion of the foreigners, Mexican and white male captives considered too old to be acculturated into tribal life—generally around the age of twelve—were killed at the scene, or by grieving tribal women upon return to camp, rather than left to fight another day.

Mexicans, as had the Spanish before them, used indigenous captivity as a source of slaves, most of whom—after local markets were satiated—regardless of age or gender were sent south to Mexico City or Yucatan, or north to Santa Fe, where they were forced to perform agricultural, mining, or domestic labor until worked to incapacity or death. Whites took Native American children captive under the guise of "civilizing them," sometimes through informal and illegal adoptions, sometimes through domestic servitude, and sometimes through education at Indian boarding schools in the eastern and midwestern states.

Research for this book did not reveal the identity of the first Indian captured by whites in Arizona, but the identity of the first Mexican female liberated from captivity by whites in Arizona is fairly certain. While surveying the boundary between Mexico and Arizona in 1853, survey commissioner John Bartlett had discussions with Chiricahua chief Mangus Colorado in which he informed Mangus of the political changes at hand, including the U.S. government's obligation to prevent Apaches from abducting Mexicans and their livestock. "Our protection of the Mexicans he did not seem to relish, and could not comprehend . . . what business it was to the Americans if the Apaches chose to steal their mules, as they had always done, or to make wives of their Mexican women, or prisoners of their children. I told him the Americans were bound to do so and could not break their word," said Bartlett.[5]

Continuing their work, the boundary commission was then visited by "New Mexicans," led by one Peter Blacklaws, who had a young female Mexican captive with them. They had acquired her from Pinal Apaches, a sub-band of the Western Apaches, and were intending to sell her into servitude. But "as all kinds of traffic of this kind . . . [were] strictly prohibited by the treaty with Mexico, I deemed it my duty, as the nearest and highest representative of the government of the United States in this region, to interfere in the matter."[6]

Bartlett went on to quote the treaty provision that authorized him to take action to "rescue them and return them to their country or deliver them to the agent or representative of the Mexican government." Armed with authority, Bartlett notified the commission's military escort, which immediately endorsed Bartlett's position. Blacklaws was the only man of the party of twenty to possess the necessary trading license, and insisted it gave him the right to purchase any of the Indians' wares. Lieutenant Craig, however, disagreed. The girl, Inez Gonzales of Santa Cruz, Mexico, was liberated by the military escort and taken under the protection of the boundary commission before being returned to her family.[7]

Despite the treaties of Guadalupe Hidalgo and the Gadsden Purchase, Mexican children continued to be enslaved by Indians and whites in Arizona. In 1858 an early white pioneer, Palatine Robinson, lived in his Tucson home with his Mexican wife and children and a nine-year-old Mexican servant girl, Ramona, most likely an orphan. Ramona lived with the Robinsons in Tucson for a year before Palatine moved to the Rio Grande, "taking the girl Ramona with his family in the stage with him. He returned to Tucson after an absence of five or six months, and told me himself that he had sold her (the girl Ramona), also stating the price he obtained for her, but I have forgotten the amount," an acquaintance officially testified in 1862. For some white Southerners in Arizona, the privileges of slavery died hard.[8]

Before introducing the captives selected for this work, some thought regarding terminology—which can be problematic in Arizona history—is in order. So as not to encumber the narrative with scholarly technicalities and specialized language—and to maintain academic focus on the captives in the foreground of the work—this book reduces several concepts to their simplest terms.

For example, the term "whites" is used here to indicate emigrating citizens of the United States, although it is understood that this same class of people represented scores of differing national origins from Europe and the States, and not all were U.S. citizens. Moreover, during the era under discussion, Mexican Americans were considered "white" for purposes of the federal census. Similarly, this work distinguishes between the terms "Mexican" and "Mexican American" to indicate those of Mexican descent who opted to remain in Arizona after the Gadsden Purchase—and who embodied a distinct social class in Tucson and southern Arizona—and those who continued to identify as Mexican nationals. Finally, concerning issues of race, this work uses the terms "Indians," "indigenous," and "Native Americans" interchangeably, fully aware that Columbus was in error, and that many nonindigenous people consider themselves "native" Americans. In sum, the ideology and effects of imperialism were monolithic, but the historic actors were diverse.

Regarding nomenclature, this work introduces Mexican American captives by their traditional Hispanic names—Mercedes Sais Quiroz, for example—but subsequently refers to them by their more common names: Mercedes Sais, or Mercedes Sais Shibell. Native Americans have also been referred to by their most common historic appellations—Apache Kid instead of Hacke-bay-nay-ntayl—in most instances. To balance this latitude, *Captive Arizona* takes care to identify specific indigenous clans and bands among the Mojaves and even more so among the Western Apaches, in order to clarify previously murky history.

Therefore, for example, the White Mountain, Cibecue, and Aravaipa bands of the Western Apaches come under close scrutiny in this work, while the Tontos and Pinals receive less attention, as captivity demands.

The text also ascribes clan affiliations in order to more narrowly identify the common, broader historic conception of Western Apache band identity. Of the sixty Western Apache clans identified by anthropologist Grenville Goodwin in the 1930s, five come into focus in this work: the *nadots-usn* headed by Hacke-idasila of the Eastern White Mountain Apaches, the most powerful Western Apache chief as the era of white imperialism broke; the *ti-uk-a-digaidn* clan of Cibecue headmen brothers Miguel and Diablo from Carrizo Creek; Pedro's *tca-tci-dn*, driven from the Carrizo by Miguel prior to the arrival of whites; the *ti-sie-dnt-i-dn* of clan head Nayudiie of the Western White Mountain Apaches; and the *biszahé* of his son, John Rope, all of whom except the *tca-tci-dn* were forcibly relocated to the San Carlos reservation from the Fort Apache reservation in the White Mountains. This technique illuminates the internal tensions gnawing at Western Apache social relations during the territorial era.[9]

Likewise, simplifications apply to place names. Military installations—whether white or Mexican—changed names and designations with dizzying regularity in Arizona and Sonora; therefore, this work refers to them by the names most commonly used in the present era—for example, Santa Cruz, Fort Apache, Fort Bowie, and Fort Lowell, but Camp Grant and Camp Verde. Similarly, the indigenous people of Arizona used several universes of language to convey place names, but for simplicity's sake this book refers to geography using common terminology.[10]

The study of captivity in Arizona confounds the boundaries of conventional military histories or tribal studies. Where military histories—battle histories—may traditionally appear to be the loci of racial interaction in Arizona, captives—the illegitimate stepchildren of war—offer an alternative view. Tribal histories, of necessity, must focus on the core members and movements of any indigenous society, rather than the marginal or peripheral. The captives alone have the ability to transport historians to the camps and firesides, the hearths and homes of territorial Arizona, for an intimate look at the social relations of empire. This book presents enough historical contextualization to orient scholars who are new to Arizona history, but not enough to bore those who are already familiar. Even then, captivity gives new meaning to old facts.

Captive Arizona makes no apology for utilizing the manuscript collections and other archival sources housed in research libraries across Arizona. In fact—although this book applauds the incorporation of Native American oral tradition into the canon of historical sources—it would argue that historians who reject conventional sources formerly used to construct imperialist presentations of Western American and Native American history are doing themselves a disservice, for hidden behind the fabrications of "great men" lies something closer to the historical truth, if one if willing to venture through the labyrinth of documents necessary to find it. Once across the Mississippi River, the government of the United States quickly realized, as had the Spanish before them, that far-flung empires are governed through massive bureaucracies built of paper. Within this paperwork lies the proof, as recorded by the invaders themselves—a step-by-step documentation of the systematic dispossession and selective genocide of indigenous Americans. As an alternative historical interpretation, *Captive Arizona* gives voice to the silenced, liberating them from their historic bonds.

Some of the indigenous accounts utilized here rely on oral histories collected by early anthropologists Alfred Kroeber, Grenville Goodwin, and Ruth Underhill. These scholars recorded their material, and interpreted it, in an academic era that cannot withstand postmodern scrutiny. Therefore, this work probes these sources only deeply enough to illuminate captivity, and shies away from references to sacred knowledge, out of respect for postmodern Indian nations. To coin an oddly appropriate old phrase, documents don't kill history—historians do, through careless interpretation.

Whenever possible, this book frees the captives to share their own experiences in their own words, in order that historians might better understand their worldview and behavior. As a methodology, the captives' lives have been set against a background of territorialization, the process by which post-Revolutionary "states" were born and united. This process utilized many of the earlier features of colonialism, such as westering mercantilists of European descent posing as frontier trappers and traders. These were followed by expansionists intent on dispossessing indigenous Americans: the military, miners, white pioneer families, settlers. With them came the settlers' infrastructure: wagon roads, fortified settlements, and, most important, military protection, which in the territorial era had the additional advantage of telegraphs and railroads. Whereas British colonialism had led to Anglo rebellion, revolution, political independence, and the removal of indigenous people out of the former colonies and into the American West, territorialization provided for the systematic federal bestowal of "state" status based on white population figures, and full incorporation into the United States for whites. For indigenous people, territorialization meant the establishment of Indian reservations on reduced homelands. From the captives' perspective, territorialization takes on highlights and undertones not visible in the master narrative.

Without women and children, white males in Arizona were merely adventurers and mercantilists, transitory features in the indigenous landscape. Accompanied by white women and children, however, they were transformed into pioneers and settlers, with a vested interest in real estate and secure property. In this sense it was white women and children, not men, who drove the Arizona territorial process on the one hand, while raising the stakes for white males on the other, men who felt compelled by a code of patriarchal honor to protect their families from Native Americans, a "privilege" encoded in the U.S. doctrine of Manifest Destiny. But whether white, Mexican American, or Indian, the captives of Arizona exercised personal agency under the most trying of circumstances.

As Carlos Montezuma, Mike Burns, and Merejildo Grijalva illustrate, the captives examined in this work represent only a portion of the captives known to Arizona historians. Miner Daniel Ellis Conner's memoir, *Joseph Reddeford Walker and the Arizona Adventure*, alone refers to at least four nonindigenous captives whose identities and historical significance are waiting to be recovered. The first, a nude, starving Mexican girl freed from the Apaches, was taken to Prescott by whites, given the name Lucy, and became a celebrated member of the community. The second was a Mexican boy who ran into Prescott, was adopted by the community, and found work at a blacksmith shop. The third and fourth were brothers. While trailing Apaches with the King Woolsey party in the early 1860s, the party attempted to communicate with an indigenous group while camped near the conjunction of the Gila and Aqua Fria rivers. "The savages came in sight and showed themselves under a white rag. . . . They presented to view two little red-headed white boys, evidently captives. . . . These children were evidently too much alike not to be kin to each other, and were probably brothers." When negotiations broke down, the Apaches—and their captives—seemingly disappeared from history. Furthermore, the oral histories published by Eve Ball, Jason Betzinez, Sherry Robinson, Grenville Goodwin, and others contain numerous accounts of indigenous captivity that deserve to be better understood by historians.[11]

Chapter 1 opens the era in 1851 with a reexamination of the life of Olive Oatman, Arizona's most familiar historic captive. As discussed above, her recent biographer,

Brian McGinty, considered legitimate academic issues surrounding Olive's life, which *Captive Arizona* continues to pursue. In a larger sense, however, Olive's life encapsulated and foreshadowed a social "captivity complex" that held Arizona in an uneasy grip for the next five decades, setting the tone for the book.

Captives Larcena Pennington, Mercedes Sais Quiroz, Feliz Tellez Martinez, and Nah-thle-tla, 1855–61, are the subjects of chapter 2. Pennington's captivity experience of 1860 functions as an informative contrast to that of Olive Oatman. Both physically scarred for life by their ordeals, the young white women processed their experiences differently, illuminating class distinctions between the two. Mercedes Sais, a Mexican American girl taken captive by Apaches with Pennington, draws the reader into the delicate negotiations of redemption between Indians and whites in 1860s Arizona, while Tellez's capture in 1861, which ignited the infamous Bascom affair, lays the foundation for decades of warfare between whites and the Chiricahuas. Like the captivity of Olive Oatman, the captures of Larcena, Mercedes, and Feliz would result in whites unfairly implicating the wrong indigenous captors, adding to the social chaos in Arizona Territory. Nah-thle-tla, a young Chiricahua woman captured by Mexicans in 1855, did not have the advantage of an army to come to her rescue. Her resilience and self-liberation illustrate the contrast in worldviews between indigenous and nonindigenous female captives in Arizona.[12]

In chapter 3, the incursion of whites into Apache territory after 1864 created increased opportunities for the liberation of captives. One unnamed Tohono O'odham woman, taken captive by Western Apaches and self-rescued, returned to the O'odham community at San Xavier only to be enlisted by her tribesmen as a guide into Apache territory, a tactic simultaneously being employed by the U.S. Army. In Prescott, young Yavapai captive Bessie Brooks, captured by whites in 1869, grew to womanhood in the home of a territorial judge, but territorial law would ultimately betray her. Chapter 3 closes with the infamous Camp Grant massacre of 1871, when the white, Mexican, and Tohono O'odham families of the southern Arizona captives and victims vented their rage on the Aravaipa Apaches. The search for the Aravaipa captives taken during the raid would lead white federal authorities into the web of intercultural power relations governing Tucson and southern Arizona in the post–Civil War era.

Feliz Tellez returns as the captive/scout "Mickey Free" in chapter 4. Liberated by the military in the 1860s, Tellez quickly enlisted as an Indian scout, and in that capacity returned to his adopted people at Fort Apache in 1871, positioning him for a historic role as Mickey Free, the foil of Geronimo. Miss Harris, a young white captive of the Chiricahuas, is redeemed by the army in chapter 4, but chooses to return to her captors, confounding white society, while Chiricahua warrior Chatto's family is captured by Mexicans and sold into slavery, compelling Chatto to break with Geronimo and join forces with Mickey Free. The Chiricahuas would never forgive either man. While power relations shifted on the battlefield, Mrs. Andrew Stanley, a young Eastern White Mountain woman of the *nadots-usn* clan and niece of chief Hacke-idasila, would inadvertently find herself the captive of Chiricahua warriors. Although her relatives—acting in the capacity of army scouts—searched for her relentlessly, it would be up to Mrs. Stanley to rescue herself, as had Nah-thle-tla and the unnamed O'odham woman before her. Her resilience would sustain her, but her reentry into White Mountain society would be problematic.

Chapter 5 continues to follow developments on the battlefield through the lens of captivity. Now engaged in all-out war with Geronimo, Mickey Free and the Western Apache scouts track the leader's band into Mexico in 1883, searching for young white captive Charlie McComas, whose fate would remain a mystery for almost another century. In Mexico, chapter 5 observes Dji-li-kinne, a captive white man raised with the Western Apaches who became Geronimo's father-in-law and a prominent Chiricahua warrior. Dji-li-kinne's ultimate loyalties would cost him his life. Geronimo's actions in the final year of his resistance—resulting in the captures of two young Mexican Americans, Trinidad Verdin and Octaviano Gastelum, and an Irish Mexican boy, Santiago McKinn—would fly in the face of reason, leaving historians to decipher his motives. At chapter's end, Mickey Free, acting as Chatto's interpreter, implores authorities in Washington DC in 1886 to redeem Chatto's relatives in Mexico, to no avail.

Finally, chapter 8 examines captivity in the eerie silence that befell Arizona following the deportation of the Chiricahuas to Alabama and Florida. Though the whites' war with the Chiricahua Apaches was over in 1886, Apache Kid's war against whites had just begun.

His daughter, the captive Apache May, would reignite the heredity-versus-environment debate launched almost thirty years prior in Prescott with the captivity of Bessie Brooks. The book closes with a summary of the life of Yaqui Indian captive Santiago Suviate, emphasizing the social and geographical implications of *Captive Arizona*.

The captives' voices relate an underlying brutality that characterized Arizona's territorial era. Whites, Mexican Americans, and Indians alike behaved ruthlessly regarding captivity, but distinct differences lay in issues of motive. Whites and Mexicans, as colonizers, fought an offensive war of captivity against the indigenous people of Arizona. Indians, unwilling to be colonized, fought a defensive war of captivity against the invaders in response. These colliding worlds held Arizona captive for more than half a century.

Captive Arizona, 1851–1900

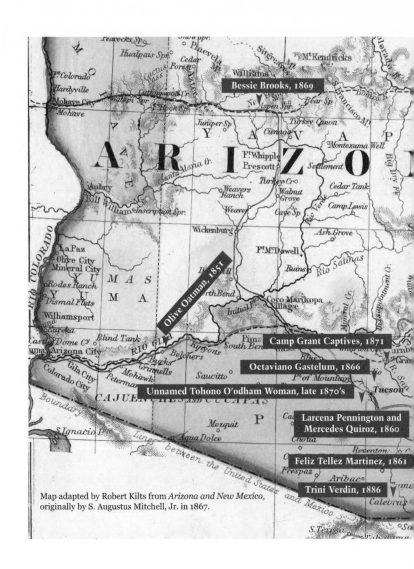

Bessie Brooks, 1869

Olive Oatman, 1851

Camp Grant Captives, 1871

Octaviano Gastelum, 1866

Unnamed Tohono O'odham Woman, late 1870's

Larcena Pennington and Mercedes Quiroz, 1860

Feliz Tellez Martinez, 1861

Trini Verdin, 1886

Map adapted by Robert Kilts from *Arizona and New Mexico*, originally by S. Augustus Mitchell, Jr. in 1867.

Captive Arizona

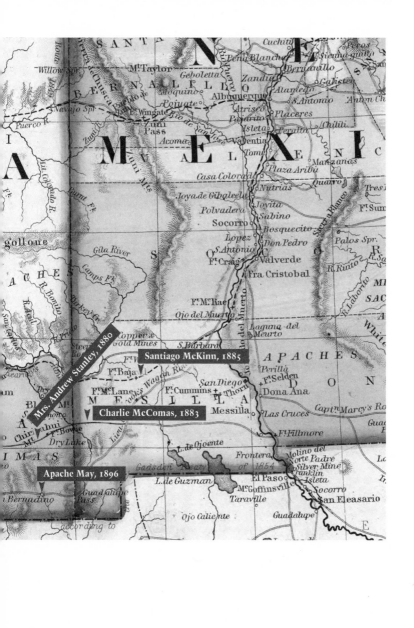

Mrs. Andrew Stanley, 1880

Santiago McKinn, 1885

Charlie McComas, 1883

Apache May, 1896

1

1851–1856

Scholars have demonstrated that colonial-era captivity narratives were important to the ways in which white expansionists used gender in the construction of race and nationalism. Embodied in these texts were the beliefs that native men were by nature sexual beasts, and as such were naturally threatening to white women. Moreover, Anglo-Americans assumed that white women who returned from captivity had been sexually "defiled" by native males. Such inferences strengthened their perception of Native American men as dangerous, and thus justifiably dispossessed and murdered. Two hundred years later, the life of Olive Oatman would prove that such racist, gendered thought had migrated west to Arizona.[1]

Olive's story began on the Gila Trail, or southern overland route, which would historically prove less heavily traveled than its counterparts, the northern overland trails. Scarce water, punishing heat, fierce summer storms, cold winter winds, scant forage, challenging terrain, poisonous wildlife, and Native Americans determined to oppose the invasion convinced most whites to try their chances farther north. Moreover, until the Gadsden Purchase of 1853, a crucial portion of the Gila Trail wound its way through Mexico, where remote Tucson's three hundred Mexican colonists provided the only relative safety that Anglo-Americans could expect to find on their way to the goldfields. Despite the challenges, by 1851 some twenty thousand whites and Mexicans had traveled the trail to California.[2]

By the early 1850s, the sight of white men in Arizona—and encounters both passive and aggressive—had become, if not commonplace, at least not unusual for the indigenous people of the region. However, the increased presence of white women and children on the southern trail to California after 1848 heightened the risk of passage for white American males, who perceived the ability to protect their women and children from Native American males as a proof of their "manifest destiny" to possess indigenous land. But Anglo-American men feared not only the potential deaths of their family members by "fiendish heathens"; worse, in most whites' eyes, was to be captured by Native Americans.[3]

Only weeks before the Oatmans entered Arizona, U.S. Boundary Commissioner John Russell Bartlett had rescued Inez Gonzales from New Mexican slave traders and liberated the captives of chiefs Mangas Coloradas and Delgadito of the Chiricahua Apaches. Regardless, Native Americans, on the one hand, and Mexicans, Mexican Americans, and Anglo-Americans, on the other, would continue to capture each other in an interminably protracted war of imperial thrust and indigenous response that would persist for another sixty years. Additionally, with the arrival of white families, the potential pool of captives expanded for Native Americans, but so did the risks as well.[4]

As the first white woman taken captive on the Gila Trail, Olive Oatman's captivity occurred prior to the establishment of a series of camps and forts later intended—in addition to posing as staging stations for the further invasion of Indian homelands—to deter Native Americans from attacking travelers on the early trails. In the absence of official protection, Olive's ordeal would serve as a cautionary tale to all who would travel the early trail from Santa Fe to Los Angeles, feeding the gendered, racist fears of whites everywhere regarding the indigenous people of Arizona.[5]

Unlike most Mormons of the era, who as a class of people did not begin settling Arizona until the late 1860s, Olive's father, Royce Oatman, didn't migrate to Utah. He chose instead to accompany a wagon train of Brewsterites—who challenged Brigham Young's rise to leadership after the death of Joseph Smith—intent on starting a colony on the Colorado River. In August 1850 the Oatman family—Royce, forty-one years old; his wife, Mary Ann Sperry; and their seven children, ages two to sixteen—left Independence, Missouri, with a wagon train headed for Yuma, joining the thousands of others heading west on the Gila Trail that year.[6]

Oatman, like many white expansionists, was no stranger to greener fields. Originally from western New York, he moved to Illinois and married the "educated, confiding and affectionate" Mary Ann, the "pride of wealthy parents," as her daughter Olive would later recall. A mercantilist, he lost everything during the "hard times" of 1842 and moved the family to the Cumberland Valley in Pennsylvania. By 1845 the family was living in Chicago. In the spring of 1850 Oatman sold all he had for $1,500, packed up his family, and started for Independence in a wagon, ultimately headed for Yuma.[7]

The train of twenty wagons and fifty people, most of them women and children, optimistically left Independence, but by the time they reached Council Grove, "religious arguments" had begun to sow dissension among the group. According to Olive, followers lost respect for their leaders. Passing through Raton Pass on the New Mexico–Colorado border, the train split, with the "malcontents" choosing the northern route west, while the eight wagons and twenty persons of the "peaceable party" continued south to Socorro. By the time the Oatmans' train reached the Rio Grande, the Mescalero Apaches had challenged the whites' presence in Apache territory. By then all plans for a colony at Yuma had been abandoned, and the party intended to push on to California. Between them and their goal, however, lay Arizona's indigenous people. While it was relatively true that by 1851 the Gila Trail was "well known" to whites, it was only so to those Americans—mountain men such as Pauline Weaver— who later functioned as guides for American exploratory parties in the Southwest and who had traveled it more than once. But to novice easterner white males such as Royce Oatman, it was a trail through an unfamiliar and inhospitable land.[8]

At last the Oatman train reached the eastern boundary of Arizona. Once in Tucson, earnest Mexicans tried to convince the party to delay. Most of the travelers agreed to remain, but three families, including the Oatmans, pressed on, fearing the "prowling savages" outside the old adobe walls. In February 1851 they reached the Pima Indian villages along the Gila River. Agriculturalists who had established amiable relations with emigrating whites—and who shared a common enemy in the Apaches—the Pimas would normally have supplied the destitute wagons. But recent Apache attacks had decimated the natives' own grain stores; they had nothing to share with the white travelers.[9]

Desperate for supplies, two families stayed with the Pimas—hungry though the tribe was—intent on waiting for a passing government wagon train. Oatman, however, stubbornly pressed on, still more than 350 miles from his destination on the Colorado River. "Mr. Oatman believed that starvation, or the treacherous savages, would soon bring them to an awful fate if they remained, and the danger of going ahead would be but little greater, anyway," Oatman biographer Royal Stratton would later write.[10]

Oatman's fears were not remarkably uncommon. For example, elderly frontiersman John Udell—who with his wife crossed Beale's wagon road in northern Arizona in July 1859—feared starvation as well. Lost, without supplies, and attacked by Indians, the members of Udell's wagon train felt victimized by the course they had chosen with an "inevitable fate." "We read and hear of the barbarous murders and treatment by savages of citizens from our beloved civilized country," Udell wrote in his diary. "We also hear of death by starvation, and perhaps we may feel a degree of sympathy for such sufferers, but we cannot realize the sensitiveness of such persons until we are placed in circumstances in which it seems to be our inevitable fate soon to suffer death by one or the other of these horrible means."[11]

Scholars have noted the incompetence of men who attempted the overland crossing. John Udell and his wife were eventually rescued, but Royce Oatman and his family would answer for their invasion of indigenous Arizona. Additionally, parental responsibility weighed heavily upon Royce Oatman's shoulders, as the folly of his actions began to weigh on him.[12]Stratton writes:

> Let the imagination of the reader awake and dwell upon the probable feelings of those fond parents at this trying juncture of circumstances . . . attended by a family . . . [,] which in the event of their being overtaken by any of the catastrophes that reason and prudence bade them beware of on the route; . . . even by their presence and peculiar exposure, give point and power to the sense and presence of danger; . . . a thousand kindred considerations, crowded upon those lonely hours of travel . . . [,] burned through the whole being of these parents with the intensity of desperation.[13]

Seven days after leaving the Pima villages, the Oatman oxen played out, unable to proceed. A lone white traveler on horseback overtook the family on the trail, promising to send help from nascent Fort Yuma, on the lower Colorado River ninety miles away. Shortly after the encounter, Native Americans robbed the man of his horse, leaving him no choice but to finish the journey afoot. He left a note on a tree trunk for Oatman to find, warning of danger, but the family failed to notice it (although in retrospect, young Lorenzo Oatman would question that assumption). By March 18, 1851, the Oatmans had struggled to the banks of the Gila River, within eighty miles of Fort Yuma.[14]

Desperate to reach the safety of Yuma, they forded the Gila River, swollen from recent rain, and dragged themselves onto an island in its center. Drenched and defeated, they huddled around a meager fire, discussing what they would do if attacked. "'I shall run,' said a timid child." Another declared he would die fighting. The oldest brother, Lorenzo, aged sixteen, planned to grab a gun or club and fight. Olive, the second-oldest daughter at fifteen, took a defiant stance. "Well, there is one thing. I will not be taken by these treacherous savages. I will fight as long as I can, and if I see that I am about to be taken, I will kill myself. I do not want to die, but it would be worse than death to me to be made a captive among them."[15]

The following morning, the family finished fording the Gila, but a "disheartening and soul-crushing despair" fell upon Royce Oatman, though Mrs. Oatman remained remarkably "calm, cool and collected." The family rested all that day. Following a "fitful night," they intended to continue on to Fort Yuma. But as Oatman hooked up the oxen, Indians appeared in camp. The scene as described by Stratton was clearly designed to invoke a sense of outrage at American victimization.[16]

The natives demanded food, according to Stratton, so Oatman invited them to sit down, though he had few provisions. It was a decision said to be in keeping with his experience. "[He] had always believed that Indians could be treated so as to avoid trouble with them. He had been among them much in Illinois and Iowa and had so often tried his theory of leniency with success that he was inclined to censure the whites for their severity towards them."[17]

Oatman shared tobacco and bread with his visitors, but they wanted more, as the story goes. When he refused, they attacked. Quicker than she could size up the situation, Olive found herself captured by their visitors; her sister, seven-year-old Mary Ann, stood nearby, hysterical. Olive later described the scene:

> As an Indian was taking me to one side, I saw them strike Lorenzo down and in an instant afterward my father also. . . . I saw my father, my own dear father, struggling, bleeding and moaning in the most pitiful manner. Lorenzo was lying with his face in the dust with the top of his head covered with blood. I looked around and saw my poor, dear mother lying on the ground with the baby clamped in her arms; both of them were still, as if the work of death had been complete. . . . The rest were almost motionless upon the ground, dead or dying.[18]

While the episode is intended to convey the victimization of the "generous" Oatman family by ungrateful "heathens," a close reading of Lorenzo Oatman's perspective suggests his father may have fatally panicked under the stress of the circumstances. Though the words are couched, Lorenzo claimed: "For one hour the night before [the attack] my father had wept bitterly while in the wagon, thinking himself concealed from his family"; and again, "At one time during the severest part of the toil and efforts of that day to make the summit of that hill, my father suddenly sank down upon a stone near the wagon and exclaimed, 'Mother, mother, in the name of God, I know that something dreadful is about to happen!'" When told by Lorenzo that Native Americans were approaching the camp, "The blood rushed to my father's face. . . . I saw too plainly the effort that it cost him to attempt a concealment of his emotions. . . . His wonted coolness and fearlessness seemed to abandon him; and *I have never been able to account for the conduct of my father at this time*," said Lorenzo, even though he had made it clear to his father, whose back was turned, that the natives were merely "slowly and leisurely approaching us in the road."[19]

According to Lorenzo, the natives asked for tobacco, and Royce smoked briefly with them, "but amid all this, the appearance and conduct of father was strange." It may have been the visitors' request for food that caused Oatman to snap, for according to Lorenzo, "Father told them of our destitute condition and that he could not feed them without robbing his family. . . . They became earnest and rather imperative . . . increasing their wild and furious clamors. Father reluctantly took some bread from the wagon and gave it to them, saying that it was robbery and perhaps starvation to his family." When his guests had eaten the bread, they asked for more. "They were told that we could spare them no more," Lorenzo said simply, but one wonders in what manner Oatman conveyed his message, for it was his refusal that led the natives to attack. In retrospect, the concepts of hunger and meager supplies are relevant, and what appeared to be scant rations to Oatman may have seemed an abundance of food to hungry indigenous Arizonans, whose natural resources strained under the intrusion of emigrants and their livestock. Panic, and an unwillingness to share resources reciprocally, may have cost Oatman his life and family.[20]

Olive and Mary Ann's captors, meanwhile, herded the terrified girls into the Gila River, forcing them to ford it once more. Olive would not be seen by whites again for five years.[21]

The raiders rifled Lorenzo's pockets, leaving him for dead. After waiting long enough to assure himself of the Yavapais' departure, the semiconscious teenager struggled to his feet, only to lurch over a precipice. Upon regaining consciousness the next morning, he crawled back to the wagon and, by sheer strength of will, proceeded before collapsing again. The following day he crossed the path of two friendly Pimas, who fed him, and then left to find help. As passing wagons neared him on the trail, Lorenzo realized it was that portion of his own train that had remained behind in Tucson months earlier.[22]

Appalled by the severely injured boy, the men of the train returned to the scene of the attack and buried the dead family before pressing on to the Pima villages, where Lorenzo recuperated for ten days. With his strength somewhat regained, Lorenzo traveled with a wagon train to Fort Yuma, recuperating there until June 1851, all the while pleading with the commanding officer to rescue his sisters. That summer a distant cousin came to claim him, and Lorenzo left for San Francisco. There he would stay for the next three years, plotting his sisters' rescue.[23]

While Lorenzo struggled to find help in the desert, Olive and Mary Ann were hustled along a footpath, keeping a rapid pace for hours. "The girls were bareheaded and barefooted, the Indians having taken off their hats and shoes. The rate of travel was much beyond their strength, but every slackening of their pace brought threats of torture from suspended war clubs," Stratton writes. Exhausted and hungry even before their captivity, the added stress nearly incapacitated the sisters, but the removal of their shoes was necessary to conceal their presence among the captors to the whites who might follow.[24]

Historians have disagreed as to the exact identity of the Oatman sisters' captors. Stratton, most disconcertingly, uses the term "Apache" as a ubiquitous euphemism throughout his book, alternating with Olive's claims that it was the "Toutos," more correctly known as the Tontos, a tribe of Apaches living on the northeastern edge of Western Apache territory, who had killed her family and taken her captive. One historian, who in all other respects has written an important comprehensive work on the Yavapais, only lightly touches upon the Oatman incident, but postulates that it was the Tontos or perhaps the Kwevkepayas, a band of Yavapais whose territory was the most southeastern of that tribe's range. But historian Brian McGinty has provided the most convincing evidence that Tolkepayas, the westernmost-ranging Yavapai band, were most likely responsible for Olive's captivity. Using mileage as calculated by Olive, McGinty demonstrates that her own estimates would have placed her captors' village in Navajo and Hopi territory, a highly unlikely event since these tribes were not known to travel to that region. More likely, in McGinty's view, was the possibility of Tolkepayas. Although the attack had technically occurred in Maricopa territory, it had been so only marginally, and the presence of Tolkepayas in the Gila Bend region would not have been unusual.[25]

After traveling some miles, Mary Ann collapsed. The Yavapais, uncertain how soon whites would follow, grew impatient. They first beat her, and then threatened to kill the girl. According to Stratton, Mary Ann "became utterly fearless of death and said she had rather die than live. . . . Then one of the Apaches removed his pack and placed it on the shoulders of another Indian, rudely threw Mary across his back, and with a vengeful look bounded on." Three days later they arrived in the Yavapais' village.[26]

The tribe turned out to greet the returning raiders. The women pushed Olive and Mary Ann onto a pile of brush, where they found themselves surrounded by Yavapais dancing "in the wildest and most furious manner," spitting on them and striking the girls with their hands. The girls survived the traditional victory dance given to returning raiders, but they would be forced to live in what they perceived as the "filth, degradation and utter abandonment" of the Yavapai for the next year. Given to the women of the tribe, Olive and Mary were compelled "to perform tasks beyond their strength, and [the women] even seemed delighted to whip the poor girls to the last stage of endurance. . . . They did everything to show their hatred for the race to whom the girls belonged," writes

Stratton, oblivious of the Yavapais' imperative to repel invaders from their homelands, and their need to absorb white captives in the most expedient manner.[27]

As was expected by her religious doctrine, Olive determined to accept her captivity as the will of God, "odious" as it was to her. After acquiring some of the Yuman language, the girls tried to teach the Yavapais how to farm like "white men" in an effort to "civilize" their captors. Young Native Americans, lacking the maturity to gauge the implications, expressed measured curiosity about the Americans' way of life. Olive and Mary were "gratified" to find that some of these younger members of the tribe "asked frequent questions, and seemed anxious to know about civilized modes of living," Olive would later recall, as if the indigenous people among whom she lived were devoid of a civilization of their own. But hunger among the Yavapais was relentless for all, and the debilitated Mary suffered.[28]

Occasionally the sisters entertained the thought of escape, but having no idea where they were, or where white settlements were, they had little hope of succeeding. The Yavapais often asked them if they wanted to escape, but in Stratton's words, "The girls soon learned that the expression of any discontent was the signal for new toils, new hardships; so they made a great effort to keep their feelings on the subject to themselves."[29]

In Arizona, captives often caught the attention of men of high social status. In March 1852 five Mohave Indian men and a young woman "not twenty years old" entered the Yavapai village. They had permission from a Mohave chief to buy the Yavapais' captives, should the tribe be willing to barter. The young woman—a chief's daughter, according to Stratton—functioned as the final arbiter of the decision, which she ultimately approved. The Mohaves relocated Olive and Mary three hundred miles west on foot, according to Olive, an eleven-day ordeal, although McGinty has pointed out that her mileage estimate would have placed her in the Sierra Nevadas of east-central California, an unlikely prospect. He speculates instead that the Mohave village was that of Wiltaika, about ninety miles from her Yavapai captors.[30]

While young Mary's debilitated condition predisposed her to a measure of accommodation with her new captors, Olive remained on the alert for them both, determined not to capitulate. Catching sight of the Mohave village (McGinty has speculated that it occupied the present location of Needles, California) strung for twenty miles along the Colorado River under giant cottonwoods, Mary voiced her relief. "Oh, isn't it a beautiful valley? I believe I shall like to live here," she exclaimed. Olive quickly admonished her little sister. "Perhaps you will not want to go back to the whites any more." Mary, rebuffed, quickly modified her position. "These awful savages are enough to make any place ugly, however beautiful, after a little time," she reassured her older sister.[31]

As is the case with her original abductors, scholars have differed on the identification of Olive's new adopted family. McGinty agrees with ethnographer Alfred Kroeber that the girls' adopted father was a Mohave *kohot*, or spiritual leader, known by the Spanish name of Espaniole and a member of the Owits clan.[32]

However, the evidence that Olive lived with the Mohave "head chief" or *pipatahon*, Homoseh Quahote, is seemingly stronger. Although Stratton records the name of the young daughter of the Mohave chief as Topeka, she was more likely known as Malika. The patrilineal Mohaves traditionally referred to all women by the names of their fathers' clans. No sources, however, have noted the existence of a clan designated as *topeka*. The *malika*, on the other hand, was a recognized Mohave clan, signifying a ground squirrel or wood rat. According to Mohave tradition, when the creator Mutavilya named the original Mohave families, he instructed them not to despise these "below-earth things," because they were wise.[33]

Furthermore, the *malika* lineage was that from which the most powerful chiefs of the Mohave traditionally descended. Malika's father could only have been the headman of the Mohaves in the 1850s, Homoseh Quahote, "Orator of the Star." It is unlikely that a Mohave *kohot* would have the authority to travel to Tolkepaya territory for the purpose of purchasing a white woman. Such an unprecedented event could only have occurred with the approval of Homoseh Quahote, who sent this daughter, Malika, in his stead as his arbitrator. And though it is true that a Mohave informant told Kroeber that Olive was sometimes known by the clan name Owits, the word also signifies clouds, winds, and rain. Not insignificantly, Olive herself recalled that the day of her family's murder had been an exceptionally windy day. Even as the family had built a fire on the island in the river, the wind had pushed the waves to shore, threatening the camp. Given Native Americans' penchant for bestowing anecdotal nicknames upon each other, she may have received the name from the Tolkepayas who captured her and who spoke a Yuman dialect similar to the Mojaves, but did not share their clan designations. Most significantly, she would be historically remembered among the Mohaves primarily as "Aliutman," not "Owits."[34]

Although the exact household might remain in doubt, Olive and Mary found their situation with the Mohaves improved. Here, they slept in the same hut as Malika, were given blankets for warmth, and shared such food as was available. They were even given small plots of their own to farm, a sure sign of their presence in the community because Mohave fields traditionally belonged to men, and tillable soil was limited along the Colorado.[35]

But despite the improvements and Malika's good intentions, Olive and Mary still felt like captives. According to Stratton, "The children were greater tyrants than their parents, and took great delight in showing their authority over the girls. Any failure to comply with their commands brought punishment either by whipping or not allowing them food. The parents seemed to enjoy seeing their children order the girls about." Mohave children clearly perceived the white girls to be of lower status than themselves.[36]

Worse, the rugged trek from Yavapai territory had destroyed Mary Ann's health, which she failed to regain in the new environment. Daily, for over a year, Olive watched her little sister slip away. More than anything, Olive confessed, she dreaded living alone among the Mohaves, yet she half-wished for death to relieve her sister of her suffering. Moreover, the drought that parched Arizona in 1853–54 only aggravated Olive's and her sister's desperation. That winter, Mary Ann died among the starving Mohaves, leaving Olive devastated: "When Olive saw she was dead her heart was almost broken with grief and sorrow. She wished, and most earnestly desired, that she too might lie down in death and be forever at rest."[37]

It may have been this occasion, the death of Mary Ann, that led to Olive's receiving the facial tattoos that would capture curious American eyes for the remainder of her life. Artfully pricked with dots and dashes in traditional Mojave style, running both vertically and horizontally across the span of her chin, Olive's tattoos cupped her young face, and would forever hold her hostage to the racism and sexism of nineteenth-century white America.

Some have speculated, and Olive later implied, that she had been marked as a slave, an idea entirely possible among a society that traditionally raided enemy tribes such as the Cocopah for women to enslave. A monogamous, patrilineal tribe, the Mojave men tattooed these women with slave marks and used them as agricultural labor. Since Olive clearly claimed to have worked her own garden, she may well have been marked as a slave. On the other hand, Mojave wives also tattooed their chins, a fact that would eventually complicate Olive's return to "civilization."[38]

Moreover, according to traditional belief, one could not enter into the Land of Death without the distinguishing tattoos of the Mohaves. Even if a child died prior to being tattooed, the soul was denied access to heaven, descending instead into a rat hole for eternity. After the Mohaves witnessed Olive's acute distress at the loss of her sister—particularly when they announced plans to cremate the dead girl according to their tradition—they relented and allowed her to bury Mary, surely a sign of the affection the tribe must have felt for the young captives. Olive may have received her tattoos at this time, if the Mohave feared that she too might die.[39]

Regardless of when Olive received her tattoos, she remained with the Mohaves another two years. By her own admission, "she delighted to steal away alone and enjoy the beautiful scenery that abounded on every side. . . . She even imagined herself happy sometimes." Meanwhile, Olive's brother Lorenzo had not given up hope of finding his sisters. In October 1854 he returned to Los Angeles, the terminus of the southern trail, to inquire from recent arrivals for news of them.[40]

Finally, in late 1855, nearly five years after their being taken by Yavapais, rumors of white women living among the Mohaves reached American ears in California. Significantly, it was said that the women were married to Mohave chiefs. Persons familiar with Lorenzo Oatman notified him in San Francisco, relaying that a carpenter working at Fort Yuma had heard of the women and was doing what he could to rescue them. He had several times searched for the girls, the rumor went, but no one would help him. Lorenzo solicited help from authorities in San Francisco, but it was soon determined that there was no grounds for legal jurisdiction. He next drew up a petition to Congress for aid in rescuing his sisters, and waited impatiently for a reply. Anxious to take action, he joined a party of whites hunting for gold on the Mohave River. Finally, five men from Fort Yuma agreed to help. After searching fruitlessly for several weeks, they disbanded, and Lorenzo retreated to San Bernardino, California, for supplies.[41]

With the increasing presence of whites along the Colorado River, the Mohaves must have feared that Olive's presence among them would be discovered. In mid-February 1856, as Olive sat grinding corn, a Mohave boy informed her that a Yuma Indian runner was on his way from Fort Yuma for the purpose of taking her to "the white settlement." As she believed they had before, Olive suspected the Mohaves were setting her up for disappointment, so she said nothing, fearing to betray any sign of hope. She had heard there were whites at Fort Yuma, but she didn't know where it was, or how far. When a subchief confirmed the report, she could barely contain her excitement.[42]

The Yuma runner, Francisco, arrived in the Mohave village, but the Mohaves hid Olive from him. They argued among themselves and sent Francisco away. He returned the following day with a number of Yumas. After he asked to speak to Olive, the Mohaves produced her. They had painted Olive a "strange color," and warned her to tell the Yumas she was not a white woman.[43]

Despite her overwhelming fear, Olive defied the Mohave chiefs and addressed Francisco in English. He handed her a letter from the commanding officer at Fort Yuma, informing the Mohaves they must release Olive immediately. Reading aloud, Olive embellished the message by informing the chiefs that the officer had threatened to "send a large army to destroy the Yumas and Mohaves and all the Indians they could find" unless she were released.

Reluctantly, the Mohaves relented. When she understood she was to be freed, "Olive could no longer control her feelings and burst into tears of great joy."[44]

As Olive prepared to leave quickly, lest the Mohaves change their minds, she tried to take with her several strings of beads and "other possessions." But "about the time they were ready to start, the chief's son went to her and took them away and all other keepsakes she had learned to prize." After a last visit to Mary's grave, Olive walked away from the Mohaves forever. Malika and Francisco accompanied her to Fort Yuma.[45]

On February 28, 1856, Francisco led the group to the environs of Fort Yuma. Timidly, dressed only in a traditional Mohave reed skirt, and naked from the waist up, Olive hung back in the trees along the river, unwilling to move closer. From among the curious throng at the fort, an officer's wife sent a white woman's dress out to Olive, and at last Francisco escorted the captive to the commanding officer's headquarters. After some negotiation, Malika was presented with four blankets, six pounds of white beads, "some trinkets," and a white horse to compensate her for the loss of her adopted sister.[46]

Meanwhile, as Lorenzo restocked his supplies in San Bernardino, he received a letter from Fort Yuma claiming that the girls had been seen among the Mohaves, and that the chief had offered to sell them to the commanding officer, but the officer had refused to negotiate. Lorenzo departed for Los Angeles again to seek help.[47]

Even as he traveled, the *Los Angeles Star* was reporting that the oldest Oatman girl was known to be alive and living with the Mohaves. The *Alta California* and the

California Chronicle picked up the story. On March 8, the *Star* reported her release at Fort Yuma. Most significantly, it reported—contrary to the earlier rumor—that Olive had "not been made a wife" of the Mohaves, a statement intended to reassure white men that a white woman had not been violated by Indian males. In Los Angeles, Lorenzo visited the editor of the *Star*, who confirmed the paper had officially received notice from the commander at Fort Yuma that the Mohaves had released Olive.[48]

Elated, Lorenzo departed for Fort Yuma, two hundred fifty miles away, on March 10. At Fort Yuma, Olive, now living with a family at the fort, was exhilarated to learn her brother Lorenzo was alive, since she had always presumed him dead. According to her biographer, a constant stream of visitors "rejoiced with her from the trying and cruel captivity which she endured so long," though it is just as probable they were there to see Olive's tattoos. At last, on March 10 Lorenzo reached Fort Yuma. Of the siblings' reunion, their biographer is curt: "A large company of Americans, Indians and Mexicans had gathered at the fort to witness the meeting of the brother and sister, which was a very affecting scene."[49]

Within weeks the *Los Angeles Star* had sent a reporter to Fort Yuma. The resulting story—said to be the most complete account of Olive's ordeal until the publication of Stratton's *The Captivity of the Oatman Girls* two years later—was picked up by most other California presses, including the *Alta California*, the *San Francisco Herald*, the *California Chronicle*, and the *Sacramento Union*. The sensational story, besides demonstrating the "interchange of news" among the nascent presses of the region, proved to be a significant "scoop" for the budding *Los Angeles Star*. Claiming two full front-page columns, the interview with Olive has been described as the first of its kind in Los Angeles journalism, propelling the little press, which would one day be known as the *Los Angeles Times*, to national attention.[50]

Significantly, one historian noted in 1947, the article was "genuine literature" that reflected the "feminine fifties" era of western literature, a period that has since captured scholars' attention. One would write that similar texts from the colonial era had "helped create and perpetuate the climate of suspicion of women who returned from captivity." Like the colonial captivity narratives of an earlier era, the publication of Olive Oatman's story unfairly demonized Native American males, particularly and erroneously Apache males—who had had nothing to do with the girls' capture—and cast suspicion on white women who survived captivity, perpetuating a climate of racist and sexist bigotry among whites in Arizona.[51]

But Olive could only guess at the lifetime of scrutiny that lay before her. She and Lorenzo left Fort Yuma, arriving in the Los Angeles area in April. The *Star* reported that the crowd was pleased with her "lady-like deportment" and "pleasing manners," words that again were constructed to reassure whites that Olive had not been "Indianized." Within months, a paternal uncle from Oregon arrived to claim them. They continued to San Francisco, where Olive granted an interview to the *Bulletin*. While there, Royal B. Stratton interviewed the two surviving Oatmans, filling in gaps the earlier press reports had missed. Two editions of Stratton's *The Captivity of the Oatman Girls* were subsequently published in San Francisco in 1857, with about thirty thousand copies sold in two years. Despite never being lauded as a literary work, and in some instances scorned, the book would be reprinted for decades afterward and devoured by readers.[52]

A biographer has questioned whether Olive would have ever voluntarily left the Mojaves on her own. With her family dead (to the best of her knowledge), Olive might not have left, the theory goes, even if the remoteness of the Mojaves were not a logistical factor. After all, she had "formed bonds with Mojave men and women." She was "bound to the land and the people by ties of familiarity and habit. The Mohave Valley had become home." Furthermore, she was "conscious that [her] Mohave tattoos and [her] background as Indian captive would make it difficult for [her] to gain acceptance in a world in which, after all, [she] no longer had any place."[53]

There can never be an answer to this question, however, only speculation. In reality, "The Oatman tragedy attained the status of legend. Hardly any American who traveled along the Gila River in the half century that followed the attack on the Oatmans was ignorant of the story or failed, at some point in the journey, to reflect on the family's plight." With the growth of the legend, whites' loathing of the indigenous people of Arizona increased as well, "undermining efforts to bring peace to the southwestern desert."[54]

While Stratton clearly wrote *The Captivity of the Oatman Girls* to elicit sympathy for two "innocent" American girls who had "clearly" been "victimized" by Native Americans, the most egregious victimization relayed by the publication of the book was Stratton's insistence on referring to most Native Americans in the story as Apaches, even though the pertinent indigenous groups under discussion were Yavapais and Mohaves, tribes geographically and culturally distinct from Apaches. His broad generalization succeeded in demonizing the Apache people of Arizona for generations to come, as the testimony of James Miller illustrates.

While visiting Oregon, Olive caught the attention of Miller, then a youth, who would twenty years later find himself in Arizona. Miller had an opportunity to observe Olive.

> She was beautiful, a well-formed woman. I was fascinated with her. She had on a dress; the color was brown, pale red and green. Could not keep my eyes off of three marks on her chin. I never saw her smile. Her youth was destroyed. She was old beyond her years. . . . She was selling a book relating the murder of her family and her captivity among Apache Indians. . . . I heard them read about the beastly, inhumane treatment she received at their hands. I grew up hating Apache Indians. Even then, Arizona, the land of mystery, was calling me, and the Gila River, the river of tragedies.[55]

Scholars assert that texts such as *The Captivity of the Oatman Girls* perpetuated the suspicion among whites that Native American males were "naturally inclined to sexual violence." Furthermore, in such a climate, a redeemed captive woman "could hardly have failed to address the question of her sexual history." Olive Oatman would find herself in just such a predicament.[56]

After a short stay in Oregon, Olive and Lorenzo returned to San Francisco and to Royal Stratton. In March 1858 the trio sailed for Stratton's home in Albany, New York, where Olive would have ample opportunity to publicly mend any damage to her reputation caused by lingering suspicion about her years in captivity and, most important, by those troublesome tattoos on her chin.[57]

In April, as Olive sailed the 18,000-mile voyage to New York, the Mohaves attacked a wagon train. After troops from San Francisco descended on them en masse, the Mohaves surrendered to American control, and by 1859 government troops were busy erecting Fort Mohave on the Colorado River. The Arizona that the former captive left behind had changed—but so had Olive Oatman.[58]

One study of captivity in New Mexico found that "women and children who crossed cultures proved remarkably adept at making something of their unfortunate circumstances." Furthermore, another has found that "the behavior required of a woman if she was to survive captivity often required transgressing gender expectation." In order to endure the scrutiny of whites—indeed, to capitalize on it—twenty-one-year-old Olive found herself confronting their curiosity by speaking on the New York lecture circuit, in an era when female abolitionists and suffragettes had only recently asserted a public feminine voice. The rigors engendered by the frontier did in fact "alter responses to the facts of rank and social class."[59]

In city after city (a biographer lists Syracuse, Victor,

East Bloomfield, Little Falls, and Rochester, New York), Olive stood before inquisitive crowds more concerned with impending Civil War than the western territories, but who were curious to see Olive's face. "Ladies and Gentlemen," she would begin, with the ritual disclaimer expected of white women of the era,

> I appear before you at this time, not as a public lecturer but as a narrator of events; events connected with my own personal experience and observation. Neither the position of public speaking nor the facts that I am to relate are in harmony with my own feelings, for my nature intuitively shrinks from both. But I yield to what I conceive to be the opening of providence and the stern voice of duty. . . . The record contains exhibitions of warmest affection, the occasion of the greatest fear, and the display of the most reckless and cruel fate. . . . It leads the anxious inquirer through the woolliest and wildest regions of the "great West."

She then begged her audience, "With these preliminaries I ask the suspension of all criticism while I give you a recital of my wrongs," with no more acknowledgement of the Yavapais' and Mohaves' right to defend their homeland from invaders than Stratton expressed in 1857.[60]

Nightly she relived the massacre of her family, the death of Mary Ann, the years alone among the Mohaves. "Poor Mary, she faded fast—her sad look; her dejected countenance, are before me still," Olive told the somber crowd. As for her tattoos: "Their captives, whether Indians or whites, become slaves. They give them the tribe's slave marks so that in case they desert to any other tribe they can be recognized at once. You perceive I have the marks indelibly placed upon my chin."[61]

But when release from her captors at last seemed imminent, Olive shared,

> Yet I could not leave the wild mountain home without a struggle. Every stream and mountain peak and shaded glen I was as familiar with as with the dooryard of my childhood home. Those grand old solitudes possessed a peculiar charm for me; denied congeniality with human society, communion with nature was sweeter than it otherwise would have been. But there was one spot in that valley to which my heart clung with a mournful affection. It was the grave of my sister. . . . I left my Indian home, leaving them under a great state of excitement.[62]

Olive, evidently—after five years of living with the Mohaves and Yavapais—did not consider them "human society."

She closed her presentation on a compelling note, one crafted to evoke guilt and outrage among white men who had failed to protect American women and children from Indians.

> [My] brother still lives in Illinois, near our childhood home, blessed with a good degree of health, although suffering at times from the effect of the terrible blow inflicted upon him. Francisco, the hero of my release, became a great favorite at the fort and lost his life in consequence of the part he played in my rescue, through jealousy of his own tribe. . . . Allow me to address a

few words to the young ladies in this audience. You have pleasant homes, kind parents, and affectionate brothers and sisters, and are in the enjoyment of the comforts and perhaps the luxuries of Christian society. I once had all these, and having experienced the frightful contrast, the other extreme, I think I now know how to appreciate the word *home*, and had I one I should know how to enjoy it. . . . May God grant that my experience may never be yours.[63]

Not insignificantly, one historian has observed that Olive's postcaptivity lectures omitted mention of her Mormon roots. Her reemergence had coincided with the Mountain Meadows massacre of 1857, where Mormons and Indians had murdered non-Mormon immigrants in Arizona, leading to a Mormon war with federal troops, which raged even as the Mohaves released Olive from captivity. She, or Stratton, may have reconsidered the wisdom of reminding the audience about her Mormon roots.[64]

For virtually the entire duration of the Civil War, 1860 to 1865, Olive shared her story publicly, promoting Stratton's book and using the profits for her and Lorenzo's education, as well as for "church-building." Only after she met and married John B. Fairchild did she retire from public speaking, living out the remainder of her life in Sherman, Texas, where Fairchild founded the City Bank.[65]

After marriage, Olive lived a "reclusive life" with Fairchild. By all accounts, despite her material comfort, she was a pained woman, suffering depression and

physical ailments—headaches, "sore eyes," and nervous-
ness. She often traveled to seek medical help, occasionally staying in a hospital or sanitarium. At one point the
pain in her eyes "confined [her] to her bedroom for nearly
eight weeks." Sometimes she had to seclude herself in a
darkened room. By 1877, due in part to an eerily incor-
rect report, it was even rumored that Olive had died in
an insane asylum, but the story was erroneous.[66]

Although the pair never had children of their own,
they adopted a daughter, Mary, later known as "Mamie"
Fairchild Laing. Furthermore, Olive Oatman did not die
in an insane asylum; she lived until 1903. Ironically, it
was her biographer, Royal Stratton, who almost met that
other unfortunate fate. In 1873 Stratton was confined to
an asylum, where he remained for almost two years. On
January 24, 1875, he died in Massachusetts. A newspaper
reported the cause of death as "disease of the brain, which
perhaps has been present for a long time."[67]

Despite her material comforts, it was remembered that
the "handsome woman always wore a dark veil around
Sherman to hide her secret." Reputedly, her husband,
John Brant Fairchild, had jealously guarded her privacy
throughout the long years of their marriage, forbidding
guests to question her about her captivity, and going so
far as to buy every copy of Stratton's book that he could
find and destroying it. Whatever their secrets, they both
died in the shadow of lingering questions.[68]

But in 1922 an unexpected bit of legal news tickled
the ears of those who still wondered about the meaning
of Olive Oatman's tattoos.[69] On April 30 the *Arizona
Republican* reported, "The opening skirmish of one of the

most interesting legal battles in the history of Mohave County was fought out today in the Oatman Court of Domestic Relations."[70] The paper continued,

> John Oatman, wealthy Mohave Indian, was sued for divorce by his wife, Estelle Oatman. Both plaintiff and defendant live near the Oatman gold camp in which the Mojave chief is heavily invested. . . . [He] claims to be the grandson of Olive Oatman. . . .
>
> In bringing her suit for divorce yesterday, Mrs. Oatman swore, both legally and literally, that her husband had reverted to "dog dinners," that he frightened her on several occasions by putting phosphorous on his body and doing the old tribal ghost dances. . . . Moreover . . . Mrs. Oatman stated that her husband had built a covered pit and filled it with gila monsters, lizards, vinagroons, scorpions, tarantulas and rattlesnakes, that he had pushed her into said pit when she objected to [a certain albino Yavapai girl] swimming the Colorado River to visit her husband.[71]

Estelle's litany of offenses continued.

> Mrs. Oatman further alleged that her husband was addicted to eating locoweed and that during the dementia following this dissipation on one occasion he had tied her into the topmost prickly pear branches of a candelabra cactus and had left her there during a scorching hot afternoon. . . . She further alleged . . . that he had threatened to feed her youngest son . . . to the Mohave sacred rattlesnake, which is fed but once a year.[72]

The *Arizona Republican* wrestled with the meaning of the accusations. By way of explanation, they offered the following: "While using dynamite in working a claim in the Oatman gold mine district in 1916, Mr. Oatman lost part of his scalp, one eye, and also sustained such severe lacerations to the lower jaw that . . . a local dentist . . . found it necessary to extract all of Oatman's teeth."

But Estelle's complaints mounted.

> Her husband had taken delight in removing his false teeth, taking out his glass eye and scalping himself by removing his wig in order to frighten both his own children and the boys and girls of the tribe. . . . Moreover . . . her husband spent most of his money buying glass eyes from a Los Angeles optical goods house. When questioned as to what disposition her husband made of the many glass eyes . . . she replied that he lost most of them at poker and that for some weeks . . . [he] had no eye at all owing to the refusal of the . . . optical goods house to extend his further credit.[73]

Estelle Oatman continued to hurl charges at her husband: during a "recent division of communal property," John had sawed the furniture in half. Estelle conceded, however, that after they reconciled he tried to nail them back together. But John Oatman had some complaints of his own. In his defense,

> Mr. Oatman stated he was tired of married life, that his wife put mud on her hair and fed him nothing but prunes and chile con carne, prunes and tortillas, prunes and enchiladas, prunes and frijoles, and prunes and

tamales. . . . He further alleges that she had broken [an old tribal taboo] by feeding him underdone jackrabbit. . . . Oatman vehemently denied that he had ever tasted intoxicating liquors or that he had made home-brew from cactus.

John Oatman went on to claim that his father-in-law had defrauded him by sprinkling ant powder on his tarantulas, thereby causing them to curl up and die during a critical moment in a wager. As a result of his father-in-law's "underhanded work," he had "wagered away all the money he made in one summer panning gold."[74]

Judge Sheffield took the Oatman divorce case "under advisement," stating he would "hand down a decision next Monday." In the editor's words, "The entire mining camp eagerly awaits the verdict," but there the print trail ends.[75]

While the *Arizona Republican* does not provide definitive proof of Olive's motherhood among the Mohave, it does raise issues regarding the acculturation and assimilation of captives in Arizona. Marriage and parenthood generally grafted white captives into the social matrix of the host tribe. These ties of affection served to bind non-Indian captives to indigenous mates in marriage, and to mixed-blood children through childbirth. Were the "possessions" Olive had attempted to take as she left the Mohave village her children? Was the chief's son who prevented her from taking her "possessions" also her husband? Was he the "subchief" who had confirmed to her that the whites were coming to take her to Fort Yuma? Did Olive leave children and a mate among the

Mohaves, willingly or unwillingly? Was the lifetime of depression she experienced postcaptivity related to the man and children she seemingly left behind?

For all Olive's insistence to the contrary, stories of her abandoned children persisted in the Mohave County area long after her death, and among the Mohave people around Needles, California, as well, where Olive had spent her captive years. As to whether she married a chief's son, as was believed by locals, and had willingly or unwillingly left children behind (the stories vary), only Olive and the Mohaves would ever know for certain. The *Arizona Republican* article reveals but a single piece of evidence, found in the first paragraph: "Both plaintiff and defendant live near the Oatman gold camp in which *the Mohave chief* is heavily invested." Given the Mohaves' system of hereditary chiefdom, John may well have been the person he claimed to be, the grandson of Homoseh Quahote's son and the captive Olive Oatman.[76]

Stratton's *Captivity of the Oatman Girls* was clearly designed to appeal to whites' sense of victimization, an attempt to justify the appropriation of Native American homelands by expansionists who viewed themselves as racially and culturally superior to their opponents. But traumatic as the Oatman ordeal was, and for all its deleterious effects upon the Apaches, the least culpable victims of Olive Oatman's life were the motherless Mohave children she left behind. Caught between a patrilineal Mohave husband who would not—could not—allow Olive to take her children with her, and a patriarchal Anglo society that could never accept Olive were she accompanied by native children, their mother had no choice but to return to white society without them, or forever relinquish hope of rescue. After all, considering the effort it had taken whites to locate her and to communicate with the Mohave village, Olive could hardly have hoped for such assistance again should she refuse the present offer. Abandoned by their mother, the mixed-blood children Olive Oatman left behind would face a rapidly changing world on the basis of Mohave terms alone, without the circumstantial mitigation their intermarried mother may have provided.

Ironically, the Mohaves historically avoided blame in the Oatman affair by pointing out that it was not they, but the Yavapais, who had murdered the Oatman family, and that in trading for possession of Olive and Mary Ann, they had rescued the girls from their harsh life with the Yavapais. Only fear of misdirected reprisal from whites, the Mohaves would claim, prevented them from returning her to the Americans earlier. Olive reinforced this view. According to a Mohave who was present at her arrival at Fort Yuma, she informed the interrogating officer there that following her captivity among the Yavapais, "Those Mohave Indians heard about us, came, took us away and kept us both. My sister died and I was alone, but they treated me well. There was not much to eat, but I helped them, and got used to it, and got along with them. They saved my life."[77]

A cautionary tale, a tale of survival, a call to arms against Apaches, and a record of white bias: Olive Oatman's story encompasses all these elements and more—orphanage, violence, revenge, and scars. But captivity posed more then an immediate physical threat to whites,

Indians, and Mexican Americans in the territorial era, for it embodied a broader-reaching array of social themes as well. Adoption, childlessness, intermarriage, biracial children, and acculturation accompanied captivity. Race and racial constructions, guilt and blame, rescues, non-rescues, and self-rescues posed issues of their own, while social reintegration, gendered power relations, and marriage partners were another hidden facet of captivity, along with concerns regarding heredity and environment. Ultimately, Olive Oatman's ordeal would curiously embody and presage the recurrent features of captivity in territorial Arizona.

2

1855–1861

As in the case of Olive Oatman, the national press would bring the dramatic details of Larcena Pennington's capture by Indians to the public's attention. But unlike Olive, Larcena had no entrepreneur such as Royal Stratton to catapult her riveting tale into a lucrative commercial enterprise. Too, Feliz Tellez's captivity—caught in an outrageous tale of army mismanagement, and in the crosshairs of Apache hatred of Mexicans—shot into the national spotlight, only to fade in the public mind with the advent of the Civil War.

Public interest in Mercedes Sais—captured with Larcena—also paled in the uproar over Larcena's astounding return to Tucson, where whites and the press were less concerned over the fate of a Mexican American child than with that of a white woman who had defied death. Too, the story of Nah-thle-tla, a young Chiricahua woman captured in Arizona Territory but enslaved by Mexicans, lived only in Apache oral tradition until published by her son, Jason Betzinez, decades later. But whether obscure or notorious, these unique experiences testify to the pervasive culture of captivity that dominated the era.

During the years of Olive Oatman's absence (which, from the standpoint of the Mohaves, was no absence at all), white territorialization proceeded. Despite the resistance of Native Americans, both Northern and Southern whites were united by a desire to incorporate the region. Arizona's indigenous people, on the other hand, kept anxious watch over the invaders, determined to retain possession of their homelands.[1]

The passage of some twenty thousand immigrants along the Gila Trail by 1850 had prompted the positioning of a military garrison in Quechan, or Yuma Indian territory, on the California side of the Colorado River. The same year, exploration for a northern route across Arizona penetrated Navajo country, precipitating the establishment of Fort Defiance in 1851, the first U.S. military post on Arizona soil. In 1852, while Olive and Mary Ann lived with the Yavapais, the arrival of steamships on the lower Colorado foreshadowed Fort Yuma's role as a pivotal U.S. military depot.[2]

Intrusive miners forged capillary excursions off the Gila trail, invading Yavapai and Western Apache lands. Scattered parties scoured the Colorado and Gila rivers for gold, while south of the Gila, copper deposits lured whites into Tohono O'odham country. Far to the north, surveyors explored the territory between the Zuni pueblos and the Colorado River.[3]

Expansionists proposed the Gadsden Purchase in late 1853 to acquire the land, including Tucson, below the Gila River. Heated controversy over the Kansas-Nebraska Act and the extension of slavery into the territories hindered any meaningful national discussion of the purchase, however, as opponents opposed slavery in the Southwest. At last, Congress ratified the treaty in July 1854, as Olive learned to live among the Mohaves without her sister. The United States now held—on paper—all of present-day Arizona. Still, 250 miles separated Tucson from Santa Fe on the east, and even more—350 miles—from the nearest California settlements in the west.[4]

With the passage of the Gadsden Purchase Treaty, exploration and expansion south of the Gila quickened. Sylvester Mowry worked the lucrative old Spanish Patagonia mine in Chiricahua territory, while in eastern New Mexico, American army units pressed into Warm Springs and Mimbres Apache territory, establishing Fort Stanton, near modern-day Riudoso, in 1855.[5]

Under the pressure of white expansion, Native Americans fought back. The U.S. Indian agent in Santa Fe—although disadvantaged by the abrasive presence of the military—attempted to reach accords with the Apaches led by Mangas Colorado, Cochise, and a young Bedonkohe shaman and warrior known as Geronimo, agreements that often fell apart due to the failure of whites to uphold them.[6]

The agent held a conference with Mangas Coloradas in July 1852, outlining through interpreters the parameters of the Treaty of Guadalupe Hidalgo: the transfer of title of the Apache homeland from Mexico to the United States; the U.S. obligation to safeguard American settlers; the need for roads and military posts in Apache territory. Adding to the Apaches' consternation, the agent informed them of the United States' newly acquired responsibility to prohibit Indians from raiding in Mexico and, even more troubling, from taking Mexican captives. The Apaches could only reluctantly acknowledge the provisions; preventing Mexicans from settling Chiricahua territory had always been integral to Chiricahua autonomy, and the trading and adoption of captives had been central to Apache economy and social organization since earliest encounters with the Spanish in the 1600s.[7]

The tenuous treaty fell apart after the winter of 1853–54, as Mary Ann Oatman starved to death among the Mojaves. Just as the Chiricahuas had feared, Mexicans attacked Apaches on U.S. soil, killing one of Geronimo's two wives and a child; they took captive four female relatives of his band as well. Years later these women would escape from slavery in Sonora and rejoin their people, but in 1855 they had simply vanished. One Chiricahua woman, Nah-thle-tla, who would afterward become the mother of author Jason Betzinez, shared her captivity story with her son.

> [She said] that during the march toward Chihuahua, the Mexican commander . . . was kind to most of his prisoners. He was a bit harsh with one Indian woman who boasted that her husband was one of the fighters who had made the recent raid to Namiquipa. The general forced this woman to walk all the way to Casas Grandes, a distance of a hundred miles, instead of riding a horse or a mule like the other captives. He didn't realize that such a hike was no hardship to an Apache woman.

In Mexico, as in U.S. territory, the objectives of colonists and military officials did not always agree; a desire for revenge competed with military objectives: "[At Namiquipa] . . . the inhabitants, still in a fury over the recent Indian attack, urged that the general turn over to them his prisoners to be slaughtered. The commander refused, so as the column pulled out, the Mexican women ran alongside the vehicles, screaming curses and throwing rocks."

But the Mexican officer's motives were not born of benevolence, for as Nah-thle-tla told her son, when the command arrived in Chihuahua, his "kindness" turned to something else. "At Chihuahua the captives, who had been well treated, were turned over to various Mexican families in the city. Nah-thle-tla's children were taken from her and she never saw them again. But on the whole, the captives were treated kindly, even being taken on sightseeing walks through the town," an activity designed to announce the presence of indigenous slaves for sale in the city and to impress the captives with the "progress" of Mexican "civilization."

More than a testament to Nah-thle-tla's personal strength, her account also illuminates the expansive Mexican slave-trade network that continued to stretch from Chihuahua to Santa Fe even after the Gadsden Purchase. As often happened to the Mexicans' indigenous captives, Nah-thle-tla's captors groomed her for a life of domestic servitude before retailing her to the buyers' market. "After several months spent in working as a slave for a Mexican family, Nah-thle-tla was sold to a wealthy Mexican from Santa Fe, New Mexico. She and another young woman were loaded into an oxcart for the long journey north to her owner's home. . . . Tied to a pole at the front of the cart trotted a large, mean dog to assist in preventing the escape of the prisoners."

Once in Santa Fe, Nah-thle-tla bided her time, awaiting an opportunity to escape. "The journey was continued to Santa Fe. . . . Nah-thle-tla did her best to be a good houseworker. . . . The whole family were kind to her. . . . [One time] the young people of the household held a big dance which lasted nearly the whole night. The second night they slept so soundly that Nah-thle-tla saw a chance to escape . . . [, and] she climbed through a window."

Nah-thle-tla eventually reunited with Loco's band and her family. "During this amazing flight my mother had covered at least two hundred and fifty miles mostly on foot and in very rugged country," Betzinez remembered. In Arizona white captives and Mexican Americans could take hope that military forces would follow their trail, but Nah-thle-tla would not be the first, nor the last, indigenous captive who would have to rely on her own resourcefulness to rescue herself.[8]

In the summer following the deaths of his wife and child and the capture of his relatives, Geronimo organized a war party that successfully carried out the first attack on an American pack train, while Olive Oatman learned to plaster her hair with mud and weave Mohave skirts from grass. Encouraged by his success, Geronimo led repeated raids on Americans over the next several years.[9]

By the spring of 1855, U.S. troops in New Mexico Territory numbered over a thousand. Tensions between Anglo-Americans and Apaches increased when the whites discovered a permanent spring in Chiricahua territory. Apache Pass, as whites called it, remained a focal point of contested ground until the establishment of Fort Bowie there in 1862.[10]

The Indian Bureau continued to assert pressure on the Apaches. In 1855 it appointed Dr. Michel Steck as Indian agent in New Mexico. Steck and department commander General Carlton disagreed on Indian policy (Carleton wanted a return to captive Indian servitude, while Steck worked for peace treaties), and the Anglo-American populace soon found itself polarized, emphasizing the lack of agreement among white Arizonans regarding "the Indian problem."[11]

Steck held a council with Warm Springs and Mimbrenos Apaches at Fort Thorn on the Rio Grande, resulting in the Chiricahuas ceding access to fifteen thousand square miles of homeland. Expecting the United States to honor a reservation on the remainder of their land, Congress's refusal to ratify the treaty (which would have placed mineral lands in Indian control) embittered the Apaches and left Steck short on credibility.[12]

Territorialization had proceeded at the cost of Native Americans' homelands during the years of Olive's captivity, but the Apaches' defensive war was far from over. Even while Olive Oatman bewitched little Jimmy Miller in Oregon in 1857, another young white woman was about to meet her own destiny on the Gila Trail. Like Olive, Larcena Pennington was the daughter of a restless man. Her father, Elias Green Pennington, had been born in Virginia in 1809 to a Valley Forge hero, Elijah Pennington. For his service Elijah received land in Virginia, where he made his wealth growing tobacco.[13]

Elijah held his eight children—of whom Larcena's

father, Elias, was among the eldest—to a strict rite of passage. As each son came of age, he was given a rifle, a dog, a horse, a saddle, and $2,100 in silver and was informed he no longer had a home, but must go out into the world and make one. As each daughter decided to marry, she was given the same and warned that she should no longer consider her father's home her own. Pennington descendants were proud of claiming that out of the sixteen marriages, not one ended in separation or divorce.[14]

Elias married Julia Ann Hood, and the pair settled on a South Carolina farm before moving to the Nashville. In Tennessee, Elias's first four children were born, including Larcena in 1837, but the family moved to Fannin County, Texas, in 1839, where Julia bore him eight more children before dying of malaria in September 1855.[15]

In the spring of 1857, Elias and his children left for California on the Gila Trail. But the three ox-driven wagons lumbering into newly established Fort Buchanan in June carried a very ill Larcena, who was suffering with "chills and fevers." Availing themselves of the post surgeon, the family camped while Larcena recuperated. When Apaches ran off the family's oxen, Elias had no choice but to stay put.[16]

The region offered the solitude from intrusive whites that Pennington craved, but the environs of the fort were not ideal for family life. Situated twenty-five miles east of Tubac, Major Enoch Steen commanded the remote outpost, manned with four companies of the First Dragoons. Nearby, Paddy Graydon's Boundary Hotel and saloon catered to the needs of the soldiers, as well as a handful of ranchers who had accompanied the dragoons from Santa Fe. Larcena, now twenty years old, would eventually choose her first husband from among Paddy Graydon's patrons.[17]

Despite their precarious circumstances in Chiricahua territory, the Penningtons stayed. Elias and his oldest child, James, cut wild hay to sell to the post and built the family a shelter, while the oldest daughters tended to the needs of the youngest children and performed domestic chores. But in 1859 Jack met the patrons of Paddy Graydon's bar.[18]

He befriended the Felix Ake family, early settlers on the Sonoita. The Akes and their hired man, John Hempstead Page, had rushed east from California in the spring of 1857, hoping to join the Crabb filibustering expedition, which intended to establish an unauthorized American colony in Sonora. But by the time the Akes reached Fort Buchanan, Mexicans had killed all but one member of the Crabb expedition. Infuriated, the Akes and company, including Jack Pennington, organized a posse, roaming the border for Mexicans.[19]

They found them at a mescal distillery in the spring of 1859. Riding camp to camp, the Ake posse gunned down three Mexicans and a Yaqui Indian. The citizens in the area protested the vigilante action, and it wasn't long until most of the gunmen were apprehended. Bill Ake escaped to California, but Jack was compelled to testify against five of the conspirators. Because of his age, charges were dropped against him, but the others paid an aggregate fine of $900 and were released.[20]

Meanwhile, at the Pennington house, Larcena's oldest

sister Caroline married Charles Burr, most memorable for a duel fought with the volatile Paddy Graydon. After Caroline's marriage, "Old Pennington," as Elias was known, moved the family to Calabasas, on the upper Santa Cruz River near the Mexican border. After working for a time with the newly formed Butterfield Overland Mail—which linked Tucson to El Paso and Los Angeles—Jack rejoined his family at Calabasas. Larcena, however, married John Hempstead Page.[21]

By December 1859 Page was working for government contractor William Kirkland, felling lumber south of Tucson in the Santa Rita Mountains. According to Kirkland, after Larcena married Page, her husband departed for the Santa Rita Mountains in Chiricahua Apache territory.[22]

Soon, Page requested that Larcena move fifteen miles closer, to the Canoa ranch on the Santa Cruz River south of Tucson. There, a Mrs. Heath ran a station for travelers and the mail. William Kirkland objected to the idea, as the women were particularly vulnerable to Apache attacks. Moreover, in Tucson, Larcena had been tutoring a young Mexican girl, Mercedes Sais Quiroz, the ward of William Kirkland. "I regarded the move [to Canoa] as an unwise one on account of the Indian situation, and was particularly sorry because it would deprive little Mercedes Quiroz . . . of the advantage of her tutor. Mercedes was a bright young girl and I had been glad to have her taught something by Mrs. Page," Kirkland recalled.[23]

Against Kirkland's advice, Page insisted that Larcena move to Canoa. Shortly, he arrived at Canoa to take Larcena to the lumber camp in Madera Canyon, unaware that Mercedes was now in Larcena's care. Said Kirkland, "Finally, against my will and my better judgment, I consented for Mercedes to accompany Mrs. Page, so anxious was I that she should secure the benefit of Mrs. Page's instruction."[24]

They arrived at the camp on the morning of March 16, 1860. When Page walked away to retrieve some tools, the only other man in camp went to "look for a deer," leaving Larcena and Mercedes alone. Many years later, Larcena's daughter Georgie would describe what happened next, her detail attesting to the vibrance of the tale in her family's oral tradition:"[Page] had been gone a half hour perhaps, when five Apaches came into the camp. Mamma was sitting down, after having knocked down some oak balls for the little Mexican girl who had accompanied her. . . . The little dog jumped up and down and began to bark and Mamma scolded him and told him to lie down; just then the child screamed and started to run to Mamma, but the Indians caught her."[25]

Unlike Olive Oatman, who had not had time to react to her captors, Larcena responded instantly: "Mamma sprang to the bed for the pistol but as soon as she took it in her hands one of the Indians snatched it away from her, and when she started to run they caught her. They then told her, by signs and in Mexican, that they had just killed Mr. Page. . . . Mamma began to scream and one of the Indians put his lance to her breast and said if she did not hush he would kill her."

The Apaches made clear their feelings about the presence of white men, and white men's women, in their territory. "They then cut open the flour sacks, and poured the flour out on the ground, and destroyed the rest of the provisions. They took the feather bed up on a little knoll and scattered the feathers on the ground. Mamma again began to scream and they again threatened her with the lance."

Both Olive and Larcena were in charge of young girls at the time of their captivity. Like Olive and Mary Ann, Larcena and Mercedes were hustled along a footpath, their captors unsure of how quickly white men would follow.

They started along the side of the mountain, traveling almost north. Mamma told the child, Mercedes, to tear off pieces of her apron and drop them along the way as she was doing and to then bend the twigs from the trees so that their pursuers could follow them. One old Indian took Mercedes and went on ahead, while another returned to see if they were being followed. He came back and said that he could see the white men coming, and then they hurried them dreadfully. As they went up a very narrow ridge of the mountain with a steep slope one side they told Mamma to take off her waist and heavy skirt.

As had been the case with Olive's Yavapai captors, the Apaches used the situation to protest the whites' unwelcome intrusion into their territory.

They then retold her that lots of their people had been killed by her people. . . . They had told them this before during a short rest they had taken, and one of the Indians hid behind a bush and threw rock and made believe he was shooting white people. Mamma thinks they were trying to make her understand that they intended killing her.

Larcena's response to her captors differed markedly from Olive's, however, assuring her role as a "heroine" to the Tucsonans she returned to, rather than as a tragic victim, as Olive had been remembered by all who knew her.

When she had taken off her waist and skirt, which they said were too heavy and impeded her progress, they motioned to her to go on. She turned and started and then felt the first lance in her back; she sprang forward and fell down the side of the hill. As she rolled they followed and pierced her back each time she turned, and struck her with rocks. At last she struck against a big pine tree and one of the Indians struck her in the head with a rock, rendering her insensible. She was pierced by fifteen or sixteen lances, once in the head, and was struck with seven rocks as the marks afterwards showed. They then dragged her around the tree and removing her shoes, left her there.

Larcena then demonstrated the difference in fortitude between herself—a seasoned young woman who had already proved her ability to survive in Indian territory, the daughter of a stubborn "mountaineer" father—and Olive, a girl from the Midwest with no prior exposure to indigenous people, except possibly the militarily defeated and emotionally demoralized eastern Indians with whom her father had reputedly exhibited judicious behavior, and was reputedly reluctant to murder. "When Mamma recovered consciousness three days later," her daughter continued,

> she ate a little snow, and pulled the clots of blood from her head and put snow on it; she then rested, then ate some more snow and began to crawl down the mountainside, for she was too weak from loss of blood to attempt to stand. After getting on the level ground at the foot of the ridge she went to sleep and slept until morning. She awoke at sunrise and as the sun was just setting when she struck down she knew which direction to go. She kept on, eating wild onions and garlic, but naturally she almost starved to death. . . . Once she came to a bear's nest made of straw and wanted to sleep there because it was soft but was afraid to do so, so crawled on, digging a little hole to crouch in at night, for her arms and shoulders were bare and while the sun was hot the nights were very cold.
>
> She climbed up over the foot of the long ridges that ran down on the level to keep from going around them. Her feet were filled with small stones, her arms and shoulders blistered by the sun and her head a mass of clotted blood. . . . She was high on a ridge when she saw some men down in the valley with an ox team. She called to them and waved her petticoat but could not make them hear and they did not look up. They hitched up and drove off but left their fire burning. It took two days for her to get down off the ridge; there was a little fire there yet, so she picked up a stick afire at one end and crawled to the camp and built a

fire where she had cooked breakfast the morning of her capture.

She scraped up some of the flour left, and tearing a piece of cloth from her skirt, put the flour on it and crawled down to the creek and mixed the flour in a little pat of dough, then she got back to the fire and cooked and ate it and some of the coffee that was yet on the ground. Then she lay down and slept until morning. She then decided to go up to the lumber camp for she knew she could go nowhere else for lack of water. She could walk a little where the road was soft, so she went on to the camp.[26]

It would take Larcena two weeks to reappear in the lumber camp; her husband, meanwhile, searched for her. Alerted to his wife's abduction upon returning to the camp, Page had commandeered a horse and raced for Canoa, where his mount fell dead from exhaustion. Other men in the vicinity "took the trail of the Indians," while an additional runner was dispatched to Fort Buchanan, where a detachment mounted up under Captain Richard Ewell. Before daylight the civilian posse had rendezvoused with Ewell and his men on Cienega Creek, thirty-five miles southeast of Tucson.

Ewell presumed the captors to be Pinal Apaches whose objective in taking the women was to trade them for twenty Pinals recently captured in a skirmish and being held by Ewell at Fort Buchanan. He brought into the field with him the men among these prisoners and compelled them to serve as trailers on the search. Mercedes, now alone with her captors, shed bits of her clothing along the trail, and took care to leave occasional footprints trailside, knowing a search party would follow.[27]

The searchers scoured the Santa Rita range to no avail, and then the Catalina Mountains north of Tucson. From there Ewell sent out a Pinal Apache, "mounted on a cavalry horse, giving him a certain length of time in which to return," a surety because of the remaining Pinal prisoners. Captain Ewell sent with him "two fine blankets," supplied by William Kirkland, the guardian of Mercedes Sais.[28]

Within days the Pinal messenger returned, claiming that not Pinals, but Tonto Apaches, had possession of Mercedes, and that Larcena had been killed. Furthermore, if the Fort Buchanan hostages were released, and two wagonloads of goods supplied to the Tontos, that tribe would release Mercedes. The whites begrudged the Apaches their demands, but according to William Kirkland, "There was no hesitating about acceding to the Indians' terms, one-sided though they were, and every effort was immediately put forth to carry the agreement into effect."[29]

John Page hastened to Tucson to notify William Kirkland, who was to ride to Fort Buchanan for the remaining Pinal prisoners and deliver them to Ewell's camp. On his way to Fort Buchanan, Kirkland stopped at Canoa, where he learned that Larcena had survived her captivity. A runner left for Tucson to notify Page. By morning Page arrived at Canoa, then rode on to the lumber camp where his wife lay recovering.[30]

Captain Ewell, meanwhile, proceeded with the ransom of Mercedes Sais. According to Kirkland, who had delivered the Pinal noncombatants and was present, the bank of the San Pedro River "was literally swarming with Indians. I never saw so many in my life. A number of chiefs were receiving their prisoners and the provisions, having delivered Mercedes to Captain Ewell. Two of the chiefs wore the blankets I had sent her by the scout. . . . The first thing Mercedes said, as I rode up to her, was that she was hungry, having been given almost nothing to eat. *Otherwise she has been treated well*," Kirkland reassured his readers (italics mine). Captain Ewell "had the pleasure of handing the child to her friends. She is quite intelligent and her account fully corroborates that the robbery was made by the Tontos. Many circumstances not necessary to mention, places this matter beyond a doubt."[31]

Mercedes informed her rescuers that after their captors had thrown Larcena from the precipice, the group had moved on only a little farther before camping. Mercedes "could hear [Mrs. Page] crying during the night." But the Tontos had treated Mercedes kindly, she reported, "carrying her on their heads." They were as hungry as their captive. Once, she had to eat a rat's head, at other times roots or herbs. Ewell's report also indicated that the harsh treatment of Larcena Pennington could be attributed to the fact that "a Ranger party of volunteers had just been driven from their country, thereby exciting the Indians," an observation that did nothing to appease the rage of whites and Mexicans in southern Arizona.[32]

When the returning party descended the Catalinas and arrived at the Rillito creek, Kirkland borrowed a fast horse from Ewell and, with Mercedes behind him, rode to Tucson ahead of the command. On the way they met Mercedes's uncle, Francisco Sais, who rode back to Tucson to "alert the Mexican population." Consequently, said Kirkwell, "When I reached the Pueblo, I was intercepted by large numbers of them singing and praising Santa Maria. They stopped me and wanted Mercedes, but I refused to give her up, saying that I proposed to take her to her mother. Their insistence came near causing trouble, for my horse was spirited, and when an aunt of Mercedes grabbed her, the animal commenced to buck. This stampeded them, and I rode on into town with the girl."[33]

Like the ransom of Olive Oatman, Mercedes's liberation was bought at the price of nervous diplomatic negotiations, at a time when Native Americans and the sparsely stationed U.S. troops maintained a tenuous balance of power in Arizona. It was a balance of power that would ultimately tip in the whites' favor.

Whereas whites had eagerly anticipated Olive Oatman's arrival at Fort Yuma, and Mexican Americans gathered excitedly for sight of Mercedes Sais, Larcena's reappearance in the lumber camp defied all presumption.

> One of the men named Smith saw her coming and ran into camp for his gun. He and the others then came running out and she called to them that she was Mrs. Page. Smith said he knew better, but came up to her with the others, declaring all the while that she was a spirit. The other men were not so frightened and one of them picked her up and carried her into camp, where they got dinner for her, bathed her feet, and made her

go to bed, while a colored woman there brought in all her clean clothing and insisted on her putting it on. When she was comfortable, they sent the courier into town.[34]

As if the story were not fantastical enough, one source claims that the "colored woman" who tended to Larcena's wounds was commonly known as "Virgin Mary," yet another reason for Larcena's captivity to be "canonized" in white Arizona's lore.

Tucsonans celebrated Larcena's triumphant return. According to Larcena, she "beat" Mercedes back into town on April 17, 1860. Within weeks the national press had heard of her story and descended on Tucson; Mercedes's experience shrank in the shadow of Larcena's ordeal. Larcena, however, recounted her captivity in detail to reporters. The press could not get enough; the story appeared in papers around the nation, further galvanizing whites' fear and loathing of the Apaches of Arizona.[35]

In a curious parallel with Olive Oatman, Larcena and Mercedes's capture also succeeded in historically vilifying the wrong tribe. Whereas Ewell's report clearly held the Tonto Apaches responsible, Tucsonans would historically remember only that the Pinal Apaches had played a role in the affair. Complicating identities even more, Larcena would ultimately claim that Eskiminzin, headman of the Aravaipa Apaches, had been her captor. White and Mexican American settlers of southern Arizona would continue to hold the Aravaipa and Pinal Apaches accountable for multiple raids and attacks in the region, justified or not, for another decade. Their resentment would culminate in the infamous Camp Grant massacre of 1871.

The series of raids carried out by the Apaches in the Sonoita Creek valley against American settlers from 1859 through the early years of the Civil War were neither random nor inadvertent. Instead, they reflected the Western Apaches' historic struggle for access to Sonora.[36]

Because their territory bordered northwestern Chihuahua and northeastern Sonora, the Chiricahuas had little need to risk warriors in attacks on the Sonoita or Santa Cruz valleys, except perhaps for occasional stock raids. Furthermore, Cochise's attention was drawn increasingly to Anglo intrusion on his northern border. Although Chiricahua women supplied hay and wood at Apache Pass for the Butterfield Overland Mail, which by late 1858 maintained two hundred stations strung out between St. Louis and San Francisco, of these, five transected Cochise's territory without his permission.[37]

As a strong man of the Chiricahuas, and with white Americans virtually spanning the northern and western borders of his homeland, Cochise, as well as other Chiricahua headmen, had repeatedly explained to white officials that their people were not at war with Americans. They were interested only in raiding Mexican villages and in preventing Mexicans from settling in Chiricahua territory, so long as whites agreed to keep to their wagon roads. Furthermore, American officials implicitly supported Cochise's position, provided the Chiricahuas would refrain from attacking whites. According to one historian, "As long as the Indians kept the peace in Arizona and New Mexico, citizens, military officers, and government agencies were content."[38]

On the other hand, the Western Apaches, far north of

the border, had long used the Sonoita Valley to access Mexico. A region once occupied by Sobaipuris under the leadership of Chief Coro, it began to fall to Apaches in 1705, when Coro at last converted to Catholicism. No longer armed with weapons, but with hoes and shovels, the baptized agriculturalists increasingly found themselves unable to withstand repeated Apache attacks, and began retreating to Santa Maria Suamca, a Jesuit mission on the headwaters of the Santa Cruz River. Apaches continued to assault the Sobaipuris until 1762, when the last of them abandoned their ancient villages and congregated at the missions at San Xavier or Santa Maria Suamca, later known as Santa Cruz.[39]

With the capitulation of their Sobaipuri warrior-cousins, the Tohono O'odhams' buffer against the Apaches also eroded. The abandonment of the Sobaipuri villages cleared the way for Western Apaches, who now had virtually unimpeded access to northern Sonora and eastern Papagueria through a narrow geographic corridor that wound its way between the Chiricahua territory on the east, and that of the O'odham on the west. Throughout the following decades, Apaches attacked Santa Maria Suamca and San Xavier relentlessly, eager to bear down on their vulnerable enemies. The Western Apache memoirs recorded by Grenville Goodwin in the 1930s contain many accounts of Western Apache scouts who as men had fought for the U.S. Army, but who had served their warrior apprenticeships under fathers, uncles, and grandfathers while fighting in Sonora. The most skilled and respected of these warriors would form the pool of chiefs and influential clan heads who would eventually come to accommodation with the army. When General Crook appeared in the heart of Western Apache territory in the 1870s, these warriors and their former apprentices would enlist as army scouts, thereby continuing their traditional raids into Mexico, but under the auspices of the United States.[40]

But in 1857 the arrival of the First Dragoons in the Sonoita Valley had once again impeded Western Apache access to Sonora. Furthermore, American colonists such as Elias Pennington and a dozen others had settled along the banks of the creek, bolstering the white presence in the area. The Western Apaches renewed their fight for access to the Sonoita.[41]

In January 1861 (as Olive Oatman toured the east and Larcena, expecting her first child, kept house for John Page) the Pinal Apaches raided the Sonoita Valley. But no one—Mexican, white, or Apache—could foresee the crucial turn of events the attack would set into motion.

Like Elias Pennington, John Ward had been among the earliest whites to colonize the Sonoita Creek valley. On January 27, Apaches assailed the Ward ranch—which in addition to the family home, livestock, and farming implements also housed several Anglo-American laborers and a blacksmith shop—while Ward was absent on business. In addition to making off with the livestock, the Pinals captured Ward's young stepson, Feliz Tellez Martinez, the son of Ward's common-law wife, Maria de Jesus Martinez, and a former husband, Santiago Tellez, killed by Apaches in 1858. Jesusa, as she was known, had moved to Tubac after Tellez's death, where she met Ward, an Irish frontiersman who had probably traveled with the First Dragoons from Santa Fe, although the record is unclear. By January 1861 Jesusa had borne Ward at least three children.[42]

In 1934 Santiago Ward—Feliz Tellez's half-brother—gave the Arizona Historical Society a brief account of his brother's capture: "When he was about twelve years old and we were living at Sonoita he was stolen by Apaches and never came back. A posse of men went after the Indians but they divided into three groups. One group took my brother, a second took the cattle they had stolen from the ranch and elsewhere and the other group just kept foraging. Of course, they decoyed the men into taking the wrong trail."[43]

Runners headed for Fort Buchanan to alert post commander Lt. Col. Pitcairn Morrison to the situation, while a citizens' posse pursued the Apache raiders. As Santiago Ward remembered, the Apaches had split up, heading north to San Carlos territory with the livestock and Feliz Tellez, and eastward into Chiricahua territory, deliberately leaving signs in their wake to lure the whites who were sure to follow.[44]

George Bascom, the inexperienced second lieutenant at the head of the detachment sent from Fort Buchanan by Lieutenant Colonel Morrison, mistakenly believed reports that Chiricahua Apaches had raided the Ward ranch. He summoned Cochise to Apache Pass to demand the return of the boy and livestock. Just as the Pinals had served as intermediaries when Tontos captured Larcena Pennington Page and Mercedes Sais Quiroz, Cochise explained that he had no knowledge of the raid, but he volunteered to send runners out to ascertain the raiders and the whereabouts of the boy. Bascom agreed, on condition that members of Cochise's family remain as surety of the chief's return, much as Capt. Enoch Steen had held his Pinal prisoners in reserve a year earlier during the ransom of Mercedes Quiroz. But unlike the Pinals, the Chiricahuas did not locate the raiders. Cochise and his men returned in three days, informing Bascom that they were unable to find the boy. Convinced the chief was lying, Bascom attempted to take him into custody.[45]

Cochise deftly cut his way out of Bascom's tent and fled, leaving unfortunate family members behind. Enraged that his word had been doubted—and, worst of all, over a Mexican child—Cochise and the Chiricahuas attacked a wagon train, massacring white teamsters, one of whom was burned alive. In retaliation, Bascom hanged Cochise's family members. Cochise, the powerful leader of a culture that maintained its social equilibrium in part through a system of blood revenge, declared war on Americans in Arizona. Soon the press learned of the affair; western-ers called for more military protection, while outraged easterners decried Bascom's bungled mission.[46]

Embittered by the false accusations against them, the Chiricahuas kept the event alive in their oral tradition. "One of those who escaped was Cochise. Evidently he reacted more quickly than the others for he sprang to, making good his escape. This affair became known to the Apaches as 'Cut Through the Tent.' . . . I have heard my parents as well as others discuss it many times," wrote Jason Betzinez, the cousin of Geronimo and son of Nah-thle-tla. "For ten years Cochise exacted revenge," James Kaywaykla told the historian Eve Ball. Another historian cites Cochise reviling the incident to American authorities at least five times between 1861 and his death in 1874.[47]

Arizonans, and later, Arizona historians, would argue over the culpability of events in the Bascom affair, as they came to call it, for the next century and more, debating whether Bascom or Cochise was to blame for the disaster. But in doing so, they overlooked an essential component of the equation—the fate of Feliz Tellez.[48]

The first Mexican American boy taken captive by Apaches in white man's Arizona would survive his childhood among the Western Apaches, becoming a recognized clansman among his adopted people, and eventually a scout, guide, and interpreter for the U.S. Army. Along the way he would acquire a new name, Mickey Free, and an enemy—Geronimo. As James Kaywaykla explained to Eve Ball, among the Chokonens and Chihennes, Mickey Free would always be "the coyote whose kidnapping brought war to the Chiricahua. . . . He had, through no fault of his own, been the cause of Cochise's outbreak. Though the trouble was precipitated by the ignorance and arrogance of a young officer . . . [,] indirectly the child was held to be responsible."[49]

Historians would argue whether Feliz Tellez's captivity caused the war between Chiricahuas and whites in Arizona, or whether total war was inevitable. But it was not a child who would face the Chiricahuas twenty years later. By 1882 Feliz Tellez had transformed himself into the most influential Apache captive in Arizona territorial history.[50]

Meanwhile, the decennial census found Larcena and

John Page living in the Middle Santa Cruz settlements in August 1860, five months after Larcena's ordeal. Mrs. Page, the census enumerator noted, bore "grievous wounds" upon her body. The same enumerator found Elias and the rest of the Penningtons living closer to the border. Once again, Elias had relocated the family, this time to a tiny stone cabin a mile north of the Mexican line. By now the family enterprises included farming, freighting, lumbering, and supplying hay to Fort Buchanan. Charles Poston, a mining developer in southern Arizona who would one day call himself "the father of Arizona," described Elias's home on the Santa Cruz: "Never in my life have I seen a cabin erected in such a desolate place as the Pennington cabin on the upper Santa Cruz in 1859. . . . It was right on the road of the Apaches into Sonora, and as far from civilization as a white family could possibly reach." They moved back briefly to the Sonoita Creek, but by early 1861 had returned again to the stone house on the Mexican border.[51]

Apaches killed Larcena's husband on the road north of Tucson in the spring of 1861. Now a widow and pregnant with Page's child, she rejoined her family at the stone house on the border. But the outbreak of the Civil War meant the recall of the western army to fight in the east, leaving Arizona without military protection. Within months most whites and Mexicans had fled to Tucson for safety from the Apaches, who took advantage of the exodus, compounding the Americans' isolation by forcing the mail on the overland trail to grind to a halt. With their enemies seemingly in flight, the Apaches seized the advantage, attacking white settlements relentlessly. Before

1861 had passed, the ranches of Mexicans and whites lay ransacked and burned across southern Arizona.[52]

As Apache raids mounted, the Penningtons retreated to Sylvester Mowry's mine in the Sonoita Valley. Here, Larcena bore Mary Anne Page on September 4, 1861. Both Larcena and the baby survived an outbreak of smallpox while living in the mining camp. But Jack Pennington had had enough of Arizona; he left with the Akes for New Mexico. Elias moved the family yet again, back to Calabasas, near the Mexican line. One reporter noted: "At times [Pennington] was several days absent, and I am told that his daughters frequently had to stand guard, with guns in their hands, to keep off the Indians who besieged the premises. Still, they continue to live there today, utterly alone, seeming rather to enjoy the dangers than otherwise."[53]

At last capitulating to the Apaches, the Penningtons relocated to Tucson in 1863. There, just outside the old walls of the Pueblo, Elias and James laid timber across a wide arroyo, whipsawing lumber. In Tucson, journalist J. Ross Brown "had the pleasure of an interview with the eccentric father of the family. Strangely enough, Old Pennington is apparently a man of excellent sense. Large, tall, with a fine face and athletic frame, he presents as good a specimen of American frontiersman who knows no fear as I have ever seen."[54]

It wasn't long before Pennington relocated to the deserted Tubac, and then to the Sopori ranch, site of an abandoned Sobaipuri rancheria on the road to Arivaca, in Tohono O'odham territory. There, in a small building erected for the purpose, the older Pennington daughters conducted school for the youngest.[55]

Explorer William Bell found the family at home on the Sopori.

> [It] was built on a rock, and still further strengthened against attack by a wall of stones which completely surrounded it. On climbing up the rocks and getting over the other defenses, we found in the house five girls and one little boy. The girls were all grown up, ranging in age from seventeen to about twenty-five. They met us as if we were rare curiosities, and invited us to partake of their meal. . . . They told us that they were a family of Southerners, "and as we-uns could not live with you Yanks, father thought it best to clear out in time." The father and eldest brother were out in the Santa Cruz mountains . . . but as they had seen nothing of them for three weeks, they began to "hope that the Indians had not got them." The girls chattered away with perfect ease which strikes a stranger so much. . . . This emigrant family got along very well at first. . . . But the Apaches found them out.[56]

Unlike Olive Oatman, who privately shunned any attention to her past, Larcena shared her story, and her scars, freely with Bell. He later noted, "It is almost impossible to conceive any position so terrible. . . . She told me this in the presence of her sisters, and they were honest, homely people who would not, I am confident, say what was untrue. I saw the scars of three arrow wounds on her arms, and can well believe her when she says that on her body there are several other scars to bear witness while she lives of that terrible journey."[57]

Yet another visitor found the Penningtons at Sopori.

This time a political candidate came to call. "Old Pennington said, 'Are you one of them carpet bag fellows from Washington?'" When the guest reassured Pennington of his politics, Elijah responded, "I will take the whole family down to vote for you. We want to get clear of them varmints."[58]

Ellen Pennington soon married the visitor, Underwood Barnett, a man destined for the first territorial legislature. They moved to Tubac; not long after, sister Anne died of malaria. Brother Jack returned from Texas, and then left with sister Caroline and her husband and children. South of Tucson in August 1868, Apaches killed James while he hauled timber on the San Xavier road. The remaining Penningtons then moved to Fort Crittenden on the Sonoita, which had been built to replace Fort Buchanan after Federal troops had abandoned and destroyed it in 1861, lest it fall into Confederate hands. Finally, on June 10, 1869, Apaches killed Elias Pennington.

Like Royce Oatman, Elias was a stubborn man. Col. Thomas Hughes, eventually the president of the Society of Arizona Pioneers, remembered Pennington's death.

> Early in 1869, the ranches down the Sonoita River
> . . . were raided by the Apaches. About ten days after
> this raid, I was plowing in the field not far from the
> road leading down the valley. There I saw coming
> down this road two teams loaded with farming imple-
> ments. I also saw Mr. Pennington and his two sons
> with the teams. When they were close-up to me, I
> asked them where they were going, and he replied,
> "I am going down below to start ranching." I said to

him, "Mr. Pennington, don't go down there. You'll be killed before a month passes over your head." And he replied, "What are you doing here?" "Oh, I am farming a little, and looking out for Apaches." "Well," said Pennington, "If you can do it, I guess I can." And then he passed down the valley, and inside of ten days, he and his sons were all dead, being victims of the Apaches. They were shot down at their plows in the middle of the field while planting corn. . . . There is little doubt that the Indians intended to drive all ranchers from the Sonoita and Santa Cruz.[59]

After the deaths of Elias and his sons, the remaining Pennington daughters moved to Tucson. When the women attempted to leave by wagon for California, sister Ellen took sick, leaving them no choice but to return to Tucson, where Ellen died. In 1870 Jack Pennington arrived from Texas, hoping his sisters would return east with him. All but Larcena and her young daughter Mary Page chose to do so.[60]

Larcena's decision to remain hinged on having met William F. Scott. Born in Scotland in 1831, Scott was in New York by 1845, and eventually marched west with federal troops of the Utah expedition in the fall of 1857. In 1859 he left Salt Lake City for Arizona.[61]

Like Larcena's deceased husband John Page, Scott mined at Pinos Altos in New Mexico, and by late 1862 had joined John D. Walker's party down the Gila, and then on to the strike on the Hassayampa in May 1863, where Ed Peck, soon to figure into the captivity of Bessie Brooks, had also panned for gold before acquiring the hay contract at Fort Whipple.[62]

In 1865, as whites and Mexicans once again cautiously ventured out of Tucson, Scott formed a partnership with James Lee in a water-powered flour mill on the Santa Cruz River. Like other white men of means, he invested in silver mines in the Tucson area, but by 1867 a series of Apache raids had hit his mining operations at a cost of $1,400 in livestock. Nevertheless, Scott's wealth had grown as a result of converting his water mill to steam. He and Larcena wed in Tucson on July 27, 1870. The groom, the published nuptials confided, was one of the most eligible bachelors in Tucson.[63]

The Civil War impacted Mercedes Sais's life, too. Captain Ewell, who had redeemed her from the Apaches, "took a great fancy to her." Ewell, forty-three years her senior, made plans to send Mercedes to a school in Virginia, but "the breaking out of the war" and Ewell's subsequent resignation from the Federal army abruptly changed their plans. Mercedes was destined to spend her short life in Tucson.[64]

Like Larcena, she married well in an era when few white women were available to marry white men in Arizona. Like many other daughters of Mexican Americans, Mercedes married a white pioneer after the outbreak of the war had erased any chance she might have had for a formal education in the east. Mercedes married Charles A. Shibell in July 1868. Shibell, born in St. Louis in 1841, had arrived in Arizona as a teamster under General Carlton in 1862, two years after Mercedes had been ransomed from the Apaches. After his marriage to Mercedes, whom the Tucson press dubbed "one of the fairest senoritas in the city," Shibell was appointed deputy collector of internal revenue in Tucson, a position that required him to testify before the territorial legislature regarding Indian depredations "of which he had personal knowledge."[65]

But Mercedes Saiz Shibell passed away from complications of childbirth on Christmas Day in 1875 after bearing her husband four children in eight years. One observer reported that her funeral attracted "quite a turnout." As the "turnout" suggests, Mercedes's captivity had not been forgotten by Tucsonans, even fifteen years later.[66]

Young Mercedes Shibell, the daughter of Mercedes and Charles Shibell, would one day graduate with the inaugural class of the University of Arizona in 1895—the first Mexican American woman to do so—as white women's presence grew in Tucson, and Mexican Americans increasingly felt themselves marginalized by their white neighbors. Her father, Charles, would run the Occidental Hotel in Tucson before taking the office of county recorder in 1889, which he would retain long after he was rendered useless from "writer's paralysis." But, his historical file would one day note, loyal Republicans kept him in office anyway.[67]

Larcena Pennington Scott's oldest daughter did not fare as well as Mercedes Shibell. Larcena, her husband now a justice of the peace in Tucson, watched in 1878 as her daughter, Mary Page, married the much older Dr. J. C. Handy, a surgeon who had worked at various army posts in the region in the previous decade. By 1891 Mary Handy was heavily addicted to morphine, while her husband carried on an open affair with a neighbor woman, purposely parading his mistress on the street in front of the Handy home. The scandal reached a new level when

Mary threatened divorce. Handy publicly threatened to shoot any lawyer who took her case. Lawyer Francis J. Heney defied him, representing Mary Page Handy in her bid for divorce. An infuriated Handy made good his pledge, but Heney got the better of him, and Handy soon lay dead with a literal gut full of lead. No charges were filed in the affair. In Texas, meanwhile, Jack Pennington found it necessary to commit his mentally ill sister Caroline to the Texas State Hospital in Austin. There, diagnosed with "birth mania," she remained until her death.[68]

Although there is no indication that Mercedes Sais's captors physically assaulted her, the documentary record reveals the especially severe nature of Larcena's physical ordeal. The 1860 census enumerator noted the "grievous wounds" from which she was still recovering; William Bell had related that she showed him several scars in 1863, when he chanced upon the Pennington home in the desert. Like Olive Oatman, the visual reminders of Larcena's captivity experience indelibly marked her for life.[69]

Furthermore, beyond surviving her own brutal captivity, Larcena had suffered the death of her mother by malaria, her own brutal captivity, a smallpox epidemic, the death of her sister Anne through illness, and the deaths of her father, her first husband, and her brothers by Apaches.

In 1919 Robert H. Forbes, the son-in-law of Larcena Pennington, wrote about such women: "There were but few American women in the country in those days, and these, as a rule, not from choice, it is safe to say. Usually they chanced here through military connections or some adverse fortune that diverted them from the California road. Without society of their own kind, often without the comforts of life, without the relief afforded by active adventure, and often in danger, they had no choice but to endure."[70]

The lives of Larcena Pennington and Olive Oatman demonstrate one scholar's observation that white women "rarely enjoyed the new landscape in ways that had been promised to them." Rather, it was white men who "reaped the pleasures of the garden." Women most often found themselves "shut up with the children in log cabins; the dream of a domestic Eden had become a nightmare of domestic captivity."

Annette Kolodney wrote that the anger such women felt, "but couldn't express," toward their husbands—and by extension their fathers, as this work would suggest— who had "staked the family's future on the frontier" could be "vicariously displaced onto the dark and dusky figure of the Indian, a projection of the husband's [or father's] darker side." Larcena's rage, and that of scores of Tucsonans and southern Arizonans, would fall upon the Aravaipa Apaches in April 1871.[71]

3

1869–1871

NO CAVALRY COLUMN followed the trail of Feliz Tellez after the Bascom affair in January 1861, and no ransom obtained his release. Within months the outbreak of the Civil War prompted the transfer of troops to the east. From the standpoint of his family, Feliz Tellez had been "stolen," lost to the Apaches, like generations of Mexican captives before him.[1]

After the war, in 1867, Apaches mortally wounded John Ward while he ranched near the border. Jesusa and her children returned to Sonora. She passed away in 1868, never learning that her son Feliz had survived.[2]

In 1936 White Mountain Apache John Rope shared what little is known of Tellez's captivity. Like Olive Oatman, he was raised in the home of an influential headman. "Mickey and I were brought up together, so we called each other brothers," Rope claimed, indicating that Pinals had given the boy to his father, Nayudiie, a White Mountain *ti-sie-dnt-i-dn* clan chief.[3]

Nayudiie's wives died during Tellez's captivity. Rope remembered how his father steered him and his siblings through their grief by telling stories. "Boys," he began, "your mothers have died, and it is going to be a hard time for us now. I was raised through hard times also by my father, who used to go to Mexico for horses and cattle and bring them back for me to feed on." Nayudiie's youth had been spent in apprenticeship to warriors on Mexican raids until asked by his elders to become their clan chief at an exceptionally young age.[4]

Western Apaches' social organization identified captives or *yodascin* ("those from the outside") as members of their owner's clan—in Tellez's case the *ti-sie-dnt-i-dn*—a cultural practice that stood out in marked contrast to the Western Apaches' otherwise matrilineal clan system. Furthermore, Tellez was not the only Mexican captive among the Western Apaches. Others, such as Concepcion Brillo, Jose Maria Yescas, and Victoriano Mesta, would one day serve as the first U.S. Army guides, scouts, and interpreters in Arizona in the years ahead.[5]

As an adopted clansman, Tellez would have learned the skills necessary to the survival of young Apache males and been taught his obligations as a *ti-sie-dnt-i-dn*. Grenville Goodwin observed that this network of clan obligations vitally linked the otherwise decentralized Western Apaches. It also served to absorb captives into the tribal structure.[6]

While Feliz Tellez found his place among the White Mountain Apaches, Federal troops withdrew from the territory, and Southerners rallied to seize Arizona. By the fall of 1861, nearly 5,000 Americans and Mexicans were living in Arizona; on the other hand, so were 20,000 to 30,000 Native Americans. For political expediency following Confederate claims to the region, President Abraham Lincoln signed the Arizona Organic Act in 1861. Yet, as one historian wrote, much of the far Southwest— San Diego, Yuma, Tucson, Mesilla—was "stranded like islands in Indians."[7]

In February 1862 Confederates raised a flag over Tucson, above few objections, and Sylvester Mowery placed his resources in service to them. The arrival of 2,500 California Volunteers from Fort Yuma derailed Confederate plans, however. Mowery soon found himself in irons, with his property confiscated. What the Apaches had failed to accomplish, the Union had done for them: the removal of Sylvester Mowry from the Sonoita Valley.[8]

The return of Federal troops to Arizona transformed the territory from a Southern, states' rights, Democratic orientation to Republican control. Meanwhile, troops set about rebuilding abandoned forts and constructing new ones. Estimates claimed that Apaches had killed sixty-two settlers and relieved ranchers of $340,000 in stock during the troops' absence.[9]

While the Penningtons sawed wood on the arroyo in Tucson and Feliz Tellez lived with Nayudiie, even as Olive Oatman shared her story with rapt New York audiences, territorial officials gathered at Navajo Springs, Arizona, on December 29, 1863, to formally organize Arizona's territorial government. All agreed that the capital should be located near Fort Whipple, established only a month earlier to protect miners in the Walker District. They arrived at Whipple in late January; in May they platted the town of Prescott on Granite Creek.[10]

The Yavapais and Tonto Apaches watched the whites

erecting Fort Whipple among the cedar and pines of central Arizona, and then as Prescott rose in its shadow; by 1867 Prescott had replaced Tucson as the territorial capital. Increasingly, the indigenous people of Arizona found themselves circumscribed and endangered by the presence of whites.[11]

The intrusion dealt a corresponding blow to Native American social integrity. The discovery of gold at La Paz in 1862 forced a wedge into Mohave society, causing about one-third of Mohaves under Chief Irritaba to remove far downriver from Fort Mohave. The whites' cold-blooded murder of Mangas Coloradas in 1862 left a vacancy in Chiricahua leadership that would be filled by Victorio and Cochise, but the depth of anger felt by the Chiricahuas over the underhanded manner of Mangus's death and betrayal ran deep.[12]

In New Mexico, Federal troops constructed Fort Wingate, turning Kit Carson loose on the Navajos in July 1863. The following year the *Diné* were forcibly relocated to Bosque Redondo, far from their four sacred peaks. By 1869 most had begun to slip back to their homeland, but their military strength had been broken. In central Arizona frictions ran high between Yavapais, Apaches, and whites in the Prescott region.[13]

Significantly, as miners and settlers penetrated further into Apache country, those among the natives wishing to make their escape found whites much closer than Olive Oatman did in the 1850s. The increased opportunities for Apache captives—as well as abandoned Apache orphans, the elderly, and the disabled—to initiate contact with whites weakened traditional Apache power structures. A segment of disaffected Apaches could now look to white government agents as "protectors" and "rescuers" from a society whose social organization was increasingly frayed under the strain of war and depleted resources.[14]

For example, military field camps increased access to whites. The establishment of Camp Goodwin in 1864 opened a viable means of escape; in July 1864 young Jose Mendibles was released from the White Mountain Apaches. The boy had been a captive since 1857 and had witnessed the Bascom affair of 1861. In July, Major Thomas Blakeney, leading troops out of Fort Bowie, reported that an orphaned fourteen-year-old Apache boy ran into camp, claiming he wanted to be a white man. He wanted to live with the soldiers, provided they supply him with a hat, boots, and clothing. Deciding the boy looked "unusually intelligent for an Indian," the major offered him protection.[15]

Days later, an elderly Apache woman claimed him, but the boy wanted to stay in camp. Blakeney refused to hand him over. The same day, the Apaches forcibly recaptured him. Irked by their refusal to return the boy, Blakeney hanged "two Indian buck hostages." When Col. Edwin Rigg learned of the incident, he complained to the adjutant general's office, claiming that Blakeney's "zeal" for an Apache orphan had nearly caused a "stampede" among the Apaches. Blakeney resigned from the service; his actions had too closely echoed that of Lieutenant Bascom three years earlier.[16]

During the harsh winter of 1864–65, hungry Apaches continued to surrender at Camp Goodwin. In March 1865 a large band surrendered three Mexican captives in compliance with Colonel Riggs's general order. As a routine matter, surrendered captives were escorted to Tucson, where military and civilian authorities held them until they could be reunited with their families.[17]

Meanwhile, in 1865 the Tohono O'odham at San Xavier had sustained such heavy losses to Enemy Apaches that they agreed to make a standing force of 150 men available to the commanding officer at Fort Lowell. During one raid, the Enemy took captive with them an unnamed O'odham child, who many years later escaped her captor's camp by shedding her clothing. "The People do not wear deerskin dresses, but only a little skirt, and they travel barefoot, so she did not need those clothes. She got up in the night while the [Apache] women were asleep, and she went out," according to the O'odham oral tradition. Eventually, she came to the land of the River O'odhams, but, like Olive Oatman, "she was afraid to go there without any clothes," although she eventually communicated with a river woman, and discovered they spoke the same language. That winter, after returning to her home among the Tohono O'odhams, O'odham Enemy Slayers had enlisted her aid as a scout "to explain the enemies' ways." Like the Chiricahua captive Nah-thle-tla, this unnamed O'odham woman liberated herself from her captors. Utilizing the experience she had gained from her captivity, she turned her knowledge of her enemies' ways against them, enabling the Enemy Slayers to exact revenge upon her captors. Meanwhile, the territorial legislature, frustrated at the military's ineffectiveness in Arizona, demanded General Carlton's removal.[18]

Despite indigenous opposition, white settlers continued

to stream into Arizona. A few, "bitter" men running from a ruined South, had arrived with Carlton in 1862 and stayed behind when the California Column transferred out again. Others came with their families on the Gila trail from the east, or entered from Fort Yuma on the west, while a thin flow of Mormons trickled down from Utah, where tillable land was scarce, but the new supply depot at Yuma made commerce viable in Arizona, and as it had for centuries, the endless donkey train carrying Mexicans and their goods continued treading north out of Mexico City.[19]

One hundred miles east of Tucson, Henry Hooker secured the first lucrative beef contract with Arizona military forts, where, besides soldiers, increasing numbers of captured and surrendered Indians needed to be fed. Hooker took the precaution of conferring with Cochise before starting his cattle operation. In return for allowing the Chiricahuas to butcher an occasional cow, Cochise assured Hooker that his warriors would refrain from attacking the Sierra Bonita cowboys, an agreement sealed when Hooker presented the chief with the blanket in which the Apache would reputedly one day be buried. Hooker's subsequent material success created resentment among those Tucsonans who found themselves unable to profit from "the problem with Indians."[20]

Nayudiie may have surrendered Tellez at Camp Goodwin, for the young man next appears on the record—using the name Feliz—as an Indian scout posted at Fort Lowell in Tucson in October 1868. Now about eighteen years old, Tellez—along with other former captives—utilized his knowledge of the Apache language, culture, and geography as an enlisted scout, but his ultimate loyalties would prove to be with his adopted people.[21]

Years earlier, district commander Brig. Gen. John Mason had requested permission of the quartermaster to forgo the usual formalities associated with the hiring of Indian auxiliaries, as the captives were generally termed. Mason planned on waging an extensive campaign against Pinals and needed the services of the Mexican guides, "who having been prisoners of the Apaches, know their language and their haunts." Formal permissions, he believed, might come too late, but inclement weather derailed his plans anyway. Not until the Army Reorganization Act of 1866 would Indian scouts be formally enlisted into the army, as part of a centralized plan to "bring all Indians under the regulation and control of the United States government," according to one scholar.[22]

In 1866 orders allotted Arizona a generous portion of Indian enlistments, including seventy scouts under Pima chief Antonio Azul and Chief Juan Chivarria of the Maricopas. The department was also permitted twenty San Xavier Tohono O'odhams and *mansos*, the voluntarily de-tribalized Indians—primarily Apaches—farming on the northern periphery of Tucson. Of these, Manuel Duran would take leadership. After his enlistment as a scout in 1868 (probably under the *manso* quota), Tellez served under Duran, incessantly patrolling the mail road from Fort Bowie to Tucson against Apache raiders.[23]

In January 1870 smallpox broke out in the Tucson vicinity. To stem the epidemic, scouts were "sent away," except those who had been vaccinated. Tellez left for Fort Whipple under the command of Lt. Howard Cushing.

While at Whipple, the fair-complexioned Tellez received the nickname destined to stick with him through life and death: Mickey Free. Named for a fictional character popular in the Irish literature of the day, Mickey Free would rise to a position of unprecedented influence among the Western Apache scouts.[24]

By 1868 the Arizona Stage Company ran a regular route from Prescott and Tucson to San Francisco. Arizona had established connection with the rest of the nation, but its tarnished reputation had preceded it. As in James Brooks's analysis of New Mexico, postwar radical Republicans had not forgotten that New Mexico Territory—which at that time included Arizona—had legalized slavery in 1859. They were keenly aware that "debt peonage still held untold numbers of Mexicans and Indians captive" and that the use of captive Indians as "domestic servants" was customary, and but a "thinly veiled" form of slavery. Congress outlawed peonage and slavery in 1867, "but not until 1868 would the laws be enforced in Arizona."[25]

Scholars have found that after 1850, white women started writing themselves into western literature. In this new literature, they redefined the traditional image of "westering" white males from yeoman farmers and isolated hunters of an earlier era into "new western" males just as likely to be frontier lawyers, politicians, or doctors as frontiersmen. "No longer interested in the conquering of the west, the frontiersman had learned to turn the garden into a home." The "new western Adam" was a man committed to the simple duties of home and hearth and shared a "principled" involvement in the community around him. But he was not a fictional fabrication.

As the life of the Yavapai Apache captive Bessie Brooks would demonstrate, the new Adam was no mere ploy of clever female authors, but a direct reflection of women's experiences in the West.[26]

The seeds of white urbanization germinating in Tucson and Prescott generated a class of males who often left Indian fighting to those whose livelihoods put them in closer contact with natives—farmers, ranchers, miners, teamsters, freighters, and military men. As businessmen, doctors, lawyers, merchants, and politicians, they did not generally fight Indians.

Hezekiah Brooks was a "new westering" male. Born in Ohio in 1825, he had arrived in California in 1850. By 1854 Brooks was serving as deputy sheriff and postmaster in Yreka. After joining the Masons in San Francisco in September 1863, he left for Arizona. In October, Brooks erected the first cabin built in Yavapai territory, on the banks of Granite Creek at Prescott.[27]

Brooks wasn't the only new western Adam to participate in the Prescott dedication ceremony in May 1864. Standing with him was Charles Leib, born in Pennsylvania in 1826. Leib left the East for Santa Fe, after the Senate rejected his military appointment above the objections of his friend Abraham Lincoln. In New Mexico, General Carlton appointed him an assistant surgeon and assigned Leib to accompany the official government party en route to the ceremony at Navajo Springs.[28]

Leib's wife, Mary Catherine Smith Leib, accompanied her husband. Born near Bethlehem, Pennsylvania, in 1827, Mary grew to womanhood in a traditional Moravian home, received a seminary education, and excelled in music. In

1852 she married Charles, and the two left Pennsylvania to farm in Iowa, later moving to Santa Fe.[29]

Proud of telling how she had worn the finest leather footwear as a child, she was even fonder of telling how she had bought herself a pair of boys' boots to walk from Santa Fe to Navajo Springs and on to Prescott. Teased by the soldiers, and often implored to ride in the wagon, Mary had stubbornly walked, the sole woman on the trip. Her only fear, she insisted, was of "being separated from Charles," a thinly disguised remark signifying her distrust of her male companions.[30]

After a discharge from the army in March 1864, Leib was defeated in a bid for a seat in the First Territorial Congress. Hezekiah Brooks, now Prescott commissioner, sold lots in the Prescott town site. In June the territorial governor appointed him the first probate court judge of the district. A close neighbor to the Leibs on Granite Creek, Brooks eventually rented a room from the couple. The three lived together until January 1865, when Charles Leib passed away unexpectedly of natural causes.[31]

Mary started a school in her home; Hezekiah probably returned to his own cabin, as propriety would demand, but in February 1867 the two married. A popular couple, they were known for keeping a large garden, a small orchard, and a herd of goats. Visitors to the Brookses' home knew they would be treated to jelly cake and milk, as well as the best books and magazines available in Prescott.[32]

Mary Brooks even owned a cat, one of the first to appear in Prescott. She had begged to buy it from a miner for $17. However, it was not a cat that Mary Brooks begged for at the annual Prescott Independence Day celebration in July 1869, but rather a child, a Yavapai girl crooked in the arms of Edward G. Peck.[33]

Peck could not be numbered among the new western men. Of the old school, Peck had been born in Canada in 1835. By 1858 he was in Santa Fe via the plains, and then on to Arizona with a prospecting party through the Zuni pueblos. Arriving at Fort Whipple late in 1863, he secured the first hay contract carried at Whipple. In 1864 Peck joined the infamous King Woolsey party, a civilian outfit whose sole aim was to exterminate Apaches. A companion in the Woolsey party later said of Ed Peck, "[He] was with me—one of the best shots I ever saw."[34]

Following the Woolsey expeditions, Peck served as a civilian guide at Camp Verde and then at Fort Whipple. On June 22, 1869, he left the fort on a routine detachment to track Apaches who had hit Chino Valley—where Peck had a ranch—especially hard. After riding to Camp Verde, the troops departed again that night. The following day, they cut the trail of a "traveling party" of Yavapais west of Bill Williams Mountain. Like Larcena Pennington, Mercedes Sais, and Mickey Free, another half-orphaned child would soon fall prey to captivity in Arizona.[35]

"'Lo took to the rocks and bushes, and it is not sure that any more than four were killed, though many more were keeled over. . . . Ed Peck captured a little girl," one participant reported. In time Peck related the circumstances of the child's captivity. Dismounted at the time of the charge, he had found himself alone in the Apaches' abandoned camp. With darkness falling, he fired at a figure arising from the camp trappings, shooting a Yavapai dead. "A little Indian girl got up on a rock and I went and got her," he claimed. Not until then did he realize he had killed a woman. Dejected, the detachment returned to Fort Whipple "in rather low spirits at not getting more of the wily aborigines." They arrived in Prescott in time to help the community celebrate Independence Day.[36]

Childless, like John Fairchild and Olive Oatman, Mary Brooks coveted the toddler in Peck's arm. Judge Brooks, no doubt taken aback, asked Peck to grant his wife's wishes, but Peck's legal obligation was to turn the child over to the commanding officer at Fort Whipple. Instead, Peck took the child to his ranch. Judge Brooks visited several times, and the two reached an agreement: Brooks and his wife could have the child if the judge promised to legally adopt her and include her as an heir to his estate. His terms agreed to, Peck handed the Yavapai child over to Hezekiah Brooks on July 6.[37]

In October the Prescott *Journal Miner* updated its readers on the captive's progress, opening an academic window on white Arizonans' historic perceptions of heredity and environment.

We doubt very much if there is in the West a keener, jollier race of red people than the Apaches of this territory. The children, even, are exceedingly smart and precocious. . . . Lest our readers should doubt this, we will cite a case in point: Mrs. H. Brooks of Woodside has a little three-year-old Indian girl. . . . Well, all who know Mrs. Brooks must admit that she is a lady every way qualified to control even a savage child, yet at times, she has been at a loss to decide upon a proper course of treatment for the refractory little elf, whom she has named "Bessie," and who, true to the blood that is in her, at times becomes as stubborn as a mule. When Bessie was first taken to her present home, she wept bitterly, would not go near Mrs. B., and tried her best to get away. Failing in this, she placed her little hand to her mouth and "whooped" . . . hoping to apprise her people of her situation. She then went into the house and for a long time refused to be comforted or partake of a morsel of food. She is now in tolerable subjection, well fed, clothed and to all appearances attached to Mrs. B., yet her past fits go to show the almost untamable spirit of her race.[38]

As one Prescott pioneer recalled, Bessie Brooks would grow to maturity amid the rose bushes and orchard of Woodside estate, gradually acquiring the "impeccable" English of Mary Brooks. Another lauded Mary Brooks's tenacity in the face of Bessie's perceived innate stubbornness, implying ingratitude on the girl's part.

Mrs. Brooks' patience and perseverance with the Indian girl was remarkable proof of her character. A great many early pioneer women took Indian girls into their homes and tried to make something of them. But Bessie was stubbornly opposed to being taught. She wished to learn to read, but refused to learn her letters. She begged to be taught how to make lace . . . but balked at making chain stitch. She seemed to take a strange delight in refusing to do as she was told and was often locked up for her disobedience, yet she loved her foster parents and they made a home for her for some twenty-five years when she might have been put into an institution at any time.[39]

Bessie Brooks, the Yavapai captive taken by Ed Peck, would "to all appearances" acculturate into the Anglo community that increasingly surrounded her after 1869. Her eventual marriage in 1897 and subsequent legal battle to inherit Hezekiah's estate, however, would highlight the malleable nature of racial identity in territorial Arizona, and the pivotal role of the new western Adam in defining race.[40]

In 1890 Mary Brooks used mining stock and money inherited from a deceased brother to acquire the estate adjoining the Brookses' property. She arranged for a large frame house "with big rooms and a fireplace" to be constructed on the site, and ordered carpets and furniture from San Francisco. Just as the house was nearing completion, Mary died unexpectedly on November 18, 1891. Within months her new house mysteriously burned to the ground, reduced to ashes.[41]

For six more years Bessie and her adoptive father, Hezekiah, lived at the old family home, until Bessie met James B. Edgar, a "worthy and industrious citizen of this county" and a "stalwart son." The two decided to marry in September 1897. "Miss Brooks is a native daughter of Arizona who was brought up in the household of Judge Hezekiah Brooks and is highly spoken of by all who have met her," the paper reported.[42]

However, the impending nuptials did not please everyone in Prescott, for existing Arizona statute prohibited intermarriage between Indians and whites. But Hezekiah's good name carried weight. "When it seemed that the marriage would be thus averted, Mr. Brooks came forward . . . and made affidavit that the bride to be was his legally adopted daughter and therefore, by adoption, a white girl. On this showing a license was issued, and they were united in marriage," reported the newspaper.[43]

During the next ten years, the Edgars added at least two sons to their family. Bessie had seemingly resolved the racial divide that distinguished her from other residents of Prescott, until May 1907, when she abruptly found herself front and center of the citizens of Prescott once again.[44]

Early in the month, Hezekiah inexplicably moved the long-interred body of Mary's former husband to the Prescott Masonic cemetery, next to Mary Brooks. That done, he left Arizona and returned to Ohio, where he passed away at the age of eighty-one. The *Prescott Courier* said of Hezekiah, "He was a prince among Arizona pioneers, a man whom all loved to show the respect they felt for so good a man." Unfortunately for Bessie, her adoptive father—the first probate judge in the Prescott district—died intestate.[45]

On June 14 Bessie filed a petition for contest of Brooks's estate in response to a claim made by Van H. Brooks, Hezekiah's nephew from Ohio. Four days later, the *Prescott Journal Miner* screamed "FIGHT ON FOR BROOKS ESTATE."[46]

The drama escalated when Bessie Brooks found herself alone in Hezekiah's house with her children except for one T. L. Otis, who claimed that shortly before Hezekiah's death, he had been authorized to "take care of the place" and to "place the matter of renting the house in the care of lawyer J. M. W. Ward." Otis, holed up in a bedroom of the home, discharged a rifle-shot through the closed door, narrowly missing Bessie's children. After the shooting, the sheriff found him barricaded in the bedroom. Otis was perfunctorily arraigned and discharged from custody on bail.[47]

During the resulting court trial, Otis's lawyer testified that he was the regularly appointed representative for Hezekiah and had "ordered the Edgars off the property, except for a small plot Edgar had leased from Brooks," a position the court apparently upheld. But Bessie continued the fight for her father's estate. By June 27 she was back in court, testifying that to the best of her knowledge, she was the legally adopted daughter of Hezekiah, and had been raised in his home since childhood. But her attorney could not produce documents to that effect.[48]

On the following day, June 28, 1907, the court ruled in the matter of *Brooks v. Edgar*. "The court finds that the oral evidence . . . does not prove [Bessie's] contention that she is the adopted daughter of Hezekiah Brooks." After considering the "suitableness and competency of the persons applying for administration"—a thinly veiled reference to Bessie's race and gender—the court appointed Van Brooks the administrator of Hezekiah's estate. According to the record, the court decided the opinion "without prejudice to Bessie Brooks Edgars' right to hereafter prove that she is the next of kin and legal heir under the law."[49]

The court had denied Bessie's claim on the basis of her race and gender, but again she did not give up. In early July the inventory of the estate had been completed, consisting of "$133.57 in cash, one lot in the city of Prescott, and lands and improvements situated immediately south of the city limits, and two lode mining claims, all appraised at $4,083.50." Within a week Bessie had petitioned the district court to overturn the probate court's decision. In written testimony she claimed that she had "performed all the duties of a faithful daughter towards Mr. and Mrs. Brooks." She also insisted that Hezekiah had repeatedly told her that he had legally adopted her. She claimed that she "firmly believed" that she would be his heir upon his death. Finally, Bessie testified, Hezekiah's death and the current legal battle were the first indications she had that she wasn't his legal daughter.[50]

Four months passed before Bessie appeared in district court. On November 2, 1907, the *Journal Miner* reported that her attorney had located a letter from Ed Peck stating it was he who had captured Bessie in 1869, and he had handed her over to Mr. and Mrs. Brooks on July 6 of that year. It was his understanding, Peck wrote, that Brooks agreed to legally adopt Bessie and make her his heir.[51]

Peck passed through Globe on his way to Mexico in October 1907. He was rushed, he told a news reporter, because he had to return to testify at Bessie Brook's trial in December. After all, said Peck, "It was a bullet from my gun that laid low her old squaw mommy." Despite Peck's testimony, the district court deliberated the case for three years, eventually returning it to the probate court.[52]

On June 1, 1910, the probate court issued its final ruling in the matter of *Brooks v. Edgar*: "The final accounts of Van H. Brooks . . . [The balance of] $383.10 was ordered and distributed to one brother, three sisters, six nephews, six nieces and one great-grand-nephew."

Interests in mining shares were distributed as well. "The entire estate . . . amounts to . . . $4,569.94 . . . besides one acre of land and improvements set over to Bessie Brooks Edgar."[53]

Bessie lost her legal battle, but she retained title to the acre and improvements set aside for her. Public memory of the Yavapai captive Bessie Brooks and of her determined struggle against gendered racism in Arizona gradually receded with time. Little is found of her in the record after 1910, although it is known that her family preceded her in death. Alone in the world, and blinded by trachoma, the elderly Bessie was finally committed to "a government institution," where she apparently resided until her death. Heredity, it seemed, had defeated considerations of environment in territorial Arizona.[54]

In early spring 1871, as young Bessie learned to speak English in Mary Brooks's garden, Eskiminzin of the Aravaipa Apaches approached Camp Goodwin, asking to camp his followers in the environs of the fort in exchange for good behavior. Tucsonans heard of the matter on March 11, 1871, when the *Arizona Citizen* ran an anonymous letter informing readers that Lt. Royal Whitman had made an agreement with Eskiminzin's Apaches, who had come into Grant under a "rag of peace." Tucsonans' concern, the letter implied, lay in the notion that "the Indians have been left the San Pedro and Aravaipa valleys to cultivate."[55]

From the standpoint of Tucsonans, better land could not have been placed in less deserving hands, and a more dreaded people could not have settled closer to the old pueblo. Eskiminzin, after all, had been suspected in most of the deadly raids staged in southern Arizona for over a decade, dating at least as far back as the captivity of Larcena and Mercedes in 1860.[56]

In 1885 one pioneer recounted a long list of Eskiminzin's presumed victims. "I take for my theme some of the depredations committed by the Apache chief Eskiminzin and his band of the Aravaipa Apache Indians," he began. The speaker named a dozen or more whites who had presumably fallen to Eskiminzin, including the Penningtons. Other data indicate that unspecified Indians south of the Gila River between 1856 and April 1871 had killed approximately 1,000 whites and Mexicans, although in historical retrospect, it was not likely that Eskiminzin's men were responsible for every attack. The notion that the Aravaipas were now, in March 1871, camped under the protection and provision of the army and cultivating valuable farm land was unendurable to Tucsonans, for whom revenge was an overriding consideration.[57]

Public resentment against the Aravaipas and Whitman grew. Six whites had lost their lives in the weeks before the letter from Camp Grant was published; in the weeks following, three more were found dead. Most Tucsonans believed that Whitman had seen "that there was money in the Apache, and lost no time in the practical application of that knowledge."[58]

Indignation ignited on March 20, 1871, after Apaches killed pioneer L. B. Wooster and his wife, Trinidad Aguirre, the daughter of a respected Mexican American family, who was considered one of the great beauties of Tucson's early territorial era.[59] In the words of one pioneer, the "slaughter" of the Woosters "so infuriated the people that an 'indignation meeting' was held at Tucson. A great amount of 'resoluting and speechifying' was indulged in. . . . It was decided that a military company should be raised and 82 Americans signed their names, all swearing to kill Apaches." A committee was selected to visit General Stoneman at Florence, Arizona, to petition him for increased protection. Stoneman's infamous reply—that Tucson had enough manpower to defend itself—stoked coals of anger. The committee determined to adopt the general's recommendation.[60]

They took action in early April, when runners from San Xavier brought news that Apaches had run off with livestock. A posse took up the chase, trailing the raiders until they ran up on their rear and recovered a "tired horse" and a few cattle. Frustrated, the posse returned to Tucson, where wealthy Jesus Elias took aside community leader William S. Oury, telling him he suspected Eskiminzin was guilty of the raid. Oury suggested calling a public assembly at the courthouse so Elias could repeat his claim, but Elias declined, replying that there had been "too many meetings and resolutions." The men instead agreed to finance a "civil action." Elias promised to organize the Mexican American men, while Oury would organize the whites. "I know my countrymen," Elias reassured Oury. "If arms, ammunition and provisions, however scant, are provided, then they will be there."[61]

They sent a runner to "Chief Francisco" of the Tohono O'odhams, asking him to gather his men on a specified date. The O'odhams at San Xavier, who with the help of the returned female captive had carried out an offensive push against Enemy Apaches since 1866, then sent out runners to other villages. "They said, don't stop for food or weapons. The women at [San Xavier] will be grinding corn for you and the . . . whites will give you guns. . . . So all came. . . . The Mexicans gave them guns . . . and they led the way."[62]

On April 28, news that the O'odham warriors had gathered at San Xavier reached Tucson. "Quietly and singly, to avoid giving alarm," men left the pueblo to rendezvous with the O'odhams and a supply of arms, ammunition, and provisions provided by "an old companion, the adjutant general of the territory." By three o'clock in the afternoon, all had assembled except seventy-six of the white men who had signed the resolution. Oury remembered the moment:"During our short stay at the general rendezvous a number of pleasantries were indulged in by different members of the party upon the motley appearance of the troop, and your historian got a blow squarely in the right eye from an old neighbor, who quietly said to him, 'Don Guillermo, your countrymen are grand on resoluting and speechifying, but when it comes to action, they show up exceedingly thin.'—which, in view of the fact[s] . . . was to say the least, rather humiliating. However, everything was taken pleasantly."[63]

In all probability, men of the new western model— urban, tending to the matters of home, hearth, and business, and not usually expected to take up arms against Indians—could not afford to risk their hard-wrought material gains for a "civil action" of dubious legal status. They would leave their revenge to men of the old school, the Indian fighters. The new western Adam had, after all, an altered relationship with Native Americans.[64]

The ninety-two Tohono O'odhams, forty-eight Mexican Americans, and six whites who rode to Camp Grant took the precaution of ordering a guard to stop all travelers on the road north of Tucson. "But for this precaution our campaign would have resulted in complete failure," Oury would later reflect. Alternately, the party followed a less-used trail through the Tanque Verde pass, to the northeast side of the valley, following the trail of the Apaches who had reputedly raided San Xavier.[65]

Under a moonless night they descended into the San Pedro River flats, where they rested. Jesus Elias, taking up the march again, miscalculated the route to Camp Grant. Finally, at daybreak the raiders arrived within sight of the post. With time running out, they divided their forces—O'odhams on one side of Aravaipa Creek, and Mexicans and whites on the other—moving quickly until they reached Eskiminzin's camp. The raiders' desire for revenge could hardly be contained. "The Papagos bounded forward like deer," Oury remembered. Asleep and surprised in their wickiups, the Aravaipa camp fell quickly.[66]

According to Oury, the O'odhams attacked with "clubs and guns" while Americans and Mexicans picked off those who fled. "Within a half-hour, the whole affair was ended." Without a single man injured, the party turned back to Tucson, jubilant, bringing with them "some 28 or 30 papooses," he admitted, satisfied that "swift punishment had been dealt out to the red-handed butchers."[67]

A runner from Fort Lowell notified Lieutenant

Whitman at eight o'clock on the morning of April 30 of the attack on Eskiminzin's camp. At the site Whitman counted twenty-three dead Aravaipas. Survivors told him of the captives carried off by the attackers. "[The Aravaipas] will likely suspect treachery on the part of the military," an outraged Whitman warned his superiors in his initial report.[68]

Rumor had reached Captain Dunn at Fort Lowell on April 29 that "a large party of citizens and Papagos had left sometime during the day with the avowed purpose of killing all Indians . . . at Camp Grant." Dunn had sent a dispatch to the commanding officer at Camp Grant, ordering him to "handle it," unaware that Capt. Frank Stanwood was absent on duty in the field. Dunn's dispatcher, detained on the road by the Tucsonans' armed guard, had at last reached Camp Grant at 7:30 the following morning, "3 hours too late to save the lives of some 30 unsuspecting women and children."[69]

But the tabulation of the dead grew. According to Whitman, "The massacre is more horrible than first supposed." The total number would eventually reach eighty, and all except eight were women and children. Whitman reported to Dunn that he "did not have enough force to take back the prisoners"; he advised Dunn, "As they will undoubtedly be taken to Tucson, and the government no longer recognizes private ownership of human beings, they should be turned over to your post." Whitman also "sent a citizen to Tucson that immediate steps may be taken to save those women and children for their friends from a life of debauched servitude." He concluded by stating he hoped Dunn would "use his authority to rescue them," because the tribe had surrendered at Camp Grant prior to the attack and the captives could be "taken" as prisoners of war.[70]

By May 5 Whitman still had no resolution regarding the missing women and children, which the returned Captain Stanwood had confirmed stood at twenty-eight. Stanwood dispatched a curt letter to Dr. R. A. Wilbur, the Tohono O'odhams' Indian agent. "I demand on the part of the United States from you as agent for the Papagos, the return of these captives; if you think you cannot enforce justice among your tribe, I will assist you with the troops at my command." Wilbur, who had taken up his position following the massacre at Camp Grant, referred the matter to Arizona Indian superintendent Herman Bendell, who in turn sent it on to the military department of Arizona. Meanwhile, Wilbur proceeded with the investigation, learning that eight Aravaipa children were being held in the homes of Mexican families in Tucson, two had died since their captivity, and "the remaining twenty-one were taken into Sonora and sold somewhere in the Altar District." Wilbur added that "nothing but the best of motives induced these people [the O'odhams] to lend themselves" to the Tucsonans, "in whom they had confidence and every reason to believe that they would in no way advise them to commit a crime." Ultimately, headquarters decided that Lieutenant Whitman had the authority to issue a writ of habeas corpus for the children being held in Tucson because they had been under his official care at the time of the attack.[71]

In the interim Ed Peck of Prescott led a prospecting party into the cowed Aravaipas' territory, revealing an ulterior motive for the attack on the Aravaipas. So sure was the party of finding minerals, even the territorial governor accompanied the party. Despite a close search of the region, now widely accessible to whites for the first time, the disappointed party failed to find minerals, and soon abandoned the search and returned to Prescott.[72]

Months passed, and news of the Camp Grant affair worked its way up the chain of military command, leaked to the public, spread throughout the O'odham and San Carlos villages, and filtered onto the desks of civilian authorities. At last, on October 5, 1871, the matter appeared before the bench of U.S. District Court judge John Titus in Tucson. According to the O'odhams, "A little before winter, word came from [Tucson] that the People were wanted there for court. They spread the news, and people went from the Desert and River villages. The white people took them." One historian has found that the actions of territorial judges were particularly revealing in terms of the territorial process, and Judge Titus's administration of the Camp Grant massacre trial underscores his point.[73]

The grand jurors summoned witnesses on October 13: Lt. Royal Whitman; Manuel, "an Apache guide"; and William F. Scott, Larcena's husband. On October 16 Scott's business partner, James Lee, testified. The following day, Captain Stanwood took the stand, and on October 18 Jose Maria Yescas, who said he had been held captive by the Apaches for "nineteen years, six months and some days."[74]

On October 19 another former captive, Victoriano Mestas, stood before the grand jury, but a particularly influential Tucsonan, Sidney R. DeLong, failed to appear in court. On October 21 C. W. C. Rowell was sworn in as district attorney and G. E. McCaffrey as defense attorney. On the same day, bench warrants were issued for Sidney DeLong, William Oury, and James Lee.

The grand jury returned an indictment for murder against "Sidney DeLong and 99 Others" on October 23. On the same day—presumably as a point of honor—Raphael Sais, Mercedes's father, appeared at the court, asking to be included in the indictment, to which Judge Titus acceded. Listed with Sais on the indictment in addition were men of the Martinez and Tellez families, various relatives of the former captive Feliz Tellez Martinez.

Not only did the grand jury return indictments against the accused, but Judge Titus also issued bench warrants for Dr. Goodwin, Eskiminzin, "Jesus Lo, Manuel Lo, Juaquiri Lo, Pedro Lo, Estevan Lo and Antonio Lo." The following day, Dr. Goodwin appeared in court, pled not guilty, and was released on bail. The court assigned Grant Oury, William's brother, to defend Goodwin. Titus then dismissed the court until December 5.

He convened again on December 6, some nine months after the fact. Tensions ran high in the courtroom. Eskiminzin's people lined one wall of the room, while the O'odhams lined the other. According to the O'odhams' oral tradition,

> The Enemy chief said: "You have destroyed many people." The Mexicans said, "Why did you kill two of ours? We avenged it." Then the [Enemy chief's Indian agent] advised the Enemy to stop warring. But

the Enemy chief said it had been given him from the beginning, he could not change his ways. . . . He said it had been that way since creation. He said the Enemy had been the first to speak, the first to drink cold water. That is why they are so fierce. That chief had a rock as big as his fist. He slammed it on the table and said he would not change. The agent said: "If you disobey the law, the law will kill off the Enemy. Soldiers will come. The other Indians will help." The Enemy chief said: "If you'll give me food and all I ask, I'll stop." . . . . The White man agreed. . . . That was why the Enemy got so much. Every time the government delayed the gifts, the Enemy went on the warpath.[75]

First to testify for the prosecution was Royal Whitman. Among other atrocities, Whitman testified, "I saw the dead bodies of several woman that I recognized. . . . I'll state positively two were lying on their backs, entirely naked and shot through the breast, apparently with pistol balls."[76]

The following day, the prosecution called James Lee, who admitted that he had been among the accused party. He also pointed out to the court, "There are parties indicted who were not there at all. A portion of them were those indicted." On December 9 Guillermo Tellez testified that the "Papagos" at San Xavier perpetually feared Apache attacks. Ascencio, "the Papago Captain," charged that "the condition between the Papagos and Apaches is the same now as ever—never any peace between them." A former captive who would serve as Eskiminzin's interpreter for decades, Concepcion Brillo, testified for the defense. Sam Hughes, as the "Adjutant General of this Territory," swore that Apaches had taken government-issued arms during several raids occurring prior to the Camp Grant massacre, thus accounting for the government issue found among the Aravaipas.[77]

Gertrude Ward swore that she had known Trinidad Wooster when they both lived in Tubac, but that she, Gertrude, had moved to Camp Grant about a month before the attack. While at Grant, she had recognized Trinidad's dress, worn by an Indian woman. "The wife, an Apache Indian, of the interpreter [Brillo] had the clothing. It was a merino dress, red-striped, with black silk trimmings."

Finally, on the last day of testimony, Dr. J. C. Handy, who would one day become the son-in-law of Larcena Pennington Scott, testified that he had seen many of the same Indians at different forts, underscoring their ability to travel freely.

What the new western Adam lacked in firepower, he more than made up for in social empowerment, as the outcome of *U.S. v. DeLong et al.* would prove. As members of the grand jury and the trial jury, even as witnesses for the defense and prosecution—supported by a sympathetic judge and defense attorney, and a district attorney with a vested interest in an acquittal—the new western Adam had tangible control over the outcome of the trial.

Even as the trial had unfolded, Tohono O'odham Indian agent Reuben Wilbur reported to Lt. Royal Whitman at Camp Grant that eight captives had now been located in Tucson. Three others were living at San Xavier, including one wounded girl. Additionally, the Manso Apache guide Manuel Duran had sold one of the captives, and her whereabouts were unknown.[78]

On December 12 Judge Titus ended the evidentiary phase. District Attorney Rowell—whose anemic prosecution the witnesses had easily thrown off, some even going so far as to accuse Rowell of having participated in the planning of the affair—presented his final arguments. The following day, Titus sent the charge to the jury, virtually inviting them to acquit. In nineteen minutes they returned with their verdict: not guilty. If captivity was not simply chattel-slavery, but a contest between men over the issues of shame and honor, as one historian has claimed, Tucsonans and the Tohono O'odhams had won their battle against Eskiminzin. "After the court, the Enemy chief and the chief of the People shook hands. Four Indians were appointed to go to Washington and to tell the government there would be no more war. . . . Each of them was given a medal," according to the O'odhams.[79]

The alacrity with which Tucsonans had dismissed the Camp Grant massacre did not end the search for the Aravaipa children. In April 1872 defense attorney J. E. McCaffrey received a visit from Gen. O. O. Howard, special commander of Indian Affairs under President Grant's Indian Peace Policy. Howard was in the region to promote councils with Arizona natives, much to the consternation of the military. He requested McCaffrey's assistance in returning the missing children to their families. "And at the same time," according to McCaffrey, "Gov. A. P. K. Safford gave me a list of the children, and of the families in which they were living, and this was the first information I had upon the subject."[80]

Placed on the spot by persuasive men, McCaffrey had little choice but to comply.

I promised to assist Genl. Howard, assuring him that the return of the captives could be obtained without violence or difficulty, and at the same time asked him if he required the return of those children who had no parents living, and of those who do not desire to leave their present homes. Genl. Howard answered me in the presence of Gov. Safford that where the children were already in good hands and had no parents to claim them, he wouldn't require them to be returned to anybody else; I said further that I thought it probable some arrangements might be made in regard to those who had parents, by which their parents would agree to allow them to remain with those who had them, and Genl. Howard assured me (also in presence of Gov. Safford) that he would give every assistance in his power to effect such an arrangement if the consent of the parents could be obtained.[81]

Once again, issues of heredity and environment would play central roles in the lives of Arizona captives. On May 1 McCaffrey took "Francisco Romero and Leopoldo Carillo to see Genl. Howard about the matter—each of these gentlemen had one of these captives in his family, and each of them said that the child was considered by him as his own flesh and blood, but that he would give it up if necessary."

The general repeated to Romero and Carillo the promise he had made McCaffrey "in regard to not requiring the return of the captives who had no parents." Howard concluded the conversation by informing the trio that they must have all the captive children at Camp Grant on May 21 "to show the Apaches that we were dealing with them in good faith." Not incidentally, the Arizona territorial congresses of 1872 and 1873 would produce a spate of legislation providing—for the first time—for the adoption of orphaned and indigent Indian children.[82]

On May 21 McCaffrey and the men of Tucson known to be holding Aravaipa children met as agreed at Camp Grant. According to McCaffrey, the children present included "Lola, a girl aged about ten years, in care of Leopoldo Carillo"; "Vincente, a boy about nine years . . . in care of Simon Sanchez"; "Juan, a boy about five . . . in care of Manuel Martinez"; "Luisa, a girl about four . . . in care of Jose Luis"; "Lucia, a girl . . . three years, in care of Francisco Romero"; and "Maria, a girl . . . twenty months, in care of Nicholas Martinez."

Although General Howard had promised Tucsonans that Aravaipa children whose parents were dead could remain with their captors, according to McCaffrey, he abruptly countermanded his own order regarding the orphaned children. "At the conclusion of the talk with the Apaches, and when it had been ascertained that *none* of these children had parents, Genl. Howard ordered all the children to be delivered to the Apaches, or rather to the man with whom he was treating as a chief . . . [,] and the immediate execution of the order was only stayed because all the children struggled to get away from the Indians, and their screams were heart-rending." The following day, General Howard decided "that the children should remain at the Indian Agency at Camp Grant in charge of the agent until the matter could be referred to the President for his decision."[83]

The situation stagnated until McCaffrey wrote to territorial representative John McCormick in Washington DC on May 28, 1872, asking the politician to "do what you can to secure the return of these children because they (the children) are now Christian and it is an outrage upon Christianity and civilization to force them back into the savage heathenism of the Apaches. . . . We do not desire to take these children upon a writ of habeas corpus, as that would be claimed by General Howard to be an effort on our part to break up his negotiations with the Indians."[84]

Despite the attempts of Capt. Frank Stanwood and Gen. O. O. Howard to return the Aravaipa children, others remained in captivity. Of the twenty-eight captives reported missing in April 1871, only six were present at the redemption at Camp Grant in May 1872, leaving twenty-two captives unaccounted for. Of these, two were thought dead, and one had been sold by Duran, leaving nineteen remaining captives. Three of these were last known to be at San Xavier, in the homes of Mendoza, Lucas, and Romero, for a tally of seventeen missing captives. Like the Chiricahua captive Nah-thle-tla sixteen years earlier, the Aravaipa children were destined for a life of servitude. "The People brought some children back and kept them as their own," said the O'odhams. "When they were grown, and able to work, they were sold in Sonora for a hundred dollars a piece." Finally and most tellingly, one last captive can be traced to the household of a white man. Carlota, said to be a deaf-mute, was raised in the home of William Oury. Taken when six years old, she still resided with the Ourys at the age of twenty. Thus it was that the most disabled, least empowered captive of the Camp Grant massacre was destined to spend the remainder of her life in the home of one of the most powerful men in Tucson.[85]

While Oury would defiantly defend his comrades' actions for the rest of his life, it was Sidney DeLong alone who lived to express regret for his role in the infamous attack: "It may be said that there were many acts of cruelty perpetrated on that 30th of April that showed badly for a civilization that pretended to be Christian." The residents of Tucson had their revenge, but their guilt was inescapable. Try as they might to bury the event in the past, postmodern history has unearthed it. In the words of a recent scholar, "The massacre is not quite what anthropologists call a 'public secret' because it is not so much concealed as simply—or not so simply— disregarded" by all but modern-day Aravaipas, for whom the memory will live forever.[86]

4

1872–1882

UPROAR OVER THE Camp Grant massacre compelled
the army to transfer Lt. Col. George Crook from the
Department of the Columbia to Arizona. Arriving in
Tucson, Crook immediately lobbied for a telegraph line,
the nearest station being in Los Angeles. He then amassed
a force of some fifty civilian and Indian scouts—"some
good and some bad, the best that could be summoned
together at the time"—and rode north to Apache territory
where Fort Apache had been situated for a year. It seems
likely that Mickey Free, who had spent years among the
White Mountain Apaches and who had served his scout
apprenticeship under the chief *manso* scout, Manuel
Duran, was among them.[1]

At Fort Apache, powerful Western Apache headman
Hacke-idasila of the *nadots-usn* clan—one of the largest—
had allowed the white soldiers to erect a camp in his
territory, on the south bank of the White River. Within
two years, the arrival of Aravaipa refugees from Camp
Grant had placed further strain on resources and social
relations at Fort Apache.[2]

1. Olive Oatman. Courtesy of the Arizona Historical Society, Tucson. Photo #1927.

2. Lorenzo Oatman.
Note the wound on
the top of his head.
Courtesy of the
Arizona Historical
Foundation, Sacks
Collection.

3. Larcena Pennington
Page. Courtesy of the
Arizona Historical
Society, Tucson.
Photo #13751.

4. Mercedes Sais Shibell. Courtesy of the Arizona Historical Society, Tucson. Photo #1646.

5. William "Boss" Head and Mickey Free, ca. 1871. Courtesy of the Sharlot Hall Museum, Prescott, Arizona.

6. Bessie Brooks and other students
at Prescott Public Schools, 1902–1903.
Bessie is probably the woman standing
fourth from left in the back row. Courtesy
of Sharlot Hall Museum, Prescott, Arizona.

7. Eskiminzin and his children. The young girl may be his daughter, Chita. Courtesy of the Arizona Historical Society, Tucson. Photo #41085.

8. Charley McComas. Courtesy of the Arizona Historical Society, Tucson. Photo #43421

9. Santiago McKinn,
1885. C. S. Fly Collection.
Courtesy of the Arizona
Historical Society,
Tucson. Photo #170.

10. Geronimo. Courtesy
of the Arizona Historical
Society, Tucson. Photo
#3905.

11. Octaviano Gastelum.
Courtesy of the Arizona
Historical Society,
Tucson. Photo #1112.

12. Apache Kid. Courtesy
of the Arizona Historical
Society, Tucson. Photo
#18851.

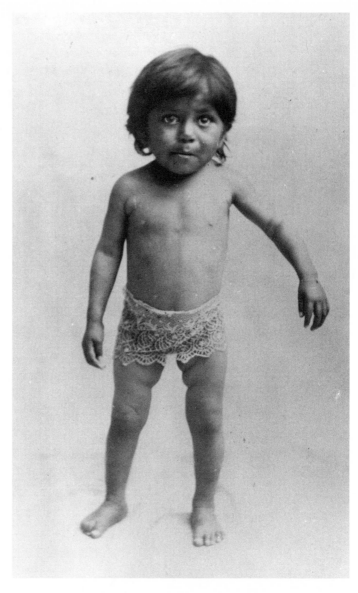

13. Apache May, daughter of Apache Kid, 1896. Courtesy of
the Arizona Historical Society, Tucson. Photo #41405.

14. John Slaughter. Courtesy of the Arizona Historical Society, Tucson. Photo #17471.

15. Cora Viola Slaughter and Apache May, 1896. Courtesy of the Arizona Historical Society, Tucson. Photo #9940.

Even prior to the arrival of the Aravaipas, the military presence had exacerbated a long-running feud among the Western Apaches. Pedro, a *tca-tci-dn* clan head whose people had been banished by the Cibecue bands at Carrizo Creek in 1850 under *ti-uk-a-digaidn* leader Miguel and his brother Diablo, had been given asylum by Hacke-idasila of the White Mountain Apaches. Internal tensions already simmered under Hacke-idasila's watch, as General Crook's entourage approached Fort Apache.[3]

Crook succeeded in recruiting Western Apache scouts there. As others have found, for most Indian males the choice was one between "extermination and domination." Apache leaders "faced a choice of accommodation or resistance." With the massacre of the Aravaipa women and children at Camp Grant and the undeniable intrusion of the military at every turn—aided by former captives—Pedro, Diablo, Miguel, and Hacke-idasila understood overt resistance was futile; they permitted their warriors to enlist. With access to Mexico via the Sonoita and San Pedro valleys now increasingly out of the question, Apache males had little outlet for traditional warrior activity other than as scouts with the white soldiers. Now, the distribution of rations—and scout wages—would replace raiding for provisions among those warriors who chose to enlist. The Western Apaches' internal social fracture was now compounded by the presence of the U.S. Army and the enlistment of scouts.[4]

Of the seventy-five men who volunteered, forty-four were mustered in, among them former captives Mickey Free, Severiano Gracias, Jose Maria Yescas, and Concepcion Brillo—all former Mexican captives of the Western

Apaches; they now found their cultural, linguistic, and geographic experience in demand. Most, like Free, married Apache women and lived out their lives among their former captors in the White Mountains while enlisted in the U.S. Army.[5]

One historian has written that frontier social boundaries were porous; some whites and Indians (and Mexicans) crossed over to live in each other's worlds, sometimes by choice and sometimes by chance. Some absorbed skills and knowledge that empowered them to serve as intermediaries in the American West. But events of April 1882 would position Mickey Free as the most influential Western Apache *yodascin* of all. Free's growing influence stemmed from years of captivity and acculturation, followed by even more years of army duty. But his position as a chief military scout, guide, and interpreter in the 1880s would intersect with his role as a *ti-sie-dnt-i-dn* clansman, posing a potent threat to Geronimo and his band. Most important, some believed, powerful medicine guaranteed that Mickey Free's enemies could not kill him.[6]

The rising tide of whites began flooding indigenous Arizona by the early 1870s. On the Salt River, Tempe and Phoenix rose from a former Mexican settlement. Below the Gila, rancher Henry Hooker, who had acquired the Sierra Bonita ranch, introducing blooded stock to the territory. Large-scale ranchers such as Hooker—who could employ hundreds of cowboys, used mail services, and required endless supplies—joined Crook in the push for a telegraph line to California.[7]

Crook, having secured the alliance of the Western

Apaches, intended to invade southeastern Arizona where—in the opinion of many whites and Mexicans—Cochise's men had too long operated with impunity along the border. But the arrival of Vincent Colyer, an emissary of the federal Peace Policy, quashed Crook's intentions. Furthermore, not only did Colyer explode in anger when he heard that some of the White Mountain scouts were enlisted "against their will," he also pitied Eskiminzin and created a reservation for starving Tonto Apaches at Camp Verde as well.[8]

Stymied, but restraining from action that could be interpreted as interfering with Colyer's mission, Crook and military supporters could not help but feel smug when the Tontos were accused of attacking a stage outside of Wickenburg. In Crook's words, "By the time Colyer reached San Francisco, his confidence was considerably shaken, and by the time he reached Washington his head was chopped off." Crook wasted no time reactivating his command. On November 21, 1871, he reissued General Order Number 10, notifying Apaches that anyone found off the reservation after February 15, 1872, would be considered hostile.[9]

But once again, the arrival of peace emissaries from the East delayed Crook's plans. General O. O. Howard, besides negotiating the attempted release of the Camp Grant captives, negotiated a reservation at Fort Grant for Eskiminzin and the Aravaipas. Howard's venture into Cochise's stronghold in October 1872—a fortress of rock enshrining sacred space in the Dragoon Mountains of southeastern Arizona—secured a reservation for the Chiricahuas on their homeland, buttressing the

Mexican border. For the first time since his outrage over the Bascom affair in 1861, Cochise reinstated relations with whites, but peace would not follow.[10]

With the Chiricahuas now "protected" by the Indian Bureau, Crook vented his frustrations on the Yavapais and Tonto Apaches, despite that fact that Delshe, one of the Yavapais' chief warriors, had been trying to initiate agreements with military agents since at least 1867. Hampered by the presence of Pima scouts, the Yavapais' hereditary enemies who attempted to kill them whenever they approached the soldier's camps, Delshe and other headmen were powerless to reach accord with the white soldiers.[11]

In December 1872 Crook once again enlisted scout companies in anticipation of the Tonto campaign. Among those mustered in were Mickey Free, Pedro's nephew Alchise, and Eskiminzin, who enlisted under Crook's request as a show of good faith. Within weeks, seven commands scoured the Tonto Basin, leaving the Yavapais and Tontos no choice but to surrender or be annihilated. By April 1873 the various bands had surrendered, fallen to a brutal campaign that gave no quarter to women and children and that placed a bounty on the war chiefs' severed heads. All but a handful of Yavapai and Tonto combatants now remained in the Tonto Basin.[12]

After the campaign, Crook praised his commands liberally, particularly the performance of the Apache scouts. John Bourke wrote that they were crafty, daring, and ambitious. In all, ten Western Apaches were given medals of honor after the Tonto campaign; but as one scholar has pointed out, white accoutrements of honor, while bolstering some Indians' status, also made it difficult for the recipients to convince their tribesmen they were "still their own person."[13]

With the increase in white population came a parallel increase in official white personnel and the propensity for heightened tensions between military and civilians. Opportunities for official corruption multiplied as well. Under the impositions, internal feuds among Apaches simmered, fueled by overcrowding and mismanagement. Rivalries riddled San Carlos, and many Western Apaches resented the seeming liberty granted the Chokonens in the south, while the Western Apaches huddled under a battery of military and civilian authorities. As if to emphasize their liberty, Nednai raiders led by Juh emerged from the Sierra Madres of Mexico in February. After wiping out the Harris family at the mouth of Turkey Creek in the Chiricahua Mountains, the Apaches took the family's teenage daughter with them.[14]

Meanwhile, Crook initiated a "civilization" program, ordering the scouts to "cultivate the soil and perform the various industries prescribed by the Indian Department, the same as other Indians." In short, they were to now "serve as the nucleus for the establishment of civil government" on the reservations.[15]

Even as Crook instilled his program, "hostiles," as defined by Crook's General Order Number 10, continued to raid. In June, Mickey Free was promoted to sergeant of the scouts at Fort Apache. Crook kept detachments in the field, relentlessly pursuing those who refused to live on the reservations. By midsummer 1874 they had stilled the Tonto Basin resistance. By November a telegraph wire stretched from Prescott to Yuma and on to San Diego.[16]

With his "hostiles" now "subdued," Crook turned to the internal management of the reservations. The establishment of Fort Goodwin in 1864 had initiated the Western Apaches into the white man's barter system: women traded hay and wood forage in exchange for flour, beans, and coffee. Then, the enlistment of scouts into the regular army brought a cash economy. Furthermore, following the Tonto campaign, Crook had paid the scouts in horses, determined they should learn to raise them rather than eat them. Bourke observed that many former captives prospered under the new economy, among them Severiano and Concepcion. The intrusion of the army at Fort Apache had wrought a new political economy among the Apaches. As the *yodascin* transformed their former status and access to power, and the warriors adapted the social order and methods of raiding in Mexico to the exigencies of aiding the white man's army; even as Apache women redefined criteria for selecting mates, the influence of former chiefs of the Western Apaches weakened under the imposed economy.[17]

At Fort Apache relations among Apaches continued to sour. One of Hacke-idasila's men shot the post brewer. The scouts attempted to arrest some men of Hacke-idasila's band; in the melee, six of his men died and fourteen were placed under arrest. Miguel's brother Diablo, a scout, killed the man who shot the brewer. Citing poor administration by the civilian agents, Crook found it necessary to occupy the agency building at Fort Apache. Then, because of continued reports of stock raiding, Crook ordered that all Fort Apache Indians must move to the vicinity of the fort. The area was the homeland of Hacke-idasila and his guest Pedro, but Miguel's Carrizo and Cibecue people lived as far as forty-five miles to the west. With the unwilling consolidation, internal White Mountain relations chafed under the cinch of alcohol, overcrowding, and resentment. In one fight, two White Mountain warriors and nine Cibecues died, including Miguel.[18]

In 1871 Tucsonans had butchered the women and children—the heart and soul—of the Aravaipas, and in 1872–74 Crook's campaign had decapitated the Tonto and Yavapai leadership. At Fort Apache the loss of Miguel transferred power to his brother Diablo, while the young Alchise had begun to speak for Pedro, even as another young warrior, Polone, represented Hacke-idasila. In June 1874 Cochise died of natural causes; his son Taza inherited his position but would die shortly. The Chiricahua and Western Apaches found themselves confined to but a nucleus of their former territory, lacking mature leadership and vulnerable to the whims of volatile tempers.[19]

Mickey Free, on the other hand, found himself at the fulcrum of change. He accompanied Crook's entourage to the Hopi villages as an interpreter and guide in October 1874. There, Crook hoped to extract promises from the pueblos that they would cease buying arms and ammunition from Mormons and Utes which they in turn had been trading to the White Mountain Apaches. But it was Free who appeared to get the better part of a bargain, according to John Bourke: "'Mickey Free,' our Apache sergeant, proved equal as a trickster to any of his adversaries and to hear him expatiate with unblushing effrontery upon the almost priceless value of the paper money in his possession one would think the knaves were not all dead yet. For two dollars, he purchased better blankets than we would get for ten, and more than that, the Moquis seemed to be under lasting obligations to the young imp."[20]

In February 1875 the Interior Department, against Crook's advice, ordered the closing of the Fort Verde reservation and the consolidation of the Tontos and Yavapais at the San Carlos Apache reservation. Functioning as interpreter for the relocation command, Mickey Free found himself at the crux of trouble when a child's game escalated into a frenzy, leaving five Indians dead and ten wounded. The commanding officer later reported that through Free, he had addressed the three leading chiefs, forcing them to end the fight. This took some time, he explained, because "the interpreter had to make all parties understand." One scholar has written that the interpreters of worlds in collision translated more than just words; they brought "comprehensibility to otherwise meaningless static." Interpreters needed not just knowledge of languages, but the ability to interpret what people believed and how they behaved. Moreover, they needed the ability to "react on the spot to every atom of incoming information."[21]

By 1875 Mickey Free had proved his worth to the whites, but he would one day have opportunity to demonstrate his worth to his clansmen as well. In July 1875 the civilian agent at San Carlos, John Clum, a proponent of the Peace Policy, obtained the closure of the Fort Apache Indian agency. He ordered all Indians there to relocate to

San Carlos, excepting the scouts and their families—most of whom belonged to Pedro, Miguel, and Hacke-idasila's bands. These were allowed to remain at the fort until their enlistments expired. By the end of July, all one thousand members of the fifteen bands had relocated to San Carlos, including Nayudiie's people—placing some 4,200 Native Americans under Clum's control. By the time the last band settled at San Carlos, Crook had relinquished command of Arizona and departed for the Great Plains.[22]

The new commanding officer ordered Diablo and his men off the post grounds two months before their enlistments expired. While Hacke-idasila's people had already relocated to San Carlos, Diablo's people were furious that Pedro had permission to remain at the fort. Diablo and his men attacked Pedro's warriors; Diablo was arrested. When released, he took his people to San Carlos. Within a year many would quietly return to Cibecue, out of sight of the soldiers at Fort Apache.[23]

South of the Gila, Chiricahuas continued to raid. In the spring of 1876, soldiers jumped a party of Apaches, only to realize they had a white woman among them. In the ensuing skirmish, the woman's baby was killed; the white woman vehemently insisted she wanted to stay with "her tribe." On the return trip, the command passed over Turkey Creek, where she told the soldiers how she had been taken captive there after the Apaches murdered her family. Only then did the soldiers realize they had the Harris girl, taken by Nednais in 1873. She took them to the scene of the captivity, where they found only "scraps and bones." Following her return to the whites, the Harris girl found herself so discontented, she was "given her freedom and she went back to the Indians." Orphaned, and her child now dead, the Harris girl chose to return to the only life she knew.[24]

According to scholars, women such as the Harris daughter who willingly breached the racial/sexual divide represented one of whites' great anxieties: the woman who got away. Not only did such a woman escape white social constraints, she also escaped the master narrative, disappearing into the unknown realm of the "dark other." Most unsettlingly, "She leaves the rest of the narrative untold."[25]

Meanwhile, forced native consolidation continued. In May 1876 Clum closed the Chiricahua agency and relocated Cochise's people to San Carlos. Raising two companies of civilian Indian police at San Carlos, he funneled the unwilling Chiricahuas onto the San Carlos reservation.[26]

In 1877 Clum relocated Victorio's Apaches from the Warm Springs agency in New Mexico to San Carlos. Doing so required that Clum "capture" a shaman-warrior already polarizing the ranks of the disorganized Chiricahua—Geronimo. With the aid of the Indian police, Clum tricked Geronimo into captivity. Against their will, the Warm Springs Apaches relocated to San Carlos. On the way, smallpox broke out among them. Terrified, the San Carlos Apaches fled from the approaching Warm Springs refugees.[27]

In September 1877 Chiricahua warriors attacked San Carlos, running off livestock and Indians, but Geronimo and Naiche, the brother of Taza and son of Cochise, stayed put until April 1878, when Nednhi warriors from Mexico once again attacked San Carlos. This time, Geronimo fled with them.[28]

Apaches lined up to enlist as scouts in pursuit of the Chiricahuas. Among them was a twenty-two-year-old known to the soldiers as John Rope, the adopted brother of Mickey Free. "My brother and I went along on one horse, riding double. At San Carlos there were lots of Indians gathered to enlist. We lined up to be chosen. My brother was the first one picked," Rope recalled.[29]

Although the scouts monitored the Mexican line, they found no trace of Geronimo. Meanwhile, Victorio too had fled San Carlos, crying "war forever" on whites. Once again the scouts combed the border, but to no avail. Surprisingly, Geronimo sent word that he would return. Angry whites and Mexicans objected to Geronimo's taking shelter once again on the reservation, but Mickey Free and John Rope and the scouts delivered him back to San Carlos. Then, in an unprecedented move, second lieutenants Thomas Cruse and Charles Gatewood received orders to take a company of scouts to New Mexico to resume the search for Victorio in February 1880. Startled at the unexpected sight of Western Apache scouts in New Mexico, Victorio's people fled to Mexico.[30]

In retaliation for having lost access to his supply base at the Mescalero Apache agency, and angry with the scouts, Victorio ordered his son Washington to head a raid on San Carlos in May 1880. Washington's men butchered an influential White Mountain scout known as Sergeant Dick and members of Dick's family. After killing more Indians at San Carlos, the raiders got away, pursued by

Mickey Free and Al Sieber, the civilian chief of scouts. On May 25, 1880, one hundred San Carlos men enlisted in the hunt for Victorio, seeking revenge for the death of their clan leader. Even Pedro sponsored a war dance to ensure White Mountain victory on the trail.[31]

On June 5 the cavalry, along with Sieber and Free, struck Washington's camp at Cook's Canyon, killing three of Victorio's sons, including Washington. Among the Warm Springs who escaped the troops was future Chiricahua author James Kaywaykla. Victorio's people retreated once again to Mexico, but on October 15, Mexican troops massacred the Warm Springs Apaches at Tres Castillos, killing Victorio.[32]

Back at San Carlos, the returning scouts learned that Pedro's nephew Alchise had killed Diablo at Fort Apache. Polone, Hacke-idasila's spokesman, was murdered too. Scouts were kept busy trying to prevent the "annihilation" of Pedro's *tca-tci-dn* by avenging *ti-uk-a-digaidn* and *nadots-usn* clansmen. The *tca-tci-dn* paid the price in February 1881 when avengers killed Petone, shot Pedro through both knees, and seriously wounded Alchise. With Petone's death, leadership of Pedro's people went to Alchise. However, another Cibecue man, Noche-del-klinne, would fill the vacuum left in the leadership of the Carrizo and Cibecue people.[33]

By August 1881 the anger and frustration of the dead Miguel and Diablo's *ti-uk-a-digaidn* had helped fuel a "ghost dance" movement, led by Noch-del-klinne on the Cibecue Creek. Frightened by the Apaches' growing interest in the new "religion," an army command was detached from Fort Apache to arrest the suspect "medicine man." But when forced to choose between their military obligations and their clan obligations, many scouts chose the latter, sparking a gun battle in which eight white soldiers and six scouts lost their lives. Shocked by the "mutiny," and ignorant of Apache clan relations, whites would never again truly trust the Apache scouts. In the aftermath of the Cibecue affair, troops rushed to Arizona to quell any further "uprisings." Geronimo and his followers, spooked by the sudden increase in military presence, fled San Carlos on September 27, 1881. They rode for Mexico with $20,000 worth of Henry Hooker's horses, but left Loco's reluctant band behind.[34]

Mickey Free had not been present at the Cibecue "mutiny," and the army had never questioned his integrity. Sergeant Fred Platten described the Mickey Free familiar to most soldiers at Camp Verde.

> H Troop had an Indian company of thirty scouts under Mickey Free. Mickey Free, sometimes called Kid Indian, was said to be the indirect cause of Cochise going on the warpath years before. . . . [He] was kidnapped by a band of White Mountain Apache who raised him. . . . Cochise tried to reason with the soldiers and explain that it was not his tribe but another that kidnapped the boy. But . . . his protestations availed him nothing. . . . Cochise was still exacting his "eye for an eye" nearly twenty years later. . . . To H Troop, Mickey Free was a valuable ally. When it came to tracking, or other scouting duties, he had no peer.[35]

In January 1882 San Carlos heard that the Chiricahuas were coming for Loco. Mickey Free and Al Sieber hurried with Gatewood to New Mexico, hoping to cut the Chiricahuas at the border. They crossed the raiders' path in late March, but too late to prevent Geronimo, Naiche, Chihuahua, and a heretofore relatively unheard-of warrior, Chatto, from racing to Ash Flats, east of San Carlos.[36]

At Ash Flats they rode into the rancheria of civilian guide and interpreter George Stevens and his White Mountain wife, Francesca. Stevens employed several White Mountain men, including the former *yodascin* Victoriano Mestas, who was married to a White Mountain woman. Dja-la-ta-ha, or Ear Tips, the brother of Sergeant Dick who had been killed by Geronimo earlier, stood by as well. When Ear Tips refused to hand his whiskey over to Geronimo, the angry chief butchered every Mexican on the ranch—nine men including Victoriano Mestas, as well as women and children. Mestas's son they spared at the insistence of Francesca, on the grounds that the child's mother was Apache. The Chiricahuas fled Ash Flats, dragging White Mountain captives with them.[37]

As they approached San Carlos, they devised a scheme to murder the Indian police, but then they abandoned the plan. Creeping into camp, they found Loco's people prepared to leave. After beheading the chief of police, Albert Sterling, they cut the telegraph wires and released their White Mountain captives. The Chiricahuas then fled, but not before running off agency livestock, including that belonging to Nayudiie, the Apache father of Mickey Free.[38]

Furious, the old chief and his clansmen pursued Geronimo and his warriors to the banks of the Gila.

There the raiders had helped themselves to the goods on a freight wagon, including a barrel of whiskey. Refreshed, Geronimo and his men crossed the river. Nayudiie and his men soon followed, but lost the trail and turned back to the scene of the demolished freight wagons, where they finished the whiskey. That night, Nayudiie and another of Mickey Free and John Rope's relatives died in their sleep. When the *ti-sie-dnt-i-dn* at San Carlos heard the news, most believed that Geronimo had poisoned the barrel.[39]

John Rope, who had been serving as a policeman at San Carlos, remembered that all the scouts were called together, and the Apaches living at Fort Apache were transferred to San Carlos for close watch. "It was at this time that they issued a gun and belt to me and put me on special duty. I no longer was a policeman. I was just carrying arms to shoot the Chiricahuas if they should come. Sieber said that the Chiricahuas had killed some of my relatives, and so he was giving me this rifle to guard myself with."[40]

Geronimo had garnered the rage of the San Carlos Apache scouts once again, but this time Nayudiie's clansmen had an obligation to exact revenge. Among the most powerful of these was Mickey Free, the "coyote" who had the ears of the white soldiers in his grasp.[41]

Upon learning of Loco's outbreak at San Carlos, Al Sieber had rushed Gatewood and his men back to San Carlos. After enlisting and arming the scouts, they were back in the saddle. According to Tom Horn, Mickey led the way for a detachment commanded by Capt. Tullius Tupper. Mickey "was so reckless and loved to fight so well that he would have led those troops right into any kind of trap and come out alright himself, for the fellow seemed to bear a charmed life," Horn wrote. The detachment caught up to the "broncos" after surreptitiously crossing the Mexican border. "Tupper was spoiling for a fight, and anyone that went where Mickey would go in a scrimmage was bound to see the biggest part of it," according to Horn. The detachment and scouts punished the Chiricahuas below the line, killing at least fourteen Apaches and capturing their sizeable pony herd. Free's reputation was enhanced once again.[42]

The Chiricahuas reeled under the scouts' wrath. According to Geronimo's biographer Angie Debo, the "utterly exhausted" Apaches "dragged themselves across the level Janos Plains." The following day, Mexican forces attacked the band. "People were falling and bleeding and dying on all sides of us," Jason Betzinez remembered. Although a party of warriors nearby could have fended the attack, they took no action. Angie Debo speculates that internal tensions had begun corroding the Chiricahuas' cohesion, because the warriors rode off, offering no aid.[43]

Geronimo and his band regrouped on a mountainside as Mexican troops attacked repeatedly, trying to dislodge them. Heavy fire continued until dark. Preparing to slip into the night, James Kaywaykla heard Geronimo call out to his men, "If we leave the women and children we can escape." One warrior shot back a reply. Raising his rifle to Geronimo, he said, "Say that again and I'll shoot." Geronimo turned and disappeared.[44]

Debo questions Geronimo's performance under fire,

citing three battles that he escaped while his wives and children perished. She wonders, Was this merely a series of circumstances? After all, Kaywaykla stood by his story, and "it gained some credence throughout the tribe," persisting into the 1930s. Furthermore, Betzinez also reported that some Chiricahuas did abandon "the babies." Others gave their permission to the warriors to choke them "so that they wouldn't give away their movements by crying." The raid to liberate Loco had cost the Chiricahuas dearly, in Debo's view. But when viewed through the lens of captivity, the historic cost went beyond dead babies, for Geronimo had now drawn the personal wrath of the *ti-sie-dnt-i-dn* scouts on the one hand, while his leadership crumbled on the other.[45]

The Chiricahua survivors resumed their flight to the Nednais in the Sierra Madres. After some days of recuperation, they ventured to Casas Grandes, where Juh had preserved nominal trade relations. When Mexican soldiers saw they were drunk, they attacked them. Geronimo, Juh, and Betzinez escaped, but twenty Apaches died, and thirty-five were carried into captivity. Among these were the wife and children of Chatto and one of Geronimo's wives. The loss of his family would soon distance Chatto from Geronimo.[46]

In early summer 1882, as the flesh decayed on the dead Apaches scattered along the trail from the Animas Valley to Janos, a small party of Chiricahuas silently approached one of the massacre sites, where the clothing and remains of the dead still lay strewn about. Among the travelers was a twenty-six-year-old Western Apache woman, known in documentary history only as the person who would one day become Mrs. Andrew Stanley. She was the maternal niece of Hacke-idasila, Eastern White Mountain chief of the *nadots-usn* clan, and she was about to escape her Chiricahua captors.[47]

Mrs. Andrew Stanley was orphaned before the age of two in 1858, after which she and her siblings were raised in the home of an uncle near the White Mountain site that would one day be occupied by Fort Apache. At first, expected to comfort her baby brother, she poked sticks at him instead. She pined for her mother and wandered back to her old camp, "but it was destroyed. I sat about there and cried. That's the way I kept the people awake at night. . . . That woman used to pick me up and carry me about. . . . After awhile I quit grieving."[48]

Her uncle, Hacke-idasila, "used to come over once in a while and tell me how to do. 'Your mother will never come back, so don't cry,' he told me. 'Are you sure she will never come back?' I said. 'Yes, she will never come back,' he said and cried about her, so I did also." Her relatives worked hard to raise her and her siblings, "but I couldn't say that I had all I wanted then. I had [a] hard time because I lost my mother when I was little."[49]

As she approached puberty, one of her deceased mother's sister's came to claim her. "I told them, 'You ought to have taken me away long ago. Now I am big.'" But she moved with her aunt, who proved to be a strict disciplinarian. Hacke-idasila scolded the woman for making the girl jump into water that was too icy, saying, "When I had that child I did her no harm." Mrs. Andrew Stanley admitted that she did not sleep well either, because her aunt made her awake at dawn to run. "She dragged me right out of the wickiup sometimes to make me do it. I thought it was awful then." She frequently warranted discipline, which her aunt dispensed liberally. "I used to get whipped most every day . . . because she said, 'You don't mind what I say.' I can see now that it was the right way to do for me. . . . Now I know that she was right."[50]

When she got older, one of her uncles wanted her to accompany him on a visit to another Apache camp, but her custodial uncle did not want her to go. "While he was off hunting, I and one of his daughters went." But Mrs. Stanley's uncle caught up to the party and ran her back to her home at the sharp end of a rope. "When we got home [he] wanted to string us up by the wrists all day, tie us up, because we had done a bad thing in running away. But . . . he did not."[51]

After returning to the White Mountains, Mrs. Stanley's family had to flee when "some of our people killed some white people and so we have enemies again with them." The family headed to Cibecue, where headmen gathered. "Then, a lot of them started out to make peace with the whites at Fort Apache. They made a flag of white cloth and held it up on their way. This way they made peace with the whites again there."[52]

But in 1874 some of Pedro's *tca-tci-dn* killed two of her *nadots-usn* relatives, and her people scattered again to the Gila Mountains. When orders were given to all outlying tribes to consolidate around Fort Apache, Mrs. Stanley's people once more returned to the fort. There, an unwelcome suitor—Tca-gudi, a *tca-tci-dn* clansman— wanted to marry the eighteen-year-old. "If you don't marry

me, I'm going to kill another of your relatives," he told
her. She left Fort Apache and returned to Fort Bowie,
"where I had kin," until at last her brother took her back
to Fort Apache.[53]

At Fort Apache, Stanley married for the first time, but
it was not to Mr. Stanley.

> My older brother . . . gave me to this man, saying that
> he did not want me going off all over any more at all.
> . . . I lived with this man I don't know how many years.
> . . . I was still a young girl then. . . . He taught me lots
> of things, improved my mind. But he finally got killed.
> This was two great troubles in my life; first my mother
> died when I was small, then this man I was married
> to got killed. That's how I had a hard life.

Following her marriage, Stanley's relatives learned that
tca-tci-dn scouts and soldiers were planning to kill them,
so they removed to the Indian agency at Fort Bowie, where
they camped with the *nadots-usn* among the Chiricahua.
"That's where I always stayed down there, among the
hai-a-ha when at Bowie," she said.[54]

But trouble arose again, and Mrs. Stanley lost her husband. The Chiricahuas, with whom they had reconciled,
made a dance. "There in the dance, one *hai-a-ha* girl
came with one bottle of tulibai and gave it to my husband
there." After finishing the drink, Mrs. Stanley's husband
wanted more. "Then he said to his brother, 'Let's go and
fill this bottle up for the girls at my camp . . . ' but his
brother said, 'No, you should not be fooling with girls
like that.'" In a brawl, his brother stuck a knife in his
side. He lived, but then the Chiricahua women cursed

him, and "in four days he died. The *hai-a-ha* must not have liked us being there," Mrs. Stanley concluded.[55]

For some time Mrs. Andrew Stanley and her brother left the Chiricahuas at Fort Bowie, visiting other relatives in the area. When they contemplated returning to the Chiricahuas, they heard they had been moved to San Carlos. One day a woman of the party told Mrs. Stanley of a rumor that an elder wanted to marry Stanley. "'This old man is not the kind that would suit you,' the woman said, 'so let's get my horse and yours and pull out.' . . . So we did." The girls headed to Fort Bayard, New Mexico, and the Warm Springs Apaches. At last they arrived at a Chiricahua camp, where Mrs. Stanley had a brother. "We had only been there two days when I heard that the girl I had come with married a man there. I guess the two loved each other well—that's why she went all that way to him."[56]

After about a year with her brother's camp, Mrs. Stanley's brother died of a pistol shot. She lingered at the Chiricahua camp until a Chiricahua woman suggested they go visiting. After collecting various companions along their route, the group decided to return to the Chiricahua camp where Mrs. Stanley's brother had died. They sent advanced runners, who learned that the camp had been moved to San Carlos.[57]

Without her husband or brother, Mrs. Stanley found herself traveling alone with the Chiricahua woman, who wanted to return to the Fort Apache agency, but Mrs. Stanley wanted to go to Fort Bayard. They reunited with the runners sent to the abandoned Chiricahua agency, and they eventually agreed to go to Bayard. When they arrived, the Chiricahua camp was abandoned, and the men with Mrs. Stanley killed the Mexicans living in their stead. Mrs. Stanley and two other women lived with the Chiricahua men at the Bayard camp for "a long time . . . just the five of us. . . . Then I talked to these two men. 'Don't kill any more Mexicans . . . that is the way they trouble us,' I told them."[58]

The group eventually headed west, and Mrs. Stanley told her male companions, "I have a lot of people living over to the west here, and I don't want you to kill any of them at all. You must mind me, because I am alone with you and am like your captive. So you ought to do what I say." They traveled until they arrived at an overhang overlooking the camp of Naiche, Cochise's son, at San Carlos. "Hey, compadre, I want you to come down here," the chief called out to Mrs. Stanley, but the others in the party declined, and the group, including Stanley, moved on. "It was from that time on that I was a captive to the Chiricahua," said Mrs. Stanley.[59]

Mrs. Stanley's position among the Chiricahua men grew precarious as they increasingly ordered her about. Once, the men killed a Mexican. His horse bolted, catching the dead man's foot in the stirrup. "Go catch that horse," they told her, "so I did. Then they said, 'Take the dead man's foot out of the stirrups,' so I did. Then they said, 'Get up on him and ride him,' so I did. . . . I had to do just as the *hai-a-ha* told me now, as I was just as if a captive to them."[60]

"Those men were pretty mean all right," she continued. "[They] were not afraid that anyone would follow them because they thought they were great fighters, and so they never looked back. Now all the women were like slaves to these men." After a series of skirmishes with whites and Mexicans, a remorseful Mrs. Stanley thought about the woman who had gotten her into the situation. "If she had not told me to go along in the first place, I would not be in all this trouble that I was. I had a lot of *nadots-usn* kin up at Fort Apache, and it was on account of me that a great number of them enlisted as scouts, so as to bring me back from the *hai-a-ha*, but they never got me," lamented Stanley, underscoring one scholar's observation that Indian males sometimes enlisted to directly intervene in their own families' welfare.[61]

From that point, the Chiricahua began to worry that the Apache scouts would find them. "It was true that my people as scouts did come through there, and [my uncle] was there and hollered my name, but I never heard him." Once, the Chiricahua men overheard one of Mrs. Stanley's relatives among the scouts ordering the other men, "If you shoot some *hai-a-ha* be sure and call out the name of that woman, she might be around there and be sure not to shoot her, please." When the Chiricahua men returned to camp, they told Mrs. Stanley, "'When those scouts shoot, you will be shot by us first, so you will have to die.' So I said to them, 'All right, kill me right now.'"[62]

In the spring of 1882, the men considered heading to Mexico, but "if we had gone down [there] we would have been killed sure, for all those *hai-a-ha* were killed down there." The small party of Chiricahuas, with Stanley in tow, instead "went from one place to another, living on tops of mountains, zigzagging back and forth." The group moved yet again; this time "they told us we were going to see the ocean."[63]

On the way to the Gulf of California, the party's path brought them to the Chiricahua skeletons lying on the ground before them. "We stayed about six days there, but those two [Chiricahua] men spent most of the time down there where the dead people were and cried there. It was the scouts [Mickey Free] from San Carlos that had done this killing, and I don't know why those *hai-a-ha* there did not kill me right there. But I had two revolvers in a belt on my waist, one on each side, and a lot of cartridges in the belt, and the revolvers loaded, and I told the other women that if the men made a move to kill that I would kill one of them first."[64]

They continued to the ocean. "We got to a big mountain and went on top of it. . . . I liked it a lot, seeing the ocean there. It sort of rose and fell, just like lines of soldiers marching along." When they headed north again a month later, a fork in the road afforded Mrs. Stanley the opportunity to separate from her captors undetected. Traveling at night, she arrived at the outskirts of Tucson and came upon a white man's cabin. Like Larcena long before her, Mrs. Stanley found some sustenance in the abandoned camp. "I found lots of things, sugar and coffee. I had never seen coffee before and did not know what it was. The sugar I stuck my finger in and tasted it. It was sweet." Stanley helped herself to supplies, especially matches, and continued by night.[65]

After traveling for weeks, Mrs. Stanley at last arrived in familiar territory on the south side of Mount Graham. From here she traveled by day, until she met a Mexican couple whom she had known years before. They hid her, then sent her off again in new clothing and Mexican beads and hair braids. After many days wandering, she came to a camp. "It was some scouts and soldiers from San Carlos and the White Mountain people who had captured some *hai-a-ha* and were taking them back. . . . They had the dance there. . . . I don't know what put it into my head; I guess I must have been crazy, for I decided to go to the dance."[66]

Mrs. Stanley dressed in the finery her Mexican friends had provided and slipped into the dance unnoticed. Two Chiricahua girls danced beside her. "I danced that way two times and then walked off." The troops moved on, and Mrs. Stanley prepared to reunite with her family. Like Olive and the captive O'Odham woman, she was of two minds regarding her reappearance among her people. "I did not want to go right among my people, as I had been by myself so long. . . . I was too wild, like a deer." She camped on the mountainside above the *nadots-usn*, who in her absence had returned to Fort Apache from San Carlos. When ready, she hobbled her horse to prevent him from leaving camp, and then descended to her people below. The first person she met was the uncle who raised her, watering a pinto horse she had ridden as a child. "He talked to me in the Chiricahua dialect and asked me where I came from. I spoke back to him in the same dialect. I asked him how his daughter was and called her by name. He had not known me before that. Then he knew me and ran to me and caught me there."[67]

As with Olive Oatman, Mrs. Stanley's reintegration into her natal society was fraught with complications.

Her family was overjoyed to see her, "but I had been alone so long that they all smelled bad to me, and I could not stand it. I vomited because of it. They gave me food to eat, but I could not swallow it. I was not used to this. I slept a ways apart from the rest, so as to avoid being too close to them." Her aloofness confused her family. When she returned from her mountain camp the following day after retrieving her horse, they had abandoned the camp, except for a woman too elderly to travel. "She told me, 'While you were away, those people said that you had gone after the *hai-a-ha* so they left here right away.' I told the woman, no, that I was all alone and all right and that I traveled two months to get here." Mrs. Stanley's return defied all expectations, as had Larcena's. "The old woman said[,] 'It was as if you were dead. But now you have come back, so stay.' Those people thought that I was dead long ago, and now, when I came back, it was like a ghost coming back to them." But Larcena's kin had not feared that she was bringing the "enemy" with her. Eventually, Mrs. Stanley's family saw that she was not with the Chiricahuas, and they accepted her. "That's the way it used to be in the old days; whenever a person returned who had been captive to the enemy, their relatives were always afraid that they would lead the enemy to them, as this had happened before."[68]

But Mrs. Stanley could not anticipate that Apache men, fascinated by the brave woman who had returned from the dead, would complicate her reintegration. She had only been in the camp for days when one of the men insulted her. Mrs. Stanley told how she "had a rock in my hand that I had been rubbing the hide with, and so I took it and hit him in the face with it. The blood came down. . . . I said, 'There is no right for anyone to call me that way. I have had a hard time and so no one should bother me.'" Her assailant reported her to the agent. When he returned, he told her, "They are going to send you away from here for two years." When she faced the agent, he laughed and asked the assailant, "What did you fight that good little girl for? She has had a hard time for a long time. . . . The next time you bother her then you will be sent away for two years."[69]

Despite the protection of the agent, Mrs. Stanley continued to attract unwanted attention. Once when she went for water, the suitor she had rejected many years earlier, Tcagudi, tried to pull her off her horse. Mrs. Stanley escaped Tcagudi in that instance, but he was persistent. He appeared at her camp with a horse, saying, "I am the man who wanted this girl long ago . . . but now I would like to have her." But Mrs. Stanley rejected Tcagudi. "He was a pretty mean man and thought that he could get away with it, that the other people were scared of him." One of her female relatives returned the horse. Again, he grabbed her hair and dragged her to a tree, where she struck him with a limb. "If I had had my knife there, I would have killed that man," she claimed. She sliced him with a child's knife in the throat. "I cannot marry even a brave man, for I am a brave woman also," she told him. "I have run off from the Mexicans and Whites many times down to the south, so I cannot marry you." He countered by confessing that it was he who had murdered her brothers years earlier. "Well, I am going to kill you sometime," Stanley told him. Troops arrived; they took Tcagudi to the agent, who mocked his bloody face: "'Don't let me hear any more about you bothering her. You will be sent away or killed if I do.' . . . But that man still thought about me," Stanley remembered.[70]

Tcagudi continued to pursue her, telling others, "I am going to get that girl sometime. I will not give her up." Mrs. Stanley's relatives reported the threat to the agent, who told them to move closer to the fort. There Mrs. Stanley made the acquaintance of scouts Mickey Free and Andrew Stanley. An officer thought she was a Chiricahua woman, but Mickey Free explained her circumstances to him. Mrs. Stanley distanced herself from the fort, but the officer sent the Indian scouts after her, still unsure if she was Chiricahua. Stanley told the scouts, "I have traveled with the *hai-a-ha* many times and was captured by them, but I ran off from them and I can't go back any more. . . . The officer who wants me, let him come to me himself." Soldiers came for Mrs. Stanley, who insisted to the captain, "I guess I look like a Chiricahua woman to you, but I am not. I belong to here." Again the captain sent for her. Stanley told him in detail about her captivity. Finally the officer replied that "now he would look after me. . . . I had rings on and a lot of beads about the wrist and neck, so I guess that was why they thought I was Chiricahua." She was now under the watch of the guard and could not leave the post.[71]

Still the men came after her. One convinced the captain she was his sister and carried her away, intending to marry her to a Chiricahua man. "I am not going to marry anyone. Why did you take me up here? If I marry anyone we will both go dead there," Mrs. Stanley told him indignantly. A scout saved her, and the agent apologized for the confusion. Her brother tried to convince the captain to allow her to leave; finally, she lived with him at the scout camp. For two years, Mrs. Stanley said, "there used to be a lot of single men . . . but I did not want any of them. . . . I told those men that they were just as well to cut me up in little pieces and divide me between them. Then the captain told me if I didn't get married soon, that he would marry me himself. He was joking." Mrs. Stanley tired of the unwarranted attention, telling the men, "I don't eat well when anyone is watching me. You men come about me every evening, so that I can't eat well." After more months of turning down prospective husbands, one scout in particular, Andrew Stanley, who had saved his scout wages "because he was thinking that he would use it if he got me, which he had planned to do for a long time," gained her approval. Like Olive Oatman, Larcena Pennington, and Mercedes Sais, the former captive married well. The two lived together the rest of their lives.[72]

Following Tupper's fight, Mickey Free fought at Chevlon's Fork in July 1882, where troops cornered "renegade" Western Apache warriors associated with Noch-del-klinne's aborted "ghost dance" movement the previous fall. More than a dozen Canyon Creek warriors lost their lives at Chevlon's Fork; Noche-del-klinne's movement was dead.[73]

Horn recounted the disposition of the captives: "Some of the soldiers afterwards said that there were a couple of wounded bucks, but that Mickey had stuck his knife into them. . . . I don't know if Mickey Free did this deed or not, but I am afraid that he did."[74] Free, it seemed, felt a special need to distinguish himself from the scouts who had "mutinied" at Cibecue.

The battle of Chevlon's Fork cut the last artery of Western Apache resistance to white expansion, the final major confrontation between Apaches and the military on Arizona soil. Military focus would now lock on the Chiricahuas, and the Western Apache scouts would work the situation to their own advantage. Most pointedly, the events of April to July 1882 marked Mickey Free as a *ti-sie-dnt-i-dn* wolf for the blue soldiers.

5

1883–1886

railroad

THE ARIZONA OF 1880 was not that of 1870. After 1877, daily mail and stage lines, as well as a telegraph network, connected Arizonans to the "States," and in 1878 the first telephones in Arizona linked Camp Thomas with San Carlos. But the arrival of the Southern Pacific railroad in Tucson in March 1880 eclipsed even these markers of territorialization.[1]

In Prescott, Ed Peck, the captor of Bessie Brooks, had made good on mining claims. Hezekiah Brooks had prospered as well, selling mining interests in June 1877 for $10,000. By 1878 the *Arizona Miner* could report that "Mr. and Mrs. Judge Hezekiah Brooks of Woodside are justly proud of their nice flower garden, thrifty fruit trees, beautiful gravel walks and grass lawns."[2]

But Ed Peck's fortune did not last. In November 1877 it was reported that suit had been brought against Peck for the recovery of almost $14,000 in assay expenses. In May 1879 a reporter followed up: "The Peck mine of Yavapai County is again in trouble. E. G. Peck, President of the Peck Mining company, took forcible possession of the mine, mills, etc., last week, holds the same with armed men and refuses to surrender without a fight. Superintendent F. W. Blake, employed by the Board of Trustees, went up to the mine and demanded admission but was told that by the aid of powder, lead and pluck, Peck would 'hold the fort.'"[3]

While life in the U.S. communities had acquired some sense of permanence, the repeated Chiricahua outbreaks from San Carlos and the ensuing chaos throughout the rural region compelled headquarters to recall Crook to Arizona in September 1882. In lieu of his long-standing civilian guide Archie McIntosh—who was struggling with alcoholism—Crook turned to Al Sieber. For his part, the returning John Bourke described how the arrival of the railroad had changed the logistics of war and eclipsed the primary need for wagon trains. The Department of Arizona ceased to fret over the availability of ammunition and supplies to its troops. On the other hand, according to Bourke, the railroad had also brought with it an influx of "coarse Americans" who had "diluted much of the quaint charm" of Tucson.[4]

Crook held long discussions with the leading men of the Fort Apache reservation in the autumn of 1882. They indignantly informed him of the grievances they held against the corrupt agents and traders that had tyrannized them since Crook's departure. Bourke noted that Pedro now relied on an ear trumpet, while an Apache woman fed her baby from a bottle. As he observed, "The world does move."[5]

Crook reclaimed control of the reservation when headquarters promised he could exercise full authority.

Next, he received permission to officially invite the former White Mountain bands to return to their homeland, although many already had. Having mollified the long-standing tension between the warriors of the *ti-uk-a-digaidn* and Pedro's *tca-tci-dn*, Crook placed Lt. Charles Gatewood in charge of Fort Apache. Gatewood set to work, allotting land to the returning families.[6]

Like other captives before his time and after, Free now found himself caught in white man's obsession with the merits of heredity and environment. At the time of Crook's return to Arizona, Free had been enlisted in the San Carlos Indian police, a move often undertaken by discharged scouts. Officially, the enrolling agent recorded the blue-eyed, reddish-haired *yodascin* as a "half-blood." Less than six weeks later, Free was discharged for "disrespectful language to the chief," and ensuing events indicate the altercation may have concerned his "real" identity, for on the following day Free reenlisted, this time as "Irish-Mexican."

On November 30 Agent Willcox notified the Indian Commission office regarding Free's behavior and the change in his racial status. Willcox received his reply on December 13: Free was to be fined five dollars, in addition to his demotion (from sergeant to private). A question accompanied the order:"Heretofore, Mickey Free has been reported simply as a half-breed. In the descriptive list he is [now] reported as 'Irish and Mexican.' Is he an Indian and a member of the tribe, as required by the rules governing the U.S. Indian Police Service?" Willcox replied on January 5, 1883: "He is of Irish and Mexican parentage, was born in Mexico, stolen by Indians when a child, adopted as a member of the tribe, a position he now holds in full fellowship."[7]

Mickey Free's racial heritage would continue to confound historians for more than a century. Many, like agent Willcox, ascribed to the notion that Free was the son of his Irish stepfather, John Ward. Al Sieber described him as "half Mexican, half Irish and whole son of a bitch." Even Tom Horn said his "mug . . . looked like the original map of Ireland." More incredibly, John Connell, the enumerator responsible for the 1880 census at Fort Apache, claimed he was half Pinal Apache.[8]

Free's physical appearance only added to the speculation and bigotry. Tom Horn described him as having "long, fiery, red hair," and John Rope agreed. Census enumerator John Connell claimed Free had "long, tawny hair, straight, ragged and unkempt." Santiago Ward, Free's half-brother, would say Free had brown hair and gray eyes. Tom Horn said he had "one blue eye, the other having been hooked out by a wounded *deer* when he was twelve years old." One historian speculated he had lost his eye to trachoma, a common occurrence in the dusty Southwest. Another claimed, "Mickey had grown to manhood, his beardless face permanently disfigured in combat with a *bear*, in which he lost an eye, his red hair long and tangled as an Apaches, and as thoroughly inhabited, too." Connell summarized the whites' viewpoint: "[Free] usually allowed his hair to fall over the affected eye, but his appearance . . . [,] his ugly features and sneering countenance, gave him a decidedly repulsive appearance." As one scholar has written, interpreters' and guides' powerful positions as culture brokers placed them on the periphery of their own communities.[9]

In fact, Free's racial heritage was a product of the settlement of Mexico's far northern frontier. Radbourne demonstrated in 1972 that Free was descended from Mexican settlers. Further research indicates his paternal grandparents, Juan Abad Tellez and Tellez's wife, Syriaca, may have traced their roots to Mideastern descent. Compounding the issue, Syriaca and her sister, Luz, bore the surname of "German" on the 1831 Sonoran census. As Cynthia Radding has written, the far Mexican frontier was the product of "wandering peoples."[10]

Meanwhile at San Carlos, Crook had placed Crawford in military command, with Lt. Britton Davis in charge of the San Carlos scouts. Mickey Free resigned from the police to become Davis's interpreter, and Sieber served as chief civilian scout. Finally, Crook reissued his order declaring "hostile" all Indians found off the reservation. Of all the whites present, only Sieber had any inkling of the war of retribution raging between the Chiricahuas and the San Carlos scouts under Mickey Free. Warily, he predicted a protracted war.[11]

Crawford led the new command to the border. There, throughout the winter of 1882–83, they patrolled a vast frontier, where Mickey Free enjoyed the camaraderie of his peers, even if he confounded them. Tom Horn shared an incident from the field.

> The sergeant with them came up to me and saluted
> me, as they had always seen the Americans soldiers
> do, in a very business-like way. Mickey said to him,
> "Why do you salute your chief? He is no soldier. He
> is a citizen. I am the ranking soldier of this outfit and

if you want to salute, I am the one to be saluted." "I can't salute you," retorted the scout, "There is too much mixture in you for me to attempt it. You are part Mexican and part something else, and I don't know what that part is. I know I never saw anyone else like you. I know only Americans, Mexicans and Apaches. You are none of these and you are all of them, and as I am only an Apache, I will have to balk."[12]

Horn explained, "This is the kind of talk and josh that you could always find in the Apache scouts' camp."

In January, word had it that Mexicans below Janos had attacked Juh's band, killing women and children, including Juh's wife. Following the defeat, the Nednai chief retreated deep into the Sierra Madre, severing ties with Geronimo.[13]

Despite their patrols, the scouts failed to see the Chiricahuas coming. On May 21, 1883, raiders led by Chatto and Josanie crossed the border. Midway on the road between Silver City and Lordsburg, the family of Judge Charles McComas found itself in the Chiricahuas' path. Earlier that morning, McComas and his wife had left their daughters at the family home in Silver City, intending to take their six-year-old son Charlie to visit two older sons living south of Lordsburg. McComas, of Virginia, had previously practiced law in Kansas before marrying the daughter of an "important" Fort Scott family. The couple then moved to Arizona, where McComas practiced law and invested in mining.[14]

Jack Devine, a freighter, drew to the side of the road to make room for the McComas's wagon, traveling in the same direction. "Likely, Devine and his companions were the last to see Judge and Mrs. McComas alive. . . . The boy waved a small hand to them as they pulled up to let the spring-wagon pass," wrote an acquaintance of Devine's years later. Within moments, the McComases lay sprawled on the desert floor, dead. Riding on, Chatto's raiders took little Charlie McComas with them.[15]

At San Carlos, Britton Davis received the telegraph reporting the Apache raid in New Mexico. Responding to a commotion at the Chiricahua camp at Turkey Creek, he was surprised to find a warrior, Tsoe—a Canyon Creek man married to a Chokonen woman—in their midst. After arresting him, Davis learned that Tsoe had deserted the Chiricahua raiders. All agreed that he would lead Crook's command to the Chiricahuas in Mexico.[16]

With the disappearance of Charlie, Crook found the excuse he needed for official entry into Mexico. In Tsoe he found his guide. After securing permissions in July, Crook prepared for the invasion. At vulnerable Tombstone, men organized themselves as Rangers. Meanwhile, Gatewood hurried to San Carlos to recruit seventy more scouts and promptly trotted them to Willcox. From there, Crook's expedition started for the old San Bernardino land grant sprawled across the border in southeast Arizona. With its natural springs, the old hacienda would serve as the base camp for the amply provisioned expedition.[17]

On May 1, 1883, Crook's commands—the scouts' heads wrapped in red to distinguish them from the Chiricahuas—dropped below the southern horizon. Some who watched them wondered if Crook's scouts would not mutiny and attack the vulnerable white forces in Mexico.

But Crook, who held a particular respect for Alchise and his White Mountain men (a mere fraction of the total scouts), proceeded confidently, buoyed by the scouts' enthusiasm.[18]

The San Carlos scouts were particularly conscious of their mission. That evening, after the Western Apaches had penetrated Mexico—some for the first time—the scouts held a sweat bath to cleanse themselves of negativity that might impede the hunt. Afterward, a war shaman performed eagle medicine to assure them of catching their enemy. Following the war dance, they had even refrained from participation in the "big drunk" hosted by Al Sieber at nearby Bacerac. At Mickey Free's urging, John Rope declined the opportunity. "My grandson," Free advised his brother, "don't go over where they are drinking. There is liable to be some trouble."[19]

According to Rope, the scouts had also brought a sacred medicine bundle with them on the trail. But on the second day, when a photographer accompanying the command caught an owl and tied it to his saddle, the scouts' hopes suddenly collapsed, for the shadow catcher had captured an omen of death. At Tesorabi the scouts anxiously approached Crook, imploring him to order the man to release the owl or risk misfortune on the campaign. Apparently to placate them, Crook obliged. But the concession came too late for Frank Randall, the shadow catcher who had enslaved death. On May 9 the mule transporting Randall's equipment fell over a precipice, shattering the photographer's camera.[20]

On May 11, deep in the Sierra Madre, Crook detached Gatewood and the scouts to locate and initiate contact with the Chiricahuas. On May 15, as the detachment attacked a rancheria, scouts who were "too eager to engage in battle" and "very much excited" broke rank and fired, killing nine Chiricahuas. Rope captured three children, one the grandson of Naiche. One scout, a "good friend" of Naiche, badgered Rope to sell him the boy. Ever cautious, Mickey Free interceded in the confrontation. "Don't ask for the boy like that. We are on the warpath now and don't know for sure if this boy belongs to the daughter of your friend or not," Free ordered.[21]

After the firing stopped, Crawford interrogated a female captive who informed him that a boy named Charlie had been with the women prior to the attack. Crawford ordered her to return to the scattered Chiricahuas with an invitation to come into camp. Crook's men waited anxiously for a reply. The following morning, as Crook wandered from camp to hunt, Chiricahua men surrounded him, angry at the white presence on Mexican soil. Hearing the commotion, Free and Severiano ran into the fray. With offerings of food and tobacco they calmed the indignant men and convinced them to talk with Crook. The interpreters sat on the ground for hours, translating, as Crook argued to Chihuahua that the attack had been a mistake. Unconvinced, Chihuahua and his family left the conference, leaving women and children behind. But on May 18 he suddenly reversed his decision and agreed to return to San Carlos.[22]

On May 20 Geronimo cautiously approached the command. Crook challenged the chief to make his choice—peace or war. In what has been characterized as "the tensest period of the most dangerous expedition ever undertaken in Mexico," General Crook, with Mickey Free translating, convinced Geronimo of the futility of war. Geronimo, understanding that Mexico would never again be impregnable, at last agreed to return to San Carlos. His close associate, Kayetannae, also agreed to return. On May 23 old Nana came in, and three days later, Loco. Soldiers watched the crowds carefully, but none spotted Charlie McComas. Rumor had it that Charlie had fled with the women as the camp came under attack, but no one had seen him since.[23]

Although the scouts had avenged their clansmen—to the extent that they could, given the proscriptions of army enlistment—they remained wary under the pall of the owl omen. As John Rope remembered, after the surrender of Geronimo, a Chiricahua shaman sponsored a dance to mark the occasion. Lit by the fire and moonlight, the Chiricahuas danced, inviting the scouts to join them. Suspicious, Sieber forbade the scouts to attend.[24]

Sorely disappointed at not finding Charlie McComas, the command, with Severiano and Mickey Free in the lead, escorted the Chiricahuas back to San Carlos. Only Juh, chief of the Nednais, remained in the Sierra Madre. On May 24 the command departed, their numbers swelled by almost four hundred Chiricahuas. While Nana, Bonito, and Loco were among those returning, Geronimo and Chatto had promised to make their way to the border at their own pace, rounding up stragglers in the surrounding hills and driving their cattle slowly to the line.[25]

Again, as the command reentered Arizona and camped at San Bernardino, the Chiricahuas insisted on holding a dance. But the occasion, said Rope, was merely a ruse to slaughter the scouts. According to Rope, only the intervention of a White Mountain warrior named Dji-li-kinne—a White Mountain *yodascin* who had married into the Chiricahuas and become Geronimo's father-in-law—prevented the planned attack. Like Mickey Free, Dji-li-kinne found himself pressed against his clan affiliations. Forced to choose between his clansmen and his in-laws, Dji-li-kinne angrily confronted the Chiricahuas.

> I won't join in this because the White Mountain people are like relatives of mine. . . . You chiefs don't mean anything to me. I have been with you many times and helped you kill Mexicans and whites, and that's the way you get the clothes you are wearing now. I am the one who has killed these people for you and you have just followed behind me. I don't want to hear you talking this way with me again.[26]

Thwarted, the Apaches held their dance anyway, but once again Sieber kept the scouts in camp.

The expedition returned to San Carlos on June 15; mounted behind them were Chiricahua women. Whispers surely followed, for Apache women were known for their modesty, and riding behind a male implied familiarity. Staging their entrance, the scouts silently hurled the insult at the Chiricahua men.[27]

Dji-li-kinne, however, was not among those who returned. According to the Chiricahuas, Mexicans had shot him in Mexico. But Rope confided that the scouts believed the Chiricahuas had executed the little warrior—whom Rope described as no taller than a long rifle—in retribution for foiling the attack on them in the Sierra Madres.[28]

On his return to the reservation, Mickey Free found a visitor—his biological half-brother, Santiago Ward, a mere baby when Free had been captured in 1861. Santiago remembered the reunion: "I did not know him at first but he looked very much like his sister, fair with grayish eyes. They called him Mickey Free. I do not know why." Santiago spent the next year with Free, helping him escort the straggling bands of Chiricahuas to San Carlos as they sent word of their arrival at San Bernardino.[29]

Traveling the long miles together, Santiago would have shared with Free their parents' fate. He would have told how their mother had passed away in Magdalena, never learning that her son Feliz was alive. "Mother and father both died thinking brother had been killed," Santiago remembered.[30] "I came back to Tucson in 1878 with a man named Jesus Munguia and went to work in his meat market making soup in order to support myself and my sister Maria. . . . She died in 1880. . . . A friend of the family told me that he had seen my brother at San Carlos; that he had grown up as an Indian and was an interpreter for the government, so I went to San Carlos to see him," Santiago said.[31]

After the Sierra Madre campaign, Crook had commended Mickey Free and the scouts for their service in Mexico. Jubilant Tucsonans had toasted the general, sure the Apache "menace" had ended. At Silver City, Judge McComas's law partner, John M. Wright, had circulated a photo of Charlie and offered a reward for information leading to his recovery.[32]

In late October 1883, while Free and Ward were camped at Fort Bowie, word came of a captive white boy among

Bonito's stragglers. Once again, Free and Britton Davis scanned the milieu for Charlie, but found only a Mexican boy. Free promised Davis that "he can find out something in a little while."[33]

On October 28 Free reported that a Chiricahua told him Charlie was alive, held by Geronimo in the Sierra Madres. The chief was holding him as a "sort of hostage" until the Chiricahuas sent word that all was as promised at San Carlos. Naiche informed Free that Geronimo intended to bring the boy with him when he returned to the line.[34]

Kayetenne, from Geronimo's band, crossed the line into Arizona on November 5. Captain Rafferty, in charge of the escort, reported that Lieutenant Davis and Mickey Free had spotted a white boy among the returnees. Cautious of spooking the Chiricahuas before the return of Geronimo, the pair asked no "embarrassing" questions. Having been advised of the situation, Crook wired pertinent parties in New Mexico of the situation. The *Tombstone Republican* reported the development on November 17.[35]

Crawford had settled Bonito's people at San Carlos by the next day but advised Crook he would make no attempt to ransom the boy until Geronimo returned. But Mickey Free returned to Crawford with a report that Chatto had Charlie in Mexico. No one, however, had seen the child since the scouts' raid.[36]

At Silver City, lawyer John Wright heard that a captive had arrived at San Carlos. Rushing to Arizona, Wright was crushed to find that the child was not Charlie but the Mexican boy, who was returned to his family in New Mexico. Furthermore, he learned that Bonito claimed to have taken Charlie to Mexico and "raised him in his wickiup" until the scouts had fired on the camp. Discouraged but not defeated, Wright retraced his route back to Silver City.[37]

At last Chatto crossed the line in February 1884. When he arrived at San Carlos, he slaughtered a mare in honor of Britton Davis, whom he claimed had earned the Chiricahuas' respect through fair treatment. Shortly afterward, Chatto enlisted as Davis's first sergeant of scouts. At San Carlos he shared a wooden house with Mickey Free, a singular event, as scouts generally lived in their own wickiup camps at some distance from the soldiers. Chatto may have feared retaliation from the Chiricahuas, who reputedly viewed him as a traitor to Geronimo. His new alliance with Mickey Free shook the Chiricahua to the core.[38]

In March the *Silver City Enterprise* reported that John Wright had received a letter from Crawford, stating that Chatto's band had arrived on February 29 and that Geronimo's had followed on March 16. Crawford informed Wright that Chatto did not have Charlie and that Geronimo had only a Mexican boy. Crawford told Wright that he himself believed Charlie was dead. Shortly afterward, Wright received a letter from Crook, reiterating the belief and effectively terminating the hunt for Charlie McComas.[39]

In 1959 Jason Betzinez would tell Eve Ball that Ramona (a daughter of Chihuahua with whom he was educated at the Carlisle Indian School) had told him that a warrior had shot Charlie after the raid because his mother had been killed by a scout. Ramona later denied having told

Betzinez the story. In 1955 Sam Hauzous, the grandson of Mangus, said that while two Apache women were making their way to Crook's camp, they happened upon Charlie, lying seriously wounded in the brush. Fearing that the soldiers would blame them for his death, they passed him by and never knew his fate. Like Olive Oatman and the Mohaves decades earlier, the Chiricahuas feared misplaced blame for Charlie's fate from the whites.[40]

Despite Chihuahua's assurances to Geronimo, tensions at San Carlos heightened. Crawford railed constantly against the inept administration of the civilian agent. Henry Hooker had contracted to supply the Apaches with breeding stock, but had purchased "an inferior kind of Mexican cattle" instead. Alchise reported that "the Great Father had sent him up [some cattle]. Some were yearlings, others were older than this world, and had not a tooth in their heads. . . . Those that did not die of cold, died of foot disease or of hunger because they had no teeth to eat with." The same report claimed that "Mickey, the interpreter, got one cow. He was away with the general at the time. When he got back, they told him there was a cow for him. He put it out to pasture, but only owned it four days, of which two were spent hunting for it. At the end of four days, it was found dead."[41]

After the last of the stragglers returned to San Carlos in May 1884, Santiago informed Mickey Free that he would be returning to Tucson. Ever perceptive, Free intuitively understood that such a return would be impossible for himself. "I tried to get him to come home and see the family but he never would do it, always made some excuse. He wanted me to stay with him," Santiago later remembered. Free remained at San Carlos, the only possible home for a man such as himself.[42]

Tom Horn and Mickey Free spent the Christmas season of 1884 at Fort Apache. A month earlier, Al Sieber, rheumatic and unable to scout any longer, had arranged for Horn to take over as civilian chief of scouts. While there, Gatewood relayed that some of "his" Chiricahuas were missing; it didn't take Free long to learn that the warriors were raiding for horses in Mexico.[43]

Horn, Free, and the scouts left for the line as 1885 dawned. Although they lacked official permission to invade Mexico, Horn reasoned that as a civilian, he could breach the border. Crossing over, he camped until he spotted Apache signal fires across the valley. Returning to Arizona, he stationed scouts at pertinent points while he and Free watched for the Chiricahuas to cross back into the territory. As they waited, cowboys from the San Simon and San Bernardino ranches joined them, eager for a shot at the Indians. Horn attached Free to the San Simon boss, who asked if Free were a timid man. "I told him that if Mickey Free acted timid, to come back and tell me and I would shoot him. . . . A more recklessly brave man than Mickey Free never did live at any time, and as the cowboys wanted to fight so bad, I knew that if they followed Mickey they would be in it," Horn remembered in 1904, indicating the stature to which Free had risen among the white men who knew him.[44]

The detachment had their fight with the Chiricahuas, but a San Bernardino cowboy lost his life, while two were wounded. Two soldiers sustained wounds as well, and Mickey Free suffered a "big gash" in his left arm. But twelve Chiricahua lay dead, so all counted the losses and injuries worthwhile. In the weeks following, the San Simon boss "pressed" Horn and Free to make a visit to the ranch. In Horn's words,

> There were ladies there also . . . and one of them [said,] "All the cowboys say your man Mickey is one of the greatest scouts alive and one of the bravest men, but I am sure he looks like a villain." I told her that Mickey was a gentleman and a scholar, and that I considered him a judge of beauty, as he had told me that the white lady with blue eyes and blonde hair was the prettiest woman he had ever seen. Next day, I noticed she had Mickey in her house, feeding him sweet cakes and giving him lemonade.[45]

Back at San Carlos, discord filled the air. Agent Willcox adamantly opposed Crook's system of Indian juries. He especially disliked the traditional clubbing of murderers to death, calling the practice barbaric. But the U.S. Supreme Court had ruled in 1883 that the federal government held no jurisdiction over an Indian who assaulted another Indian on a reservation. If Crook were to push forward a "civilization" plan at all, it rested in the success of Indian judges and juries. Nevertheless, the agent continued to complain about the lack of respect for his authority, and Crook had to defend himself to the adjutant general in April 1885. In June the Indian Commissioner recommended that Crawford's authority be restricted only to policing the reservation.[46]

Caught between rival civilian and military agencies, and forced to live among the Western Apaches and the scouts who despised them, the Chiricahuas mulled their options. On May 14 Chihuahua and Geronimo hosted a tizwin drunk at Turkey Creek. Hearing of the infraction, Davis called the chiefs to his quarters for a discussion—interpreted by Mickey Free—centered on wife-beating and drunkenness.[47]

The Chiricahua men were livid over the challenge to their behavior. Chihuahua spoke angrily to Free and Davis pressed him for a translation. Reluctantly, Free conveyed the chief's message. "Tell Fat Boy that he can't advise me how to treat my women. He is only a boy. I killed *men* before he was born. . . . We drank tizwin all last night. . . . What are you going to do about it?"[48]

Alarmed by Chihuahua's belligerence, Davis wired Crook that trouble was afoot, but the message got no further than Al Sieber. Sore from his rheumatism, and drunk, Sieber tabled the message, confident of Davis's ability to handle the situation.[49]

Davis spent Sunday, May 17, 1885, umpiring a baseball game while waiting for a reply that never came. Late in the afternoon, Mickey Free and Chatto reported that the Chiricahuas had fled the reservation. Davis immediately took the field. By late August he, Chatto, and Mickey Free headed a column trailing Geronimo high into the Sierra Madres, but lost it. Twenty-five days and five hundred miles later, Davis's column descended the eastern slope of the mountains, a mere one hundred miles from El Paso. Exhausted and in no good humor, they rode to Fort Bliss. Upon his return to Fort Bowie, a disillusioned Davis tendered his resignation, preferring to try his hand as a ranch manager in Chihuahua.[50]

Meanwhile, the Chiricahuas eluded the whites. In the Mimbres River country east of Silver City, Geronimo's warriors struck again on September 11. That morning, John McKinn had started for Las Cruces, intending to load up on provisions for the winter. Traveling with a party of wagons, a premonition caused him to turn back, but not soon enough to protect his family from Geronimo. In his absence the Chiricahuas had raided his ranch. Finding young Irish Mexican Martin McKinn and his brother Santiago tending cattle in the fields, they seized the pair. Forcing his brother to watch, they murdered Martin and stripped him of his clothes. As they mounted to leave with Santiago in tow, the boy frantically insisted, "Me Apache! Me Apache!" But Geronimo pulled his hat off, exposing the boy's blonde hair. The raiders fled the scene, taking the terrified Santiago with them.[51]

As John McKinn pulled his wagon into his yard, excited laborers rushed to tell him that Martin and Santiago were missing. Around nine o'clock the next morning, they found the body of Martin, but Santiago was gone. The boy, meanwhile, rode with Geronimo and his men, sometimes for days at a time, stopping only to eat horse meat. Later he would say it was good, if one were hungry. At night, his captors bound him with rope to the leg of an "old woman."[52]

Geronimo continued raiding for weeks. As Santiago gathered firewood and herded horses, he made the acquaintance of the men in Geronimo's band. He learned to keep his distance from the chief, however. Angry that the boy couldn't understand his instructions, Geronimo had clubbed him brutally on the head with his gunstock.

Santiago, in turn, worked hard to learn the difficult Apache language throughout the fall and winter of 1885–86.[53]

By October 1885 the hunt for Santiago McKinn and the Chiricahuas had run its course. With their supplies exhausted, those of Crook's troops still in Mexico returned to the border to reorganize. Crook stretched a heliograph system across the region to facilitate another upcoming campaign. In November the Chiricahuas attacked a White Mountain camp, killing twelve Indians and taking six captives. Consequently, by mid-December Crook's men had penetrated the Mexican line once again.[54]

On the evening of March 11, Crawford's command stumbled on Chiricahuas camped on the Rio Aros. Hidden in the hills, they waited until daylight to attack. Tom Horn's recollection of the battle testified to the determination of the San Carlos scouts to exact complete revenge upon Geronimo for the killing of their relative in 1882. "One thing that worked against me was the eagerness of my scouts. I talked to them, and warned them to try to keep from starting the fight as long as possible to give us better light, but they were all mad because of the raid that the renegades had made on the reservation and the killing of the women and children," Horn wrote, indicating the *ti-sie-dnt-i-dn* had not forgotten their mission. The troops attacked at dawn, capturing Geronimo's pony herd and supplies. The chief had little choice but to negotiate a return to the reservation.[55]

The following morning, a company of Mexican troops composed of Tarahumara Indians accidentally shot into the military camp, mistaking the scouts for Chiricahuas. Before the situation could be clarified, the Mexicans shot Crawford through the head. Hearing the gunfire, Chiricahuas descended on the camp, anxious to fire on their enemies, the Mexicans. Despite the confusion, Lt. Marion Maus and Tom Horn managed to negotiate a ceasefire. The American command hurried to Nacori to bury Crawford, but not before extracting promises from Geronimo to meet with Crook at Canyon de Los Embudos in March, some seven weeks later.[56]

At the agreed-upon time, Chihuahua and Geronimo confronted Crook twenty miles south of the border near the old presidio of Fronteras. Geronimo, wary of Mickey Free, began by insisting that Concepcion interpret. Crook agreed, but only if the other interpreters were present, in order to "act as checks on each other." Geronimo then talked to Crook for hours, explaining why he had left the reservation in May 1885:

> I was living quietly and contentedly, doing and thinking of no harm, while at the Sierra Blanca. . . . I don't know what harm I did to those three men, Chatto, Mickey Free and Lieutenant Davis. I was living peaceably and satisfied when people began to speak bad of me. . . . I hadn't killed a horse or a man, American or Indian. . . . Sometime before I left, an Indian . . . had a talk with me. He said, "They are going to kill you[,]" . . . and I learned from the American and Apache soldiers, from Chatto and Mickey Free, that the Americans were going to arrest me and hang me, and so I left.[57]

Clearly, Mickey Free and the San Carlos scouts had made life on the reservation untenable for Geronimo.

The exasperated general, in no mood to listen to accusations against men he understood to be reliable, denounced Geronimo, and retired for the night. Even as the conference had been under way, soldiers watched for Santiago McKinn. One officer spied a white child with the Apache women, wearing a "dirty white rag" on his sandy hair. But even the dirt couldn't hide his freckles. When approached, the captive shied away, "wild as a coyote," remaining silent.[58]

The following day, Crook and Geronimo resumed their negotiations but made little progress. C. S. Fly shot a single photograph of the captive boy. In March 1886 it could serve as a document that could be shown to authorities and the McKinn family, should the Chiricahuas scatter with the captive before he could be liberated.[59]

On the next day, Geronimo and his men surrendered. That night a trader sold them whiskey. In the morning most Chiricahuas were gone; only Chihuahua had remained behind. He escorted the captive white boy to the soldiers, and the command departed for Fort Bowie. They arrived on April 2. Like other former captives' experience, McKinn's reintegration to his natal society proved troubling. For the next four days, the captive dodged the white men, refusing to speak. Charles Lummis, a reporter, saw the boy at Fort Bowie, but was unaware of the trauma associated with Santiago's need to learn the Apache language. As with Olive Oatman and Mrs. Andrew Stanley, Santiago's "return" would be complicated. "This poor child, scaly with dirt, wild as a coyote, made my eyes a bit damp. He is a pathetic case. The sorrow of it is that he has become so absolutely Indianized. He understands English and Spanish, but it was like pulling teeth to get him to speak either."[60]

On April 6 troops placed Santiago in a wagon bound for the Bowie depot. Lummis described the scene: "When told that he was to be taken back to his father and mother, Santiago began boo-hooing with great vigor. He said in Apache that he didn't want to go back; he wanted always to stay with the Indians. All sorts of rosy pictures of his home were drawn, but he would have none of them, and acted like a young wild animal in a trap. When they lifted him into the wagon, he renewed his wails, and was still at them as he disappeared from our view," words that could only have chilled Lummis's readers, obsessed as they were with the environment/heredity divide.[61]

As with General Howard's return of the six Camp Grant captives, it is difficult to interpret the reactions of Santiago McKinn. Was he reluctant to return to his father because he had actually acculturated into the Chiricahuas? Or did he fear Geronimo's wrath if he were caught trying to "escape"? Did he refuse to speak either English or Spanish for fear of Geronimo, who had brutally insisted on his speaking Apache? Surely, it was a troubled boy who left the military encampment with his relieved father. Despite Santiago's notoriety, when McKinn met his son at Deming, he found he would have to pay his son's train fare. The newspaper described Santiago as being in "deplorable" condition, although his father insisted he looked good. A family friend bought the boy a new suit of clothes, and father and son boarded a wagon for home. As they approached the ranch in the evening, McKinn allowed his son to fire his father's rifle. The reunion with his mother was bittersweet, however, as the relief at finding Santiago had been tempered by the loss of his brother Martin.[62]

Little is known about the remainder of Santiago's life. He married a Mexican woman named Victoria and had four children. For some time he worked as a blacksmith in the area, but the advent of the age of automobiles "caused the demise of the blacksmith trade." He spent his final years in Phoenix, living in obscurity.[63]

Back in Arizona, citizens were in an uproar over Geronimo's latest flight. Crook, disgusted with the Department of Arizona, submitted his resignation and left the territory. In early April, Nelson Miles arrived to replace him; within days, Geronimo struck again.[64]

In need of supplies, Geronimo's band had crossed the border near Nogales and approached the ranch of Albert Peck. Trinidad Verdin, the orphaned ten-year-old cousin of Peck's wife, found herself a captive of the dreaded chief.

> My cousin, Mrs. Peck, was sitting in the house. It was about nine o'clock in the morning when the dog began to bark. . . . Mr. Peck and his vaquero were out looking after cattle and my cousin, hearing the noise, said, "Trini, look out and see what the dog is barking at." I ran out to see and saw an Apache sitting down near the corner of the corral. I called to my cousin and told her an Apache was there. My cousin ran out of the house, her baby in her arms. The Apache shot and killed both. After killing my cousin and the baby, the Apache called out to other Apaches—a large band

of them—who were behind the corral. Those other Apaches then came up and all of them ransacked the house and took me prisoner. A little later I saw [Mr. Peck]. He was also a prisoner, in the hands of the Apaches. He spoke to me, asking me where the baby was. I told him that the baby was dead. The Apaches told me to shut up. I don't know what became of Mr. Peck after that.[65]

Al Peck, too, survived the attack. On the day of the raid, Peck and his hired man had gone to check cattle about a mile from the house, unaware that Indians were in the area. "I had just layed in a large stock of groceries and supplies. We usually brought in things to last a half year or so," Peck remembered. Spotting an Apache on a ridge, Peck's partner shot him dead. In the gun battle that followed, Apaches shot Peck's horse from under him, dropping him to the ground, where he lay stunned as Apaches stripped his clothes. When they saw his red flannel underwear, however, they abruptly left the scene. Some have speculated that the Apaches mistook the flannel for blood and left Peck for dead. Leonard Wood, an army officer under Miles's command, wrote that "the terrible ordeal rendered him temporarily insane, and as the Apaches . . . stand in awe of an insane person, they set him free." Others hold that when Peck worked in the Sonoran mines, he used to roll his shirt sleeves up over the same underwear, and the Indians who liked him called him Red Sleeves. Now, they recognized him.[66]

"I remember seeing . . . Trini," Peck told his family in later years, "but they wouldn't let me talk to her. She was crying." "At the time I was captured I was wearing a black hat trimmed with black ribbons," Trini recalled, perhaps indicating she had only recently been orphaned. "The Apaches took this off from my head as soon as they captured me." Releasing Peck, the Chiricahuas rode off with Trini Verdin.[67]

The raiders flew to the Dolores River Valley. As with Santiago McKinn, Geronimo and his wife kept Trini at their side. But when attacked by Mexican soldiers, Geronimo took a bullet in the arm and slid from his horse, knocking Trini off behind him. Dazed but free, she ran to the Mexicans and was rescued on June 17. Like Santiago's, her captivity under Geronimo had been harsh. "The Apaches have treated me very badly," the ten-year-old reported. "They have half-starved me and have beaten me. The old man . . . gave me this blow between my eyes," she said, pointing to an ugly bruise. "He would tell me in the Apache language to do something and I would not understand what he wished me to do, and then he would strike me."[68]

In answer to the unspoken question clouding her rescuers' minds, one Mexican officer wrote, "From her own indications and obvious innocence in the face of questions put to her by her relatives, we deduced that she was not violated at any time, probably out of respect for her tender age." As had been the case with Olive Oatman and Mercedes Sais, reassurances that the girl had not been raped by Indians was imperative to those of her own community.[69]

The *Arizona Daily Star* reported Trini's rescue on June 25, 1886. Confirming it had received a letter from

Captain Lawton in the field, the *Star* wrote, "The girl is looking quite well but has had very hard treatment." Trini Verdin was taken to Magdalena, where Peck picked the child up and returned her to Arizona. Family legend claims that the experience left her a hunchback for the rest of her life. Like those of Olive Oatman and Larcena Pennington, Trini's scars would be with her forever.[70]

General Miles, meanwhile, had entered into Mexico. On May 5 Miles left Nogales with thirty Apache scouts. Other detachments combed the Arizona side of the border, watching for Apaches. Nevertheless, on May 22 Geronimo struck again, this time in the Tanque Verde Mountains east of Tucson. Riding up on the ranch of Juan Tellez, Geronimo snatched young Octaviano Gastelum. "Mother and I were milking the cow when we were notified by the noise that the Apaches were near. They saw us, so they came after us and grabbed me by the arm. Mother tried to get me away. They . . . knocked her down the canyon." Like Santiago and Trini, Octaviano would be victim to Geronimo's short temper. "Because I was crying they took a tin can and hit me right in the mouth."[71]

The attack had occurred at seven-thirty in the morning. By that evening, his uncles had rescued Gastelum and returned him to his home. Geronimo retreated to Mexico, bereft of captives.[72]

While inspecting Fort Apache on July 18, Miles learned of Ky-e-ta, a Chiricahua who expressed a willingness to lead troops to the hostiles in Mexico. Recalling Gatewood from Fort Stanton in New Mexico, Miles sent the command south. After a grueling 1,000-mile march through the most rugged portions of northern Mexico, Gatewood,

Tom Horn, and the scouts under Ky-e-ta's guidance located the Chiricahuas. Gatewood informed Geronimo that his wife and family had been sent east, to Alabama. Geronimo agreed to meet with Miles in Skeleton Canyon, east of the San Bernardino ranch. There, on September 4, Geronimo once again tried to convince the army that Mickey Free and Chatto had caused his flights from the reservation. As Crook had also, Nelson Miles rejected Geronimo's arguments.[73]

Forced to choose between a chance at liberty in the Sierra Madres or a chance of reunion with their families in the East, the Chiricahuas surrendered for the final time. Defeated, Geronimo and his band camped once more at the San Bernardino ranch. While there, Geronimo presented a "wooden spoon of fine workmanship" to the mother-in-law of San Bernardino rancher John Slaughter, perhaps to reassure the woman that he intended her no harm. The spoon remained a "highly prized" souvenir of the Slaughter family for decades.[74]

The command moved on to Fort Bowie. On September 8, stripped of arms and horses, the Chiricahuas were loaded into wagons and transported to Bowie station. There, throngs of whites gathered to watch the event. Among the crowd were the Tevis sisters, daughters of the station keeper who had helped liberate Merejildo Grijalva from Cochise in 1858. In the words of one who knew Minnie Tevis, "Just before being placed on the heavily guarded train which was to take him east, the old Indian chief became intrigued with the striped silk ribbon ornamenting her sister's Leghorn hat. He tried to talk her sister into giving it to him, but she refused his whimsy."[75]

Another girl, Addie Slaughter, the daughter of John Slaughter, was there too. According to an observer, while waiting for the train, Geronimo motioned to Addie. When she stepped up to him, he took a strand of beads and "gently placed them about the girl's neck and bowed to her." Geronimo's war of resistance had ended. It would be white women and children, not Chiricahua, who would call Arizona home.[76]

Meanwhile, General Miles must have been aware of the personal animosity between Mickey Free and Geronimo, for he had taken the precaution of sending Free to Washington DC as the translator for a contingent of Chiricahuas, including Chatto, prior to the conference with Geronimo. The delegation hoped to persuade the Secretary of War not to deport the Chiricahuas out of Arizona, a process already under way. Chatto used the situation to make an appeal for the rescue of his family. With Mickey Free translating, Chatto begged the "white father" to find his family, sold into slavery in Mexico in 1882. "The favor he wants to ask of you is to ask for his land as if he was asking a favor from God. . . . He says he has a wife and two children in Chihuahua. . . . [He asks] that these children may be given back into his hands, so he can take them to his heart again, and have him with them at Camp Apache."[77]

Secretary William C. Endicott agreed to have photographs of Chatto sent to George Crook, who apparently knew the whereabouts of Chatto's family in Mexico. After the photography session at the Smithsonian, the delegates traveled to the Carlisle Indian School in Pennsylvania, where Loco visited his son. Afterward they journeyed west by rail to Kansas but were abruptly detained at Fort

Leavenworth and rerouted to Fort Marion, Florida. Chatto, Loco, Kayetannae, Noche, and Toklani, all scouts, were arrested as prisoners of war and placed in confinement with the other Chiricahuas arriving from Arizona. None would ever see Arizona territory again.[78]

As a Mexican American captive, Mickey Free could not be held as an Apache prisoner of war. He returned from Florida, arriving at Fort Wingate, New Mexico, on October 15, 1886, where he requested and received a discharge from the scouts. Mickey Free's war with the Chiricahuas was over.

Of all the men who fought for Arizona during the territorial era, Geronimo's character has been most questioned. A brave, bold, determined shaman-warrior, he nevertheless earned many Apaches' distrust, and lost a critical portion of their respect. Whites feared and reviled him, even as they praised him for his cunning, and damned him for his "lies." The Western Apaches hated him for murdering their relatives, while the San Carlos scouts and Mickey Free ensured that living on the reservation was out of the question for Geronimo's band.

Yet, ironically, according to one school of thought from the era, even Geronimo was a captive. A *Socorro Bullion* article claimed that he was born to a Mexican family in La Joya, New Mexico, where his biological father, Jose Louis Peralta, was well known as a musician who supported the family by playing at "fandangos." Supposedly, when he was thirteen and returning to Socorro from a musical engagement, the family was attacked by Navajos, who later sold Geronimo to the Bedonkohe Apaches, with whom he remained.[79]

Yodascin or Apache, lingering questions hang over Geronimo's actions in the year leading up to his surrender at Skeleton Canyon. Why would he expend limited resources in a flurry of fruitless raids when the capture of white and Mexican American children heightened white aggression against him? If he wished to punish his enemies, why not kill the children rather than capture them? If supplies were the purpose of his raids, why take children? Surely he must have realized that the final days of the Chiricahuas' traditional lifeway was drawing to a close. The situation called for mobility; then why handicap the band's logistics with nonindigenous children? Gone were the days when *yodascin* could be incorporated into the tribe at leisure; there was no time to train children on the trail, and no rancheria to sponsor a victory dance and absorb the captive. Had Geronimo hoped to force acculturation on the young captives at a brutal pace, desperately needing warriors? Or were his actions simply born of blind rage?[80]

One possible answer to Geronimo's inscrutable motives rests in the notion that he had intended to cache them away in the Sierra Madres with the Nednais and presumably Miss Harris, where the only hope of a continued traditional lifestyle lay out of sight of the known world. The captives' presence could help augment numerical strength and biological diversity for generations of hidden Chiricahuas. If so, Geronimo's intentions slipped away with the lost captives.

6

1896–1900

AFTER THE DEPORTATION of the Chiricahuas, whites celebrated the "end of the Apache wars." "With the removal of these worst offenders, it was officially considered that the Indian troubles were at an end in Arizona," they felt. Although there is no doubt that Geronimo had led the Chiricahuas to the bitter defensive end—a patriot in the truest sense, and the last indigenous leader to surrender to the U.S. military—it is not true that he was the last "free" Apache in Arizona. In truth, Hacke-bay-nay-ntayl—a name that was said to translate to "brave and tall and will come to a mysterious end" but that otherwise referred to a young man known as the Apache Kid—should be considered so, for despite the absence of the Chiricahuas, he waged a resistance of his own in southern Arizona long after the Chiricahuas were gone. Although he was never caught or proven dead, Apache Kid's liberty would cost him everything, including his captive daughter.[1]

An Aravaipa Apache from the Canyon Creek band at the San Carlos reservation, Kid's father had moved the family to nearby Globe, once a portion of the reservation, but in 1875 a rowdy mining town. At some point he may have been enrolled as a student at the Carlisle Indian School in Pennsylvania. Back in Globe, the Kid occasionally worked odd jobs and gradually acquired his moniker, eventually coming to the attention of Al Sieber. By 1882 Sieber had enlisted Apache Kid as a scout.[2]

By 1887 Apache Kid had married Chita, a daughter of Eskiminzin who had survived the Camp Grant massacre. But his life was about to take a turn, one that would keep him on the run forever. On June 1, 1887, a brawl broke out, and Apache Kid found himself responsible for policing a tense situation involving his own father.[3]

By the time Apache Kid arrived on the scene of the disturbance, Gon-zizzie, the brother of Sergeant Rip (a longtime policeman and scout), had shot Kid's father, Togo-de-Chuz. Decades earlier, Togo-de-Chuz had rivaled Rip for a woman's affections and won. On June 1, while the men were drinking together, the old rivalry had flared. In revenge for his father's death, Apache Kid and his people killed Sergeant Rip and Gon-zizzie before returning to face Sieber.[4]

Upset, Al Sieber attempted to arrest the Kid, and another melee broke out. In the confusion, Sieber took a rifle-shot in the foot that would hamper him for life. With Sieber already suffering from rheumatism and alcoholism, the injury only added to his ill health and disposition. Kid, meanwhile, had fled the scene, riding to the border before deciding to return and face a court-martial.[5]

In the military trial that followed, Sieber testified against the Kid, holding him responsible for his injury.

Kid denied that he had shot Sieber. Predictably, Kid was found guilty; he was sentenced to life in prison and sent to Alcatraz. In October 1889 authorities recalled Kid from Alcatraz to face civil charges in Arizona, hoping for an attempted murder conviction. At this second trial, Kid received only seven years at Yuma Territorial prison. While being taken to the prison, Kid and several other condemned Apache men overpowered the drivers of the transport wagon and made their getaway, leaving dead white men—among them Graham County sheriff Glenn Reynolds—behind. In one historian's words, the fate of the Apache Kid has been uncertain ever since.[6]

In late spring 1890, following Kid's escape, Mexican *rurales* killed three Apaches; the men found a watch and pistol belonging to Reynolds among the spoils. It was the first in a trail of evidence that whites would use to certify Apache Kid's continued presence in Arizona. As with Eskiminzin decades earlier, any atrocity otherwise not accounted for was attributed to the "renegade" Kid. Compounding white Arizonans' frustration, it was generally assumed that the Kid sometimes ran with a Chiricahua warrior named Massai. At St. Louis, Massai had jumped the train transporting Chiricahuas and made his way back to the territory. Arizonans frequently claimed to have seen one or the other "renegade," or their sign.[7]

In September 1890 two of Kid's companions surrendered and informed Sieber of Kid's whereabouts. Detachments with special funding took his trail, but still Kid continued to fight, tangling with the San Bernardino cowboys of John Slaughter in December. For a year Kid raided as needed. Exasperated military officials ordered the deportation of forty of Eskiminzin's people, including the chief, Kid's mother, Kid's wife, Chita, and his children, to Mount Vernon Barracks with the Chiricahuas—a move designed to pressure the family into talking or Kid into surrendering. The ploy failed. Eskiminzin denied that he knew of Kid's whereabouts, and Kid's activities continued unabated.[8]

With his wife deported to the east, Kid captured the youngest wife of Tonto Bill at San Carlos, forcing her to leave her children behind in late July 1892. An official report stated that the young woman was about twenty years old and "remarkably white for an Indian." This "remarkably white" woman may or may not be the same captive one observer reportedly saw tied with her feet underneath her horse, racing at Kid's side. Kid hustled his new woman off, her husband in futile pursuit.[9]

Publicly, the Indian agent worried about Kid's influence on the San Carlos Apaches. "Kid's presence affords a constant temptation. . . . [His repeated escapes] have created the impression among the younger Indian men that he is a very smart fellow . . . looked upon as a kind of hero favored by fortune," he wrote.[10]

Apache Kid's wife, Chita, returned to San Carlos with the help of John Clum in the late fall of 1892. In November 1892 a scout posted at Fort Bowie received a handwritten message from his brother-in-law at San Carlos, confirming rumors regarding Eskiminzin: "Kid's wife came back about 7 days ago." The public braced for Kid's reaction. On November 19 the *Globe Silver Belt* strongly urged the legislature to offer a reward for Apache Kid to hasten his apprehension, suggesting a jackpot of $3,500.[11]

By late February 1893 Chita had apparently made her way to Fort Bowie. As was the case with Mrs. Andrew Stanley some dozen years earlier, Chita's presence posed a problem. An officer wrote curtly to the agent at San Carlos: "I do not desire to have the Kid's squaw here. I am anxious to get rid of all the squaws, besides, I consider her an element of danger with all the Indians here."[12]

Kid continued raiding. In early 1894, near Mammoth, he fought with a frontiersman called Walapai Ed Clark. In the scuffle an Indian woman sustained a shot through both legs and bled to death. Dan Thrapp, biographer of Al Sieber, claims Apache Kid was never sighted again in Arizona after this point. Yet Arizona had not heard the last of Kid. Sporadic raiding continued, though exactly under whose Apache aegis, whites could not be sure— Kid, Massai, or others.[13]

Intriguing word came of Apache Kid in the fall of 1894. According to Judge J. C. Hancock of Bisbee,

In the fall of 1894 . . . myself and a boy that was working for me was hunting horses in the upper San Simon valley. . . . We met the young squaw that had made her escape from the Apache Kid and was trying to get back to her people on the San Carlos reservation. She had been captured by the Kid two or three years before, when he made a raid on the reservation at San Carlos and killed . . . the girl's mother, and taken the girl captive. . . . She kept on pointing back towards the Skeleton Canyon country and said, "*muchos broncos*," and pointed to our cartridge belts and said, "*mucho*" and also put her hands on her breasts and said, "Me momma." I . . . did not realize that she was trying to tell us she had a baby and that she left it in the camp with the other Indians when she made her escape. . . . She said she had to abandon her baby and that the Kid was a very sick man. . . . After we had passed the girl and had ridden on several miles in the direction she had come, we ran into fresh unshod pony tracks, following the girl's trail, which indicated that some of the Indians, probably the Kid himself, had tried to overtake her when they found that she had got away from them, and had turned back when they found she had too much of a start or else had seen us and concluded to give up the chase. . . . So we thought it advisable to turn back.[14]

Another person present at the encounter later added that the child the woman had left behind was three months old. Like Hancock, this man rejected the idea of rescuing the Indian woman's baby, escorting the woman to Fort Rucker instead.[15]

After the woman returned to the reservation, "She found her buck and papoose, which her grandmother had taken care of. She said that Kid was a very sick man. . . . She had a papoose by the Kid and had abandoned it when she made her escape." Though seemingly lost to history, the abandoned child would surface again.[16]

Apache Kid raided as necessary in the spring of 1896, attacking a wagon near Solomonville, where he killed a local farmer, Merrill, and his young daughter Elizabeth. Apache Kid's men took Elizabeth's "girlish possessions," including a white dress-waist and a "brown woolen shawl édged with trim." Moving on, they killed sixteen-year-old Alfred Hand in the San Simon Valley in late March 1896. Ransacking his cabin, they took with them a cotton 1888 campaign poster that Hand had tacked to his wall some years earlier. Following the raid, "Friends who visited . . . noted that the poster was gone from its accustomed place."[17]

In the wake of the Merrill murders and the killing of Alfred Hand, John Slaughter and the San Bernardino cowboys agreed to lead an army detachment into the Sierra Madres in May 1896, where it was believed Kid was in hiding. Fifty miles below the border they stumbled on Kid's camp. Caught by surprise, the Apaches fled, all except one woman who ran back into the camp. As she rushed past him, Slaughter caught her by the hair. "In the struggle, she pulled him and his horse along, purposely heading for a low branch of a tree. Realizing that he would be thrown, Mr. Slaughter was forced to release his grip and so lost his squaw. She ran for her life too, and joined the rest of the Indians who fled into Mexico," wrote Matilda Hampe, a close friend of the Slaughters who lived with her husband at the comfortably refurbished old Camp Rucker in the Chiricahua mountains.[18]

After a brief chase, the whites returned to the rancheria. With the Apaches gone, the men examined the well-provisioned camp. Slaughter entered a wickiup, only to find an Apache baby asleep on the ground, "forgotten by her people." Faced with killing or abandoning the girl, or taking her to safety, Slaughter grabbed a shawl and, wrapping the youngster within, continued his search. Lieutenant Averill, in command of the detachment, expressed surprise at the amount of provisions Apache Kid's band had amassed, observing that they seemed to be preparing for an extended trip. Satisfied, the men burned the camp to ashes before turning north once again.[19]

At San Bernardino, Slaughter turned the child over to his wife, Cora Viola Howell Slaughter, a woman who had defied all expectations to become the wife of the short man with the stern demeanor, a Texas cattleman rumored to be part Cherokee, and possessing a reputation for shooting outlaws the way others put holes in tin cans. She was born in St. Louis in 1860; her father, a riverboat pilot known as "Cap" Amazon Howell, had moved the family to Montana by 1865 and on to Nevada in 1869.

By 1879 Howell was moving his family once more, this time to Texas. They entered Arizona by way of Lee's ferry, where the family crossed the path of John Slaughter, but the pair did not meet. The Howells settled outside Roswell, New Mexico, for some time, but found themselves caught in the crossfire of the Lincoln County war. While they ranched outside of Roswell, John Slaughter again crossed the family's trail, this time waiting for a delivery of cattle. Slaughter waited for his cattle for weeks, the guest of the Howells, and eventually talked Cap into ranching with him in Arizona, although it seemed he had more than a business partnership in mind. Like Mary Smith Leib, Vi Howell was a woman who knew what she wanted. "It was love at first sight," Vi remembered,

> and when we decided to get married there in New Mexico, I tried to talk to Mother, but she was very opposed: Mr. Slaughter was too old for me—he was

nineteen years my senior; I had not known him long enough; we had met in April and this was August; then there was his children to consider. He had a daughter six and a half years and a son nineteen months by a former marriage, and mother had many objections. . . . I was determined to marry so I went to my father and told him the next day Mr. Slaughter and I were planning to ride ahead to the little town of Tularosa . . . and be married, but that if he had any good excuse why we shouldn't marry, I was willing to wait a year, but I was going to marry Mr. Slaughter some day. He was on our side and said he would tell mother. . . . She cried and had hysterics all that night, but the next day we did as planned.[20]

The family continued on to Arizona, where they settled in the vicinity of Tombstone. As soon as they could, Slaughter's children came to live with them until he could make other arrangements. "I became so attached to them in just a few days that I began to dread the time when I must give them up," said Viola. "Mr. Slaughter wanted to know what was the matter and I sobbed, 'The children!' He said, 'Why Viola, don't be unreasonable. I will send them to my brother the very first chance I get.' 'I don't want them to go,' I protested, 'I want to keep them myself.'"[21]

Like Mary Leib Brooks and Olive Oatman, Viola Slaughter was childless. Viola and John Slaughter raised Slaughter's children, Addie—to whom Geronimo had given his beads at the station—and Willie, in their home. Slaughter bought the 70,000-acre San Bernardino Ranch and the family moved to the border. In 1887 he served the first of two consecutive terms as sheriff of Cochise County, in which capacity he functioned as a no-nonsense lawman with a deadly gun. But nothing had prepared him for the role the little Aravaipa captive would play in his life in 1896. A well-liked couple with no children of their own other than Addie and Will and the several orphans of different origins who found their way to the household over the years, the Slaughters probably intended the best for the Apache girl. "[John] Slaughter's love for children was one of his many fine traits," claimed family friend Mathilde in later years.[22]

The Indian scouts stationed at the San Bernardino camp were "delighted with the little wild thing" and made moccasins for her. The baby's arrival caused more than a stir of excitement, especially when it was discovered that her dirty dress was, by all accounts, very cleverly wrought from the shirt waist of Elizabeth Merrill and the campaign poster formerly belonging to Alfred Hand. Furthermore, someone recognized the shawl the child was wrapped in as also belonging to Elizabeth. There was little doubt among all that the child had come from Apache Kid's camp. Said one contemporary, "I firmly believe that the little papoose that John Slaughter found when they jumped the Indian camp was the [woman whom the men found running from Skeleton Canyon's] baby and the Kid was its father."[23]

Meanwhile, the local press caught word of the captive baby. Inexplicably, they reported that two children had been captured in the raid, a boy about eight years old and a baby girl. Their rhetoric reflects the apprehension whites felt over the ability of native children to overcome their perceived "savage" heredity. "They are lucky young Injuns, those two, far better off, so far as kindness goes, than 99 per cent of Apache children. Yet should they remain on the ranch long enough to repay the kindness, they will probably do it by cutting the throats of their benefactors and burning down the roof that shall have sheltered them for years," one editor predicted.[24]

Another offered more immediate advice. "Though it is too late now, and illegal, in that the law holds Apaches to be human beings, it would be a good job to take those young Apaches by the heels and brain them. Human life will never be absolutely safe in Arizona till the last Apache is dead."[25]

Surely, two children were carried from the Apache camp in May 1896, although the fate of the second is uncertain. An alternate source claims that a young Apache boy was captured, and after living "several years" at the San Bernardino Ranch was returned to San Carlos. The fate of the baby girl, however, whom the Slaughters christened Apache May, made her unforgettable.[26]

Patchy, as the family soon called her, created quite a stir in the household. According to a neighbor, Patchy "would eat any food that was offered to her and saw no reason for disdaining scraps picked from the ground. When thirsty, she would run to a ditch, lie face downward and suck up water from the stream. . . . The Indian scouts made her a pair of beaded boots from deerskin and in these she loved to run and play with the other children who laughed at her sign language."[27]

But according to Matilde Hampe, Patchy soon adjusted

to her surroundings. "When news of this event reached me, I put a few clothes into my saddle bag then hurriedly rode to the Slaughter ranch. On arriving Patchy was dressed in an abbreviated pink calico dress, her straight black hair hung down her shoulders, her large piercing black eyes had a look of suspicion in them. She seemed perhaps, as yet unaccustomed to white people nor her new surroundings. She showed dislike for beds, so they placed a small Navajo blanket on the floor and there she slept and was happy."

Matile Hampe approved of the baby's "progress" but could not identify with the girl's cultural attachment to her own hair.

> There was no way to definitely determine Patchy's age, but we estimated her to be about twenty months old. In a few days after her rescue, they christened her Apache May Slaughter and the little one at once became a great favorite on the ranch. When she became accustomed to her new surroundings, the little transplant savage proved to be as bright as the average child anywhere. She learned to respond to her new name, to understand much that was said to her, and to prattle volubly in English. Presently, her Indian habits were forgotten and she was eating from a plate, drinking from a cup, and sleeping in her own little bed. Mrs. Slaughter made a number of simple little dresses for Patchy, who soon learned to enjoy . . . looking "pretty." . . . She was quite vain [about her hair]. . . . Once it was cut short and she cried bitterly; but it grew again, more luxuriant than ever, and Patchy's vanity increased accordingly.[28]

Just as the *Prescott Miner* decades earlier had tracked the acculturation of the captive baby Bessie Brooks, Matilda witnessed the child's interaction with the Slaughters.

> In an undemonstrative way, Patchy showed a liking for many people . . . but there was never any doubt that Mr. Slaughter was her favorite. The little thing adored him from the very first and used to follow him about the place holding to the top of his boot to steady her wavering baby feet. . . . When he rode away on his horse, she would wait with Indian patience, perhaps for hours, watching the gate for his return. The day could hold no greater happiness for her than a ride on the horse with "Don Juan," as she learned to call him.[29]

As for Patchy's relationship to Viola Slaughter, Hampe observed, "She loved Mrs. Slaughter too, but with more reserve. Patchy liked to stand very close to her, gazing silently into her face, registering admiration. Caresses were not in her line, but her big, dark eyes dumbly expressed her affection."[30] Apache May's "admiration" for Mrs. Slaughter may just as easily have been confusion, but the truth will never be known.

However, if the Slaughter household was comfortable with their new daughter, the local community was not. As they had concerning the Yavapai captive Bessie Brooks thirty years earlier, whites resurrected issues of heredity and environment. "Many questioned the wisdom of bringing her home. Had not Apache Kid and his followers murdered Elizabeth Merrill and her father?" wrote one local historian. Furthermore, little Patchy harbored a "dark side," according to some who thought they knew her.[31]

Many of the Indian traits persisted. She slipped noise-lessly about the house, often startling some unsuspecting visitor from nowhere. She talked when necessary, but preferred silence. When she chose, her active little body became as motionless as a rock on a hillside. Though usually pleasant and obedient, she was at times sullen and obstinate. Once, resenting a reprimand from Mrs. Slaughter, she said, "When I grow up I'll kill you," and she was all venomous Apache for a moment.[32]

The perceived threat—which may have been merely a parroting of the dire predictions of the whites around her—did not go unnoticed. According to Matilda, "The story got about and pessimists wagged their heads and quoted a lot of that old stuff about leopards not changing their spots and the impossibility of making a silk purse out of a sow's ear. The old-timers insisted that once an Indian always an Indian."[33]

Complicating matters even more, the local press ran a pertinent announcement the same month Slaughter brought the baby home:

SOMETHING MORE FOR SHERIFF SLAUGHTER TO WORRY ABOUT
The Apache squaw, mother of the young papoose captured recently in an Indian skirmish is said to be back on the reservation and pining for her off-spring. Mr. Slaughter has taken steps to inquire into the matter and if the mother of the youngster who has been in his charge since its capture is back at the reservation, the little heroine will be returned to her.[34]

According to one Slaughter biographer, "[He] disputed the reports, stating his inquiries established that the mother had not returned." Nothing further was made of the matter, presumably because "the Apache woman knew little of the law, and either did not know or was prevented from doing so by circumstance." As in the case of Bessie Brooks, Arizona territorial law did not shine favorably upon Indians who dared challenge it.[35]

Meanwhile, according to Matilda, Patchy soon regained her equilibrium, "and the optimists had their inning": "They chanted, 'Bring up a child in the way that it should go and when he is old he will not depart from it,' and asserted, 'As the twig is bent the tree is inclined.'"[36]

Unfortunately, Apache May didn't live long enough to prove either side correct. On a chill morning in February 1900, while John and Viola were absent from the ranch, tragedy took six-year-old Patchy's life. "A little boy out at the ranch, one time when the Slaughters were gone, they were boiling water for wash out in the backyard and this little boy pulled a piece of burning wood out from the fire and chased the little girl and her clothing caught fire," a neighbor recalled.[37]

Another neighbor relayed what happened next. "Enveloped in flames, she ran to the house for help and here Will Slaughter, her foster brother, grabbed her and put out the fire."[38] Frantic phone calls were placed to the nearest doctor in Bisbee, fifty-five miles and several hours away, but help came too late for Apache May. John and Viola rushed home by automobile to find the child severely burned. When the doctor finally arrived, he held out little hope for her recovery. As the night passed, and it became clear that Patchy would die, the family gathered close. "Even in her pain she thought of her hair. 'My pretty hair is all burned,' she moaned. And to Mr. Slaughter she said, 'Don Juan, I'm going to die.' . . . The following morning she died, and presently her tortured little body was laid away in the San Bernardino burial plot."[39]

The press reported the tragedy on February 18, adding with a sense of contrition, "Since her captivity she has developed into a bright and interesting child." But the concession was too late. As another historian wrote, "Her tiny span of existence was spent, and Patchy passed on into the mysteries of the Future, leaving unsolved the big problem that her life here presented. Heredity or environment—which would have dominated had she lived to make the experiment complete?"[40]

Apache May's painful death shocked the Slaughter household, indeed the entire San Bernardino ranch community. But one household member seemed to take it harder than the rest. Edwin Flint Williams, an "old-time cowman," stopped by the Slaughter ranch. After sharing a meal with the family, he remembered,

> The intuitive hunch came to me that John was very keen on having me stop. He took me out into the saddle room; told me of a little Apache girl whose people had all been killed in a fight. I cannot recall the details, but I can most vividly recall John's face and eyes and voice as he told me the story. It is very hard for an old-time cowman to tell a tale such as John told me, for the cowman seems to feel that it is unethical to divulge his real tender emotions to

the world. He stopped from time to time and tried to inject a humorous incident—sort of tried to laugh it off—but the sentiment was too deep—it couldn't be laughed off.[41]

Williams grappled with the meaning of the girl's life to the distraught lawman, finally attributing it to Slaughter's Cherokee heritage.

> I reckon he gathered her up as he would have gathered up a motherless calf; carried her home; just couldn't see her hungry and homeless. And I reckon that this little Apache waif, all alone among a hostile people, looked upon John as the only living God. And I reckon that all the love and sympathy and tenderness in John's being went out to that Apache kid. And I reckon that this lone wolf and this lone cub, both congenitally bound to a tradition that demanded a stoical forbearance of sentimentality, sometimes sneaked off together and silently conveyed their mutual sympathy and devotion.[42]

But others held a less sympathetic view of the daughter of Apache Kid. "A wild Apache remains savage under all circumstances and conditions. We must agree that heredity is stronger than environment, from this experience," claimed one pessimist. With the passing of Apache May, the long war of captivity that had held Arizona in its grip passed as well, leaving in its wake a territory now "fit" for statehood.[43]

Years passed, and the fresh dirt on Patchy's grave gave way to the wind and dried in the sun in the San Bernardino graveyard. In 1890, before Apache May's captivity,

90,000 whites lived in Arizona, marking the first time they outnumbered Mexicans in the territory. The 1890 census counted 29,000 Indians in Arizona, almost as many as in 1850. But whites no longer swam in a "sea of Indians," as virtually all Native Americans struggled for survival on reservations, with the exception of the Apache Kid and Massai and their small, furtive bands.[44]

In the same year, Arizona boasted 1,000 miles of railroad and 700 miles of canals. With the "beleaguered frontier now part of the American economy," politicians held their first state constitutional convention in 1891. "Excitement for statehood grew" among whites, and unmistakable change hung in the air.[45]

William Oury, so prominent in any account of the Camp Grant massacre, died in March 1887. In July 1889 the *Tombstone Prospector* reported that Geronimo was now a church-attending Christian in the East; within a year, General Crook died of heart failure.[46]

Mickey Free had waited six months following his return to Arizona before enlisting again as a scout on May 16, 1887. John Rope, on the other hand, resigned from scouting following the deportation of the Chiricahuas, stating he "no longer enjoyed the work, since it involved simply policing the reservation instead of the long scouts to which he was accustomed." After his return to Tucson, Santiago Ward had gone to live on his relative Juan Tellez's ranch in the Tanque Verde pass northeast of Tucson, and was probably one of the cowboys who rescued Octaviano Gastelum in 1886. Ward made the Tellez ranch his home for a decade, eventually marrying Carmen Lopez and fathering a large family. In time they would move to Tucson, where Ward worked for the city for decades, sweeping the Fourth and Sixth avenues underpasses.[47]

In May 1890 Free received his final discharge from the scouts. Just as the scouts had found their inception at Fort Lowell, so would they end. In September, Colonel Clendenin, post commander, informed the AAG that the terms of the two Apache scouts at Fort Lowell had expired. He took the opportunity to ask that headquarters not send anymore, "because they are worthless as scouts" and a "source of annoyance." Clendenin wrote that he would "much prefer to hire Mexican guides . . . as emergency arises," thus delivering the phenomenon of scouting back to the point at which it had begun, with Mexicans. In 1891 Indian scouts, as such, were abolished and replaced with experimental all-Indian regiments of regularly enlisted soldiers. Free, now in his fifties, chose to enlist in the Indian Police Service.[48]

Al Sieber resigned as chief of scouts at San Carlos, allegedly over the "ill-treatment of the scouts," while in 1893 Santiago Ward, now living in Tucson, became a founding member of *La Alianza Hispaña*, the first mutual-aid society established by Mexican Americans. Like Mercedes Shibell, who graduated from the University of Arizona, Ward realized that Mexican American survival in the white man's world would call for self-reliance.[49]

In October 1894 the Chiricahua Apaches were transferred from confinement in the east to Fort Sill, Oklahoma. Among them was Chatto, whom the Chiricahuas still shunned; he was never reunited with his captive family. In 1896 army officers formed the Order of Indian

Wars, a fraternity of veterans who would not even agree among themselves as to what had transpired in Arizona. War with Indians was over, and the era of written imperialist history had begun.[50]

Following the capture of Apache May in 1896, Mickey Free tried to find Apache Kid, eventually locating a cave in Aravaipa Canyon, in the homeland of Kid's people. He found a corpse there, but due to its decomposition, he could not transport it back to the post. As the story goes, he carved a tattooed "W" from the forehead of the corpse as proof to his superiors that Kid was dead. Rumors of Apache Kid continued, however; in 1899 a Mexican officer reported that Kid headed up a "small, well-behaved band" in the Sierra Madre, but these were only two of several endings assigned the elusive Kid.[51]

According to Howard Lamar, the fight for statehood began in earnest in 1901. At issue was whether Arizona should remain in perpetual territorial status, like the Philippines and Puerto Rico, or become incorporated as a state. In the view of some, Arizona was as yet still a "mining camp."[52]

In 1903 Tom Horn was hanged in Wyoming for a murder he was never proved of committing. Al Sieber died in February 1907. While he was supervising an Apache construction crew building a road from Roosevelt Dam to Payson, a boulder dislodged from a hillside and rolled, crushing Sieber beneath it. History has presumed that Sieber, a lifelong bachelor, left no descendants. But the death certificate of a seventy-year-old Yavapai man, William Sieber, who passed away in 1966, claimed he was the son of Mary and Al Sieber. According to Sieber's biographer, the incident could be explained away—one of the orphan Indians Sieber was fond of fostering had simply taken Sieber's name.[53]

However, local historian Clara Woody claimed that a childhood friend of her son had known Sieber at both Camp Verde and Globe. Jimmy Anderson had told John Woody that "Apache women liked Al, and he had quite a cluster of sons scattered over the reservation." Anderson had another insight on Sieber as well. According to the Woodys, he claimed that "the fight with the [Apache] Kid was because of an Apache girl who preferred Sieber to the Kid."[54]

As late as 1906 to 1907, the hunt continued for Apache Kid. According to two accounts, he met an ignominious end. In the first, an informal posse composed of local ranchers tracked the Kid in September 1906 to the San Mateo Mountains. After recovering stolen horses from Kid's band, a skirmish ensued, and a male Indian believed to be Kid fell dead; one "squaw" got away. Approximately one year later, several of the men returned to the camp, among them "Mr. Thoms. E. Wilson (Pres., Wilson Packing Co.) and H. A. Ford (of Chicago Board of Trade)." The men, accompanied by the ranchers, "took the skull and I am told had it identified and it is now in the Board of Trade building in Chicago."[55]

In the alternative account, one of the same group of cowboys, John James, was said to have had a grim sense of humor, which "led to using a brush axe to cut off the Apache's trigger finger." According to this account, a "plush jewel box was prepared for the finger and it was given to an eastern woman" who "still has it in her Colorado home." Moreover, "It was also decided to decapitate the bandit and the same ax was used to carefully remove the head. Among the party were friends of Yale man John Phillips, then publisher of *American Magazine*, and through their influence . . . the head finally wound up at Yale, where it is a prize possession of Skull and Bones, [the] secret fraternal society." Finally, the prize possession of the cowboy responsible for the severing of the head "is a picture sent him by Phillips, showing the skull as it rests in the fraternal hall of Skull and Bones."[56]

In February 1909 Geronimo passed away at Fort Sill, Oklahoma. Rumors have long persisted that his bones were later dug from his grave and placed in Yale's Skull and Bones collection. If true, it is likely that Apache Kid's skull lies there too, silent testimony to the violence whites perpetrated against Indians in "captive Arizona." In the postmodern era, Native American repatriation laws and DNA testing can surely resolve the issue.[57]

In December 1910 Ed Peck—Bessie Brooks's captor—died at Nogales, very poor. "He gave the best that was in him for the advancement and upbuilding of the sun-kissed land," the newspaper eulogized. Arizona reached statehood on February 14, 1912. The act, a historian wrote, symbolized that "a satisfactory Americanization had been achieved."[58]

At Prescott, old Fort Whipple found new life as a veterans' hospital in 1913. The same year, Larcena Pennington Scott died at the age of seventy-six. The following year, 1914, William F. Scott also died. In the summer of 1914, Mickey Free passed away.[59]

Unaware that Free was dead, former reservation census enumerator Charles Connell wrote for the *Tucson Citizen* in April 1921,

> Strange that today there should live in isolation at the White River agency . . . a character who innocently was the cause of 12 years relentless Indian war in Arizona. . . . The innocent cause of murder, torture and depredations . . . is today a wandering, aged, unkempt dependant of the government, an Apache in nature, in cunning, in mind and action, knowing no other life and seeking no other status; of restless, roving disposition, and withal, more cruel, more blood-thirsty and deceptive than those of common stock, for "Mickey Free," as he is known, is a half-breed.[60]

With these words, Connell created a misinformed, bigoted characterization of Mickey Free that lasted longer than the years of war, one that denied Free—Feliz Tellez Martinez—the status he had earned among the Western Apaches and among the whites with whom he spent his career.

In 1920 Phoenix's population of 29,000 exceeded Tucson's 20,000 for the first time. The territorial world passed away and so did John Slaughter on February 22, 1922, leaving Viola a widow. Two years later, Apache Kid—long thought by some to be dead—was reported to be leading a band of horse thieves in Arizona, according to Kid's nephew. In 1927 Slaughter's foreman, Jess Fisher, who had participated in the raid on Apache Kid's camp in 1896 that resulted in the captivity of Apache May, was shot in the back "by the same Indians" while riding through the

Animas Valley. In time, whites would remember him as the last man killed by "bronco" Apaches. Apache Kid's war was over.[61]

In a most fitting ending to the era, the life of a final captive, Santiago Suviate, testifies to the geographical and cultural reach of *Captive Arizona*. Suviate died at "about the age of 134 years," at the Santa Anita Hospital in Los Angeles County in 1942. "Mudo," as he was known, was a Yaqui Indian born in Sonora who was, like William Oury's captive Aravaipa child, Carlota, a deaf-mute. He had been captured by Geronimo as an elderly man in the 1870s and then sold to a Tucson contractor, Santiago Suviate, from whom he took his name. In 1878 Suviate sold the captive to Mexican general Florencio Ruiz. According to the family history,

> Subsequently, [Mudo] would become attached to the Watts children resulting from the marriage of the General's daughter to Francis Marion Watts. . . . The Ruiz and Watts families never considered him to be a servant but a ward. He was loved, and loved in return. He lived with the Wattses in Los Angeles and Burbank [fifteen] years. . . . The University of California Medical Center in Los Angeles did perform an autopsy which confirmed his probable and approximate age at time of death. . . . Mudo may have been born a year before Abraham Lincoln, in 1808.[62]

In 1981 the San Carlos Apache Nation initiated an annual memorial service for the Aravaipa victims of the Camp Grant massacre. "Although the Camp Grant Massacre . . . will live forever in the memory of the Apache people, we are gathered here neither to forgive nor condemn. The past is gone," said Apache leader and organizer Philip Cassadore in 1984. White Mountain Apache tribal chairman Ronnie Lupe "held a sacred feather and prayed, 'It is not forgotten, it is here with us,'" he said. Descendants of Eskiminzin attended the memorial and spoke of their ancestors. Overhead, "two Air Force jets passed over at 500 feet and tilted their wings in salute." The chairman of the O'odham Nation had been scheduled to speak, but sent a message stating he had other engagements. One Apache woman, Francis Cutter, whose relatives had died in the massacre, told stories of her grandmother who died in 1945 at the age of one hundred. "My grandmother would say . . . 'Listen to me! Listen to me!' We would be driving the car past here and she would say, 'This is where it happened—a shooting! A killing!' And I wondered what she was talking about. That is the saddest part."[63]

At the 1995 Camp Grant memorial, an Apache elder, Jeanette Cassa, stated, "This is our holocaust. We were the first ones to have this happen, the Apaches. It's the same story, over and over." Another elder, Adella Swift, told how her grandfather, thirteen or fourteen at the time, hid behind the wickiups and watched as his mother was slaughtered and his sister taken by the raiders from Tucson. "He used to say the same thing over and over, how his mom was killed and they took his sister. We brought him up here in '43 or '44. He wanted to see the land once more before he faded away. His mother was buried up here." Among the Western Apaches, the memory of captive Arizona survives.[64]

. . .

In summary, captivity bound territorial Arizonans—regardless of race, class, or gender—in a network of strained social relations. Of the more than twenty captives featured in this work, nine—Nah-thle-tla, the Chiricahua woman sold into slavery in Mexico; Major Blakeney's unnamed Apache orphan; the unnamed Tohono O'odham woman; Bessie Brooks, the Yavapai captive; the Aravaipa captives of Camp Grant; Chatto's Chiricahua family; White Mountain Apache woman Mrs. Andrew Stanley; Aravaipa baby Apache May; and elderly Yaqui deaf-mute Santiago Suviate—represent indigenous Arizonans. Of these, if Chatto's family and the Camp Grant captives are excluded, five were females—six, if one includes William Oury's Camp Grant captive girl, Carlota.

Mexican and Mexican American captives are also represented in *Captive Arizona*, including four females—Mercedes Sais and Ramona, the servant of Palatine Robinson, both from Tucson; Trinidad Verdin from Nogales; and Inez Gonzales, rescued by the boundary commission, from Santa Cruz, Sonora. Three males—Feliz Tellez (Mickey Free) from the Sonoita Valley; Octaviano Gastelum from the Tanque Verde Ranch; and Santiago McKinn, the Irish Mexican boy from eastern New Mexico—were held captive by Indians.

White male captives—those least likely to be captured and acculturated—included Dji-li-kinne, raised by White Mountain Apaches but who married into the Chiricahuas, and Charlie McComas, the judge's son taken by Chiricahuas in a raid in New Mexico, as well as Santiago McKinn, if one considers him white like his Irish father.

Mormon-oriented Olive Oatman, southern mountaineer daughter Larcena Pennington, and Miss Harris of the Chiricahuas represented white female captives.

Excluding Santiago Suviate, already in his seventies when captured by Geronimo, the average age of captives was eleven to twelve years old. Nah-thle-tla, the O'odham woman, Mrs. Andrew Stanley, Olive Oatman, and Larcena Pennington were each older than fifteen years when captured. Bessie Brooks and Apache May were babies, perhaps two years old at the time. Charlie McComas was six years old, but the rest ranged in age from ten to twelve years.

Captivity concerned violence, rage, revenge, and scars. Nah-thle-tla, sold into slavery in Mexico, daily faced the threat of physical violence. Lieutenant Bascom hanged Cochise's family. Major Blackeny hanged the Apaches who dared claim "his" Apache orphan, while Mr. Otis thought nothing of firing a rifle at Bessie Brooks's children. Mrs. Andrew Stanley was attacked by Tcagudi several times after returning to her home, and Apache Kid's head was severed and put on display. "Mickey Free" was born of violence and lived a life of violence. At Chevlon's Fork he used excessive violence to punish the scouts who had left their duty posts to fire on army troops. At Tupper's fight he used excessive violence to punish Geronimo for Nayudiie's death. Santiago McKinn, Trini Verdin, and Octaviano Gastelum each felt the brunt of Geronimo's short, punishing temper. Charlie McComas died a violent death, and Olive witnessed the brutal murders of her family members and saw her sister starve to death. She, in her tattoos, and Lorenzo, Larcena, Trini Verdin, and Mickey Free bore physical scars for the remainder of their lives. And, of course, Larcena's internalized rage, and the anger of most Tucsonans, spilled over into unprecedented violence at Camp Grant.

Of the captives represented in this book, the majority were already orphaned—or half-orphaned—prior to the time of captivity, or were orphaned by the initial captivity event: Major Blakeney's "intelligent-looking" Apache boy; Bessie Brooks, whose mother was murdered by Ed Peck; the Camp Grant orphans. Chatto's children were effectively orphaned when taken from their father, and most likely separated from their mother. Mrs. Andrew Stanley was an orphan, Apache May's parents had been forced to abandon her, and Mercedes Sais was half-orphaned. Trini Verdin was an orphan. Mickey Free's father, Santiago Tellez, had been killed by Apaches—so had his stepfather, John Ward, and his adopted father, Nayudiie. Charlie McComas's parents were murdered at the time of his captivity. So were Olive's parents, and the Mojave children Olive left behind were half-orphaned too, for all practical purposes. Larcena's mother had died of illness and Larcena's oldest daughter was half-orphaned by Apaches; nine years after her captivity, Apaches killed Larcena's father and brother. Miss Harris's parents were killed during her captivity incident, and Palatine Robinson's servant girl was surely an orphan child. Ironically, at the time of Jason Betzinez's mother Nah-thle-tla's death in 1935—at the age of 112—she had the distinction of being known as the oldest mother in the United States, according to her son.[65]

But captivity posed more than a physical threat to the

vulnerable in Arizona, for it also imposed a complex of social challenges on both captives and captors. Issues surrounding adoption, childlessness, intermarriage, mixed-bloods, and acculturation coalesced around the captives. White couples in childless marriages adopted the captives Bessie Brooks and Apache May, although there is no proof that either adoption was ever legally recognized by territorial law. Olive Oatman had a childless marriage and adopted a white child—Mamie Fairchild, appropriately enough.

Captivity often led to racial intermarriage. Bessie Brooks wed Prescott pioneer James Edger. Feliz Tellez married Western Apache women, and Dji-li-kinne intermarried with the Chiricahuas. Olive was probably the wife of a Mohave man, and Miss Harris chose to return to her Chiricahua husband, while Mercedes Sais married white pioneer Charles Shibell after her return.

Issues of race and racial construction also followed the captives: Bessie Brooks, Mercedes Sais, Feliz Martinez, Dji-li-kinne, Olive Oatman, and Miss Harris all produced interracial children at a time when intermarriage—especially between whites and Indians—was unacceptable by territorial statute. Bessie Brooks was considered white enough to marry a white man, but not white enough to inherit a white man's wealth.

Other racial constructions were less obvious. Major Blakeney's Apache orphan wanted nothing more than boots and pants and to live like a white man. The O'odham woman used her accustomed nakedness to wiggle out of her Apache captors' clothing and escape, and Mrs. Andrew Stanley considered the Chiricahuas "mean." Apache May was a baby when captured, but cherished her "Indian hair" anyway; friends and neighbors attributed her fascination with John Slaughter to his Cherokee roots, as though love were bound by race, as if love nullified captivity.

Mercedes Sais, a beautiful girl who in earlier times would have married an upper-class Mexican male, married a white man, the unwitting dupe of imperialist male power relations, love aside. As Mexicans increasingly became racial minorities in Tucson, her daughter, Mercedes—like Mickey Free's brother Santiago Ward— would refuse to be labeled a second-class citizen under any circumstances.

The racial constructions continued. As they were with Bessie Brooks, issues of race were constructed around Feliz Tellez—Mickey Free—who was considered Indian enough to enroll as an Indian scout, but whose eligibility for enlistment in the Indian police was questioned by white authorities. As one scholar has found, "The legal system does more than just reflect social or scientific ideas about race; it also produces and reproduces them."[66]

Additionally, Santiago McKinn thought he *was* Apache. Dji-li-kinne was a white man who became a Western Apache clansman and then a Chiricahua warrior. Olive Oatman was a white woman tattooed with Mohave symbolism; her Mohave captors covered her with an unknown substance to hide her skin color from her redeemers. Miss Harris became a Chiricahua woman. The slave traders from New Mexico considered Inez Gonzales the "property" of the Pinals they had bought her from, and Palatine Robinson sold Mexican captive Ramona at the Rio Grande. Even Geronimo bent racial and gender lines when he relieved Trini Verdin and Minnie Tevis of their sunbonnets. Most obviously, among white captors, issues of heredity and environment challenged the tenets of Manifest Destiny—if Indians were subhuman enemies, how was it possible that they could invoke love in whites?

Guilt and blame were part of the captivity complex. The citizens of Prescott were guilty of outrageous bigotry in the case of Bessie Brooks. Whites, Mexican Americans, Tohono O'odhams, and Aravaipas blamed each other for the Camp Grant massacre. It is reasonable to presume that John and Viola Slaughter felt tremendous guilt over the untimely death of Apache May, and perhaps for having refused to surrender her to her Aravaipa mother. Olive, Larcena, and Mercedes carelessly blamed the wrong Indians for their captivities, while Lieutenant Bascom unfairly blamed Cochise for Feliz Tellez's capture and the Chiricahuas unfairly blamed Feliz Tellez for *his own* captivity. The Chiricahuas and the Mohaves hesitated to surrender the captives Olive Oatman and Charlie McComas for fear of misplaced blame. Olive most likely suffered a guilty conscience over the abandonment of her Mohave children; did she leave her children behind because she and the Mohaves feared even more severe reprisals against the tribe if whites knew of the mixed-blood children? Miss Harris blamed the army for killing her Chiricahua baby while they tried to rescue her. Mike Burns, the Yavapai captive, had a word on the notion of blame in Arizona. "And that is the very way all bloody deeds were put on the Apaches by other people: just say 'The Apaches did it.'"[67]

Other issues surrounded rescue, nonrescue, and self-rescue. Where white and Mexican American captives could hope for national press attention, and for the army to rescue them from their captors, indigenous captives had to rely on their own resources for help. Nah-thle-tla, the O'odham woman, and Mrs. Andrew Stanley—young adults—each escaped from their captors on their own. As *Captive Arizona* shows, indigenous captives had the advantage of familiarity with the geography and a lifestyle that in today's terminology would be labeled "lower on the food chain," while white and Mexican American captives could take hope only in external rescue. Bessie and Apache May, mere babies, found themselves hopeless captives of whites, as did Santiago Suviate and William Oury's captive Carlota, both indigenous deaf-mutes. Apache May's mother attempted to recover her but was ignored by the military authorities. Blakeney's Apache orphan liberated himself by running into the soldier's camp. Larcena survived her attempted murder and rescued herself without the help of the army, while Mercedes Sais, Olive Oatman, and Santiago McKinn were liberated with the help of the army. The troops and scouts searched for Charlie McComas but couldn't find him. They had tried to rescue Feliz Tellez but bungled the mission. The boundary commission rescued Inez Gonzales, while Mexican troops rescued Trini Verdin. Of the twelve nonindigenous captives found in *Captive Arizona*, three—Mickey Free, Dji-li-kinnem and Miss Harris—never returned, preferring to live with the Apaches. At least five captives—Charlie McComas, Dji-li-kinne, Apache May, Bessie Brooks, and Mickey Free—died among their captive hosts.

Once the captives were liberated, issues of social re-integration had to be confronted. The Tohono O'odham woman transformed her captivity into opportunity, leading the Enemy Slayers to the Enemy. Olive capitalized on her tattoos, but couldn't escape her memories. Miss Harris chose to return to the Chiricahuas, and Mickey Free, after serving in the capacity of scout for a decade or more, had to choose between a life in Tucson with his brother or the one he had created among the Apaches. Both Larcena and Mrs. Andrew Stanley were considered returned from the dead. Whites didn't trust that Larcena was real; displaying her scars reasserted her humanity and implied that anything that had occurred on that day in 1860 had been against her will. The *nadots-usn* feared that Mrs. Stanley had led the Chiricahuas to them. After she regained their trust, Mrs. Stanley's reputation as a "brave woman" challenged the pride of Apache men. Santiago McKinn had to learn how to speak English again.

Gendered power relations played a pivotal role in *Captive Arizona*, where war, raiding, and captivity appeared to be men's business. Virtually every captive presented in this work was captured and owned by males. Nah-thle-tla, Inez Gonzales, many of the Camp Grant captives, and Chatto's family were captured or held by slavers in the Mexican market. Chiricahua men captured Mrs. Andrew Stanley, Santiago Suviate, Trini Verdin, Octaviano Gastelum, Santiago McKinn, Charley McComas, and Miss Harris, while Western Apache males captured Larcena Pennington, Mercedes Sais, the O'odham woman, and Feliz Tellez. White men captured Bessie Brooks,

Apache May, and the Camp Grant captives—including Oury's Carlota—and Palatine Robinson sold Ramona into obscurity.

Gender relations intersected economic class considerations where captivity was concerned in Arizona. Whereas the captives were generally young, orphaned, and disadvantaged, male captors were men of some means and influence. Bessie Brooks lived in the home of a judge, Carlota lived with Tucson's influential William Oury, and Apache May lived with the sheriff of Cochise County. Civilians employed with the army had taken both Bessie and Apache May from their parents' camps. Santiago Suviate lived with the family of Gen. Florencio Ruiz—and in the home of Francis Marion Watts—while Mercedes Sais married a new western Adam-type and Larcena's husband became a judge.

Furthermore, Feliz was the *yodascin* of clan head Nayudiie, and Santiago McKinn and Trini Verdin lived at the camp of Geronimo and his wife. Finally, Olive Oatman was the adopted daughter of Mohave chief Homoseh Quahote. Conversely, the U.S. Secretary of War ignored Chatto's plea for help regarding the redemption of his family from Mexico, and the commanding officer at Fort Bowie ignored Apache May's mother's cry for help recovering her baby. Additionally, the white judge, jury, prosecutor, and defense attorney at Tucson dismissed murder charges in the Camp Grant massacre.

But if men captured, owned, and manipulated captives, women raised them. Upon their entry into camp, native women could kill the captives, if they chose. If allowed to live, captives were dependent upon native women—the food preparers—for nourishment. If adopted, the captives then shared the lives of their captors. Whatever the racial boundaries, matriarchal imagery is evident in captivity issues. Malika and her mother nurtured Olive. Mary Brooks mothered Bessie, and Viola Slaughter raised Apache May. Feliz Tellez may have been raised by Nayudii's wives. Women fed Charlie McComas, until he died, and Geronimo's woman fed Santiago and Trini while Dji-li-kinne's wife kept him fed. Conversely, images of dead mothers, too lengthy to list, also saturate the matriarchal landscape in *Captive Arizona*.

A final note regarding gender relations and captivity emerges from this study. Brian McGinty raised the issue of men who married captives, but the reverse holds just as true: captivity raises questions about whom captives chose to marry. Mrs. Andrew Stanley picked the scout who had saved his wages because he believed that she would marry him someday, if he only waited long enough. Mickey Free's Apache wives chose a *yodascin* scout as their mate; Free chose to earn regular wages from the army. Olive, Larcena, and Mercedes married white men of influence, and Bessie—with every reason to believe she would inherit Hezekiah's estate—married a white "stalwart son" of Prescott. Even Santiago McKinn married and became a blacksmith by trade. Former captives and those who married them valued material security, reflecting Olive's words: "You have pleasant homes, kind parents, and affectionate brothers and sisters, and are in the enjoyment of the comforts and perhaps the luxuries of Christian society. I once had all these, and having experienced the frightful contrast, the other extreme, I think I now know how to appreciate the word *home,* and had I one I should know how to enjoy it."

Human agency creates human history. The lives of the captives and their captors substantially influenced Arizona history, but the captives' voices—largely those of women and children—fell by the historic wayside, silenced by stories of white men and empire. Freed from the shadows of the master narrative, they inform historians of the ways in which whites, Mexicans, and Indians struggled to define and defend the differences that distinguished and divided them in *Captive Arizona.*

NOTES

INTRODUCTION

1. Ackernecht, "White Indians," 35; Heard, *White into Red*.

2. Axtell, "White Indians of Colonial America," 88.

3. See "Guide to the Scholarly Resources" microfilm edition of *The Papers of Carlos Montezuma, M.D.: Including the Papers of Maria Keller Montezuma Moore and the Papers of Joseph W. Latimer*, ed. John William Larner Jr., ASU Hayden Library. See also Mike Burns's Papers, box 82, SH; and Rockwell, "Autobiography of Mike Burns" and *Mike Burns*. Burns's enrollment is recorded in Altom, *Students at Haskell Institute*, entry #155; accompanying note indicates Burns (Apache) is listed in originating source as entry #80. Burns claimed only that he was educated at Carlisle.

5. Bartlett, *Personal Narrative*, 1: 301.

6. Bartlett, *Personal Narrative*, 1: 303–4.

7. Bartlett, *Personal Narrative*, 1: 306–7. Author A. Kinney Griffith later insisted, erroneously, that this woman was the mother of Mickey Free; see Griffith, *Mickey Free*.

8. "Testimony of Hiram Stevens," Palatine Robinson file, AHS; parentheses in original.

9. Goodwin, *Social Organization*, 600, 609, 610, 613, 619. *Social Organization* contains a critical error; researchers must understand Davisson, "New Light," before using Goodwin for historical purposes. Furthermore, it should be understood that there was a tendency for particular clans to dominate particular traditional Western Apache permanent camps over time, but these camps also included members of other clans as well, usually indicating long historic associations among a group of clans. In addition to

members of their own (mothers') clans, Western Apache warriors could generally rely on the support of their brother-in-laws' clans, their wives' clans, and their father's clans, creating an intricate network of social relations.

10. The standard reference to Apache place names is Basso, *Wisdom Sits in Places.*

11. Conner, *Joseph Reddeford Walker,* 181, 184, 317–18. See Ball and Kaywaykla, *Days of Victorio;* Ball, *Indeh;* Betzinez, *I Fought;* Robinson, *Apache Voices;* and Goodwin, *Social Organization,* for indigenous captives.

12. See also Radbourne, *Mickey Free.*

1. 1851–1856

1. For scholarship on this topic, see Wood, "Sexual Violation"; Kolodney, *Land before Her,* esp. p. 46; and Faery, *Cartographies.*

2. Lamar, *Far Southwest,* 361–62.

3. Faery, *Cartographies,* 52.

4. Bartlett, *Personal Narrative,* 1: 303–18. Inez went on to claim that a dozen Mexican women were being held by the Pinals. A. Kinney Griffith would claim in *Mickey Free: Manhunter* that Inez was the mother of Mickey Free, but Allan Radbourne corrected the record in "Salvador or Martinez?"

5. Brooks, *Captives and Cousins,* 34.

6. Stratton, *Captivity* (1909), 7–10; Lamar, *Far Southwest,* 362; Rice, *Los Angeles Star;* Walker and Bufkin, *Historical Atlas,* 28; see McGinty, *Oatman Massacre,* for details of the colony and their separation from the "Brighamites."

7. Stratton, *Captivity* (1909), 7–10.

8. Kolodney, *Land before Her,* 232; Faulk, *Destiny Road,* 71; Walker and Bufkin, *Historical Atlas,* 17.

9. Stratton, *Captivity* (1909), 20–21.

10. Stratton, *Captivity* (1909), 22–23.

11. Udell, *Journal,* 46–47.

12. Kolodny, *Land before Her,* 236; Faulk, *Destiny Road,* 75.

13. Stratton, *Captivity* (1909), 64–65.

14. Stratton, *Captivity* (1909), 26–28.

15. Stratton, *Captivity* (1909), 27–28.

16. Stratton, *Captivity* (1909), 32.

17. Stratton, *Captivity* (1909), 32–33; Lamar, *Far Southwest*, 1.

18. Quoted in Stratton, *Captivity* (1909), 33–35.

19. Quoted in Stratton, *Captivity* (1857), 82–83; italics mine.

20. Quoted in Stratton, *Captivity* (1857), 83–84.

21. Stratton, *Captivity* (1857), 35–36; see Braatz, *Surviving Conquest*, 253–54 and n. 66, for a discussion on Olive's captors.

22. Stratton, *Captivity* (1909), 40–41.

23. Stratton, *Captivity* (1909), 39–42, 106–7.

24. Stratton, *Captivity* (1909), 43.

25. McGinty, *Oatman Massacre*, 78–79.

26. McGinty, *Oatman Massacre*, 78–79.

27. McGinty, *Oatman Massacre*, 45–46.

28. McGinty, *Oatman Massacre*, 46–48.

29. McGinty, *Oatman Massacre*, 49–51.

30. Quoted in McGinty, *Oatman Massacre*, 58–62, 88.

31. McGinty, *Oatman Massacre*, 64.

32. McGinty, *Oatman Massacre*, 95–97; Kroeber, *Oatman's Return*, 6.

33. Stratton, *Captivity* (1909), 65; Sherer, *Clan System*, 15, 24, 46.

34. Stratton, *Captivity* (1909), 65; Stratton, *Captivity* (1857), 71–72, 118; Sherer, *Clan System*, 4, 25; Kroeber, *Oatman's Return*, 1, 6–7, 16n3, 17n25, 18n38.

35. Stratton, *Captivity* (1909), 77.

36. Stratton, *Captivity* (1909), 68.

37. Stratton, *Captivity* (1909), 73, 81–82.

38. Edward Pettid, SJ, ed., "Olive Ann Oatman's Lecture Notes and the Oatman Bibliography," *San Bernardino County Museum Association Quarterly* 16.2 (Winter 1968): 1–31, from AHS. Hereafter cited as "Oatman's Lecture Notes."

39. Stratton, *Captivity* (1909), 80–82; Furst, *Mojave Pottery, Mojave People*, 55, 122.

40. Stratton, *Captivity* (1909), 97, 107.

41. Stratton, *Captivity* (1909), 107–10; Rice, *Los Angeles Star*, 273.

42. Stratton, *Captivity* (1909), 99.

43. Stratton, *Captivity* (1909), 102–3.

44. Stratton, *Captivity* (1909), 103–5.

45. Stratton, *Captivity* (1909), 105–6.

46. Stratton, *Captivity* (1909), 105, 114–15; see also "Her Veil Hid Scars of Indian Imprisonment," *Sherman* [Texas] *Daily Register*, 1903, undated clipping, AHS Clippings File, Olive Oatman (hereafter cited as "Her Veil Hid Scars").

47. Stratton, *Captivity* (1909), 108–9.

48. Stratton, *Captivity* (1909), 108–12; Rice, *Los Angeles Star*, 112, 274–75; Faery, *Cartographies*, 46.

49. Stratton, *Captivity* (1909), 115–16.

50. Rice, *Los Angeles Star*, 274–75; Faery, *Cartographies*, 49.

51. Rice, *Los Angeles Star*, 112–13; Faery, *Cartographies*, 49.

52. Rice, *Los Angeles Star*, 275–76; "Her Veil Hid Scars."

53. McGinty, *Oatman Massacre*, 200.

54. McGinty, *Oatman Massacre*, 202; McGinty expands on the relationship between the legend and the Apaches. See also Rice, *Los Angeles Star*, 272–84.

55. James H. Miller, "Reminiscences," AHS MS 495. I have taken the liberty of lightly editing Miller's frontier vernacular.

56. Faery, *Cartographies*, 46, 49; "Her Veil Hid Scars."

57. "Her Veil Hid Scars."

58. Rice, *Los Angeles Star*, 277; Altshuler, *Starting with Defiance*, 43–47; Udell, *Journal*.

59. Brooks, *Captives and Cousins*, 30; Faery, *Cartographies*, 45–50; Kolodney, *Land before Her*, 139.

60. "Oatman's Lecture Notes," 1.

61. "Oatman's Lecture Notes," 17, 19.

62. "Oatman's Lecture Notes," 23.

63. "Oatman's Lecture Notes," 24–26.

64. Dillon, "Tragedy at Oatman Flat," 46–48, 54, 59.

65. McGinty, *Oatman Massacre*, 181.

66. McGinty, *Oatman Massacre*, 184, 186; the reference is to Conklin, *Picturesque Arizona*, cited in McGinty, *Oatman Massacre*, 186.

67. "Her Veil Hid Scars" and "Pioneer Girl's Tragic Tale Echoes," unknown press clipping dated September 5, 1932, both in AHS Clippings File, Olive Oatman; Namias, *White Captives*, 29; "Oatman's Lecture Notes," introduction, AHS; Dillon, "Tragedy at Oatman Flat," 59; quote is from McGinty, *Oatman Massacre*, 186.

68. McGinty, *Oatman Massacre*, 183, 186–87.

69. "Her Veil Hid Scars"; McGinty, *Oatman Massacre*, 181, 187–88; McGinty summarizes accounts of Olive's children, 190–193. Essentially, an 1893 news article supposedly sourced by Mohaves claimed she had three children, one of whom, Joe, worked in Phoenix; King Woolsey knew him and thought he might have been her child, but he might also have been the child of a Frenchman who sailed up the Colorado and taken residence with a Navajo woman. My own guess is that this is more likely; this Frenchman may even be the father of Estelle Oatman, whose name was George Bois de Vache; see "Arizona History from Newspaper Accounts" (hereafter cited as "Arizona History"), 30. In 1903 Alfred Kroeber recorded a Mohave account of Oatman children, and in 1906 Arizona historian Joseph Fish claimed that Arizona historian Sharlot Hall told him Olive had two children, one of whom still visited Fort Yuma.

70. "Arizona History," 29–30.

71. "Arizona History," 29–30.

72. "Arizona History," 29–30.

73. "Arizona History," 29–30.

74. "Arizona History," 29–30.

75. "Arizona History," 29–30.

76. Roscoe Wilson, "Arizona Days and Ways": "Did Olive Oatman Marry a Mojave Chief?" undated clipping, Oatman file, AHS.

77. Kroeger, *Oatman's Return*, 1, 5; McGinty, *Oatman Massacre*, 152–53, 192–93.

2. 1855–1861

1. Lamar, *Far Southwest*, 88.

2. Lamar, *Far Southwest*, 84, 362; Harris, *Gila Trail*; Walker and Bufkin, *Historical Atlas*, 23, 26; Altshuler, *Starting with Defiance*, 26, 67–72.

3. Walker and Bufkin, *Historical Atlas*, 23, 48; Lamar, *Far Southwest*, 365; Warren and Roske, *Historic Trails*, 76.

4. Faulk, *Destiny Road*, 51–52, 57; Lamar, *Far Southwest*, 367–68; Walker and Bufkin, *Historical Atlas*, 22, 41.

5. Lamar, *Far Southwest*, 85–86, 367–68; Walker and Bufkin, *Historical Atlas*, 22–23; Barnes, *Arizona Place Names*, 320.

6. Debo, *Geronimo*, 13.

7. Debo, *Geronimo*, 33, 46–47.

8. Betzinez, *I Fought*, 18–24; Debo, *Geronimo*, 50–51.

9. Debo, *Geronimo*, 52.

10. Lamar, *Far Southwest*, 85–86.

11. Lamar, *Far Southwest*, 109–11, 364, 381.

12. Debo, *Geronimo*, 56; Lamar, *Far Southwest*, 81–82.

13. Letter from H. F. Pennington to Florence Drachman, June 22, 1939, Pennington Family file, AHS.

14. H. F. Pennington to Florence Drachman, June 22, 1939.

15. Roberts, "Jack Pennington," 317–318, 319n4.

16. Roberts, "Jack Pennington," 319.

17. Altshuler, *Starting with Defiance*, 19; "Criminals—Sonoita Valley Murders," Ephemera File, AHS; see Thompson, *Desert Tiger*.

18. Roberts, "Jack Pennington," 321–23.

19. Roberts, "Jack Pennington," 321–23; see also Ainsa, *Crabb Expedition*, and Forbes, *Crabb's Filibustering Expedition*.

20. Roberts, "Jack Pennington," 321–23; "Criminals—Sonoita Valley Murders," AHS Ephemera File, news clippings, *Weekly Arizonian*, May 19, 1859, and June 23, 1859.

21. Roberts, *Their Own Blood*, 73; Walker and Bufkin, *Historical Atlas*, 41; Forbes, *Penningtons*, 10; Roberts, "Jack Pennington," 320; Duffen, "Overland," 356n6.

22. William Kirkland MS 1102, AHS, box 1, file 7; Barnes, *Arizona Place Names*, 271.

23. Kirkland MS 1102, box 1, file 7.

24. Kirkland MS 1102, box 1, file 7.

25. Kirkland MS 1102, box 1, file 7.

26. Georgie Scott Forbes MS 261, box 3, file 2.

27. Kirkland MS 1102, box 1, file 2; Thompson, *Desert Tiger*, 18–19.

28. Kirkland MS 1102, box 1, file 2.

29. Kirkland MS 1102, box 1, file 2; see LR, Dept. of NM, NARA RG 393, "Captain R. S. Ewell to Lt. John Wilkins, Santa Fe, March 17, 1860." The Pinals were more likely to have been raiding in the region.

30. Kirkland MS 1102, box 1, file 7.

31. Kirkland MS 1102, box 1, file 7; also Ewell to Wilkins, LR, April 10, 1860, NARA RG 393.

32. Ewell to Wilkins, April 10, 1860, NARA RG 393.

33. Kirkland MS 1102, box 1, file 2. Francisco Sais appears in the 1866 U.S. Census, Special Arizona Enumeration, in the household of Mercedes and her parents.

34. Georgie Scott Forbes AHS MS 261, box 3, file 2.

35. See *Sacramento Union*, June 16, 1860, "Mrs. Page," 2: 5, Pennington Family file, AHS.

36. These raids are listed in Radbourne, "Salvador or Martinez?" 1–26, 10–12.

37. Sweeney, *Cochise*, 119–20, 129–30.

38. Sweeney, *Cochise*, 125.

39. Radding, *Wandering Peoples*, 30, 66, 154; Nentvig, *Rudo Ensayo*, 79, 140–41; Garza, *Apache Kid*, 108, addresses the issue of Indian trails; Barnes, *Arizona Place Names*, 325.

40. Radding, *Wandering Peoples*, 38, 116–17, 154, 267; Nentvig, *Rudo Ensayo*, 79, 117–18, 140–41; Pfefferkorn, *Sonora*, 257–58, 264; Johns, *Storms Brewed*, 273; F. Smith, *Phantom*, 160; see also Basso, *Apache Raiding*, for scout memoirs, including John Rope's.

41. Altshuler, *Starting with Defiance*, 19–21.

42. Federal Decennial Census, Sonoita Creek Settlements, 1860,

lists John Ward, Jesusa Martinez, Felix (Feliz) Ward, 12, Teodora Martinez, 10, and Mary Ward 5½, but Santiago Ward claimed to have been born before his brother was captured; see John Ward file, AHS, for Santiago Ward memoir.

43. John Ward file, AHS, "Santiago Ward," 3; Charles T. Connell, *Arizona* magazine (December 1906), AHS; Connell, "The Apaches Past and Present," *Tucson Citizen*, February–July 1921, AHS, esp. April 10, 1921, 4–8.

44. One of the most useful recent chronologies is found in Sweeney, *Cochise*, 142–65.

45. Sweeney, *Cochise*, 142–65.

46. Sweeney, *Cochise*, 142–65.

47. Betzinez, *I Fought*, 40–41; Ball and Kaywaykla, *Days of Victorio*, 155.

48. Debo, *Geronimo*, 222.

49. Ball and Kaywaykla, *Days of Victorio*, 155.

50. See, for example, Sacks, "New Evidence."

51. Chas. D. Poston, "The Pennington Family," *Arizona Citizen*, January 17, 1896, AHS; Arizona Decennial Census, 1860; Forbes, *Penningtons*, 22; Duffen, "Overland," 356n6.

52. Forbes, *Penningtons*, 21–22; Duffen, "Overland," 356n6.

53. "Letter from J. Ross Brown, Tubac, February 5, 1864," *San Francisco Bulletin*, March 15, 1864, 1: 1, AHS.

54. "Letter from J. Ross Brown."

55. *Weekly Arizonian* (Tucson), March 12 and June 16, 1869, clippings in Pennington Family file, AHS; Barnes, *Arizona Place Names*, 325–26.

56. Bell, *New Tracks*, 2: 100–101.

57. Bell, *New Tracks*, 2: 100–101.

58. Poston, "Pennington Family," *Arizona Citizen* (Tucson), January 17, 1896, AHS.

59. Garza, *Apache Kid*; *Arizona Daily Star* (Tucson), June 16, 1907, clippings in AHS Pennington Family file. Only one son, named Green, died with Elias in the field.

60. Forbes, *Penningtons*, 26.

61. William F. Scott file, AHS.

62. William F. Scott file, AHS; "Criminals—Sonoita Valley Murders File," AHS Ephemera File.

63. William F. Scott file, AHS; William Fisher Scott file, AHS.

64. Kirkland MS, AHS; Altshuler, *Cavalry Yellow*, 125.

65. Charles Shibell file, AHS.

66. Mercedes Sais, Clippings File, AHS; Charles Shibell MS, AHS, esp. George Hand clipping.

67. Charles Shibell MS, AHS, file 44.

68. See J. C. Handy MS, AHS, for news clippings on this event.

69. Bell, *New Tracks*, 2: 100–101.

70. Forbes, *Penningtons*, 39.

71. Kolodney, *Land before Her*, 9, 33.

3. 1869–1871

1. John Ward file, AHS, "Santiago Ward Memoir."

2. John Ward file, AHS, "Santiago Ward Memoir."

3. Goodwin, *Social Organization*, 600, 651, 667–68; Rope, "Experiences."

4. Goodwin, *Social Organization*, 600, 651, 664, 667–68.

5. Goodwin, *Social Organization*, 95–96, 106; Basso, *Apache Raiding*, 287.

6. Goodwin, *Social Organization*, 97–98.

7. Lamar, *Far Southwest*, 100–101; Faulk, *Destiny Road*, 165.

8. Lamar, *Far Southwest*, 368–72; Altshuler, *Chains*, 24–25.

9. Lamar, *Far Southwest*, 107, 378. A census taken in the spring of 1863 counted 4,187 white people in the territory, most of Mexican descent from Sonora; the American whites were primarily southern Democrats; most were congregated in Tucson/Tubac, the Lower Gila or Colorado rivers, or at the Prescott or Hassayampa area; see Lamar, *Far West*, 380–81.

10. Lamar, *Far Southwest*, 377–78; Walker and Bufkin, *Historical Atlas*, 24, 29.

11. Lamar, *Far Southwest*, 380–81, 387; Altshuler, *Starting with Defiance*, 15–18, 63–67; Barnes, *Arizona Place Names*, 354–55.

12. Sweeney, *Cochise*, 205; Lamar, *Far Southwest*, 107–8, 381; Trimble, *People*, 398.

13. Lamar, *Far Southwest*, 107–9; Conner, *Joseph Reddeford Walker*, 170–84.

14. See V. Smith, *White Eyes, Red Heart*, for an expanded discussion on this point.

15. Scott, *War of the Rebellion*, 1:41:1, 82–86, Blackeney to Lambert, August 8, 1864; Sweeney, *Cochise*, 194, 435n29; Meketa, *One Blanket*, 55–56.

16. Scott, *War of the Rebellion*, 1:50:1, 367–70, Rigg to Cutler, September 14, 1864; Altshuler, *Cavalry Yellow*, 35, 280.

17. Scott, *War of the Rebellion*, 1:50:2, 1180, Gorman to Drum, April 5, 1865; *Post Returns*, Fort Goodwin, March 1865, NARA RG94.

18. Lamar, *Far Southwest*, 112, 387; Underhill, "Papago Calendar Record."

19. Lamar, *Far Southwest*, 113, 116; Walker and Bufkin, *Historical Atlas*, 26, 28.

20. Faulk, *Destiny Road*, 161, 163.

21. NARA RG 94, *Registers of Enlistments of Indian Scouts*, roll 70, vol. 150, 1866–74; Feliz enlisted October 24, 1868, when he was twenty-one years old (the minimum age for enlistment); see also NARA RG 94, *Post Returns*, Fort Lowell, October and November 1868; Namias, *White Captives*, 58.

22. Scott, *War of the Rebellion*, 1:50:2, 1261–63, Mason to Drum, June 18, 1865.

23. See NARA RG 94, *Post Returns*, Fort Lowell, 1866–68, for records of regular duty; Dunlay, *Wolves*, 2–3, 43–44.

24. NARA RG 94, *Post Returns*, Camp Bowie, January 1870; AHS Misc. Microfilm 0214, Clendenin to Devin, March 18, 1870, also found at Scott, *War of the Rebellion*, 1:50:2, 1180; Altshuler, *Chains*, 174, 178, 179; Altshuler, *Cavalry Yellow*, 31–32, 375; Meketa, *One Blanket*, 81. Arizona military historians may be surprised to learn that Cushing (not to mention Mickey Free) was at Fort Whipple in January 1870, but a page from a quartermaster's account book in Arizona State University, Hayden Library,

Mickey Free file, clearly shows that Cushing signed for supplies issued to Mickey Free at Whipple on February 24, 1870; Cushing biographer Kenneth A. Randall, *Only the Echoes*, has agreed with the author that the signature appears genuine. For comparison, see H. T. Ketchum, "Vaccination Report: Indian Territory," *Report of Commissioner*, 1864, in Facts on File, *American Indian History and Culture* (www.factsonfile.com), 10/6/02, for a report on Plains Indian smallpox vaccinations in 1864.

25. Lamar, *Far Southwest*, 113.

26. Kolodney, *Land before Her*, 176, 200, 221–25.

27. Hezekiah Brooks file, sh.

28. Charles Leib file, sh; Roscoe Wilson, "Arizona Days and Ways," August 18, 1957, Brooks ms, sh.

29. Wilson, "Arizona Days."

30. Wilson, "Arizona Days"; Neumann, "The Old Brooks Ranch," Hezekiah Brooks file, sh.

31. Neumann, "Old Brooks Ranch"; Wilson, "Arizona Days"; Charles Leib file, sh.

32. Wilson, "Arizona Days."

33. Neumann, "Old Brooks Ranch."

34. Edward G. Peck file, sh.

35. Prescott *Journal Miner*, July 10, 1869, sh.

36. *Journal Miner*, July 10, 1869.

37. *Journal Miner*, November 2, 1907.

38. *Journal Miner*, October 9, 1869.

39. Neumann, "Old Brooks Ranch."

40. *Journal Miner*, October 9, 1869.

41. Neumann, "Old Brooks Ranch"; Wilson, "Arizona Days."

42. Clippings File, Marriages, sh.

43. Brooks ms, sh, undated *Journal Miner* clipping.

44. Neumann, "Old Brooks Ranch."

45. Wilson, "Arizona Days."

46. *Journal Miner*, June 18, 1907.

47. *Journal Miner*, June 18, 1907.

48. *Journal Miner*, June 27, 1907.

49. *Journal Miner*, June 27, 1907.

50. *Journal Miner*, July 13, 1907.

51. *Journal Miner*, November 2, 1907.

52. Miscellaneous clippings in Brooks MS, SH.

53. *Journal Miner*, June 1, 1910.

54. Neumann, "Old Brooks Ranch."

55. *Arizona Citizen*, March 11, 1871, AHS.

56. Alphonse Lazard's "Indian Depredation Claim No. 8773, Testimony taken at Tucson, September 20, 1910," copy in Pennington Family file, AHS. The claim was conducted by Harry Peyton "for claimant." Larcena stated under oath that Eskiminzin had captured her and Mercedes; see also Roberts, *Their Own Blood*, 211–12. Roberts explains that Larcena is testifying for Lazard, but that most of the questions focus on her own experience.

57. Lazard, "Indian Depredation."

58. Lazard, "Indian Depredation"; Oury address of April 17, 1885, is in Sam Hughes MS, box 4, file 21, hereafter cited as Oury, "Address."

59. Lazard, "Indian Depredation"; Oury, "Address." See Barney, "Rescue of Julietta," 7–9, for another view of the Wooster deaths.

60. Oury, "Address."

61. Oury, "Address."

62. Underhill, "Papago Calendar Record," 36–37.

63. Underhill, "Papago Calendar Record," 36–37.

64. Kolodney, *Land before Her*, 224–25.

65. See sketch of map and rendezvous point reproduced in *Tucson Daily Citizen*, April 24, 1971, available in AHS Camp Grant Massacre file.

66. Oury, "Address."

67. Oury, "Address."

68. Whitman to AAG, April 30, 1871, in Camp Grant file, Official Reports, AHS.

69. Captain Dunn's Report, Camp Grant file, Official Reports, AHS.

70. Whitman to Dunn, May 1, 1871, Camp Grant file, Official Reports, AHS.

71. Stanwood to Wilbur, Camp Grant file, Official Reports, AHS; Whitman to AAG, May 5, 1871, Camp Grant file, Official Reports, AHS; Whitman to AAG, April 30, 1871; Reuben Wilbur file, UA Special Collections, Wilbur to Bendell, October 17, 1871, and October 28, 1871. See Wilbur-Cruz, *Beautiful, Cruel Country*, for more on her grandfather Wilbur.

72. Edward G. Peck file, SH.

73. I have abstracted, abbreviated, and compiled the trial from two original sources: "Extract from Day Book of the U.S. District Court, First Judicial Court . . . March 5, 1886–April 16, 1874" and the official trial transcript, published in *Alta California*, February 3, 1872, copies of both available at "Indians of North America—Apaches—Camp Grant Massacre," AHS Ephemera Files (hereafter referred to as Camp Grant Trial documents); Lamar, *Far Southwest*, 10, 15; Underhill, "Papago Calendar Record," 38.

74. Camp Grant Trial documents. Unless otherwise noted, all subsequent citations to the court proceedings are from this source.

75. Underhill, "Papago Calendar Record," 38–39, n. 322.

76. Underhill, "Papago Calendar Record," 38.

77. Camp Grant Trial documents; Underhill, "Papago Calendar Record," 38.

78. Wilbur file, UA Special Collections, Wilbur to Whitman, October 28, 1871.

79. Wilbur file, UA Special Collections, Wilbur to Whitman, October 28, 1871; Faery, *Cartographies*, 46–49, 52, 180, 206; Underhill, "Papago Calendar Record," 39.

80. Camp Grant Massacre file, AHS, McCaffrey to McCormick, May 28, 1872, hereafter cited as McCaffrey to McCormick, 1872. For one example of the "*farcical* nature of the trial," see C. Smith, *Oury*, 201; Underhill, "Papago Calendar Record," 39.

81. McCaffrey to McCormick, May 28, 1872.

82. McCaffrey to McCormick, 1872; Brooks, *Captives and Cousins*, 34; Howard, *Famous Indian Chiefs*, 77; Altshuler,

Chains, 209–11; Crook, *Autobiography*, 170–72, Thrapp, *Conquest*, 109–10.

83. McCaffrey to McCormick, May 28, 1872.

84. McCaffrey to McCormick, May 28, 1872.

85. Wilbur file, UA Special Collections; Underhill, "Papago Calendar Record," 37n23, 38n24; Colyer, "Peace," 32–33, claimed that all but four of the captives were returned at the meeting, perhaps meaning that only two ultimately returned to the Aravaipa; C. Smith, *Tanque Verde*, 56.

86. Sidney DeLong MS, file 2, AHS; see also Dan Pavillard, ed., *Olé* magazine, clipping in Ephemera—Apache Indians—Camp Grant Massacre file, AHS; the April 7, 1885, *Citizen* or *Star* reprinted Oury's entire address. Clipping in Sam Hughes MS, box 4, file 21, AHS; Colwell-Chanthaphonh, *Massacre at Camp Grant*, 5.

4. 1872–1882

1. Bourke, *Border*, 19, 26–27; C. Smith, *Oury*, 195–98; Altshuler, *Cavalry Yellow*, 86–88; Walker and Bufkin, *Historical Atlas*, 27A; see also Victoria Smith, "Destroying Angels: The Evolution of Scouting in Territorial Arizona," Arizona History Convention Papers, 2001, AHS, for details on the force Crook amassed at Tucson; and Bourke, *Apache Campaign*, 31–32; Duran and wife Dolores appear in 1870 census at Tucson with children Augustina and Francisco.

2. For establishment of Fort Apache, see Major John Green to AAG, Dept. of CA, August 20, 1869, and Green to AAG, December 6, 1869, and Kelly to Green, November 23, 1869, all at RG 94, LR AGO, NA MC619, reel 737, copy in University of Arizona Special Collections; see also *Weekly Miner*, September 4, 1869, for Green's full report; also Capt. William Kelly to Green, November 23, 1869, AHS Misc. Microfilm 0214, and Clendenin to Devin, January 15, 1870, Misc. Microfilm 0214; also *Alta California*, December 16, 1869, letter from Ord to Townsend; also Davisson, "New Light," 430–32; Altshuler, *Chains*, 171–72, 178, 195–98; Altshuler, *Cavalry Yellow*, 144; Bourke, *Border*, 31–32, 108–13; Thrapp, *Conquest*, 95;

Crook, *Autobiography*, 160–63. For insights into Western Apache power relations, especially as they pertain to Hacke-idasila, Miguel, Diablo, and Pedro, see Goodwin, *Social Organization*, 10, 13–14, 19–20, 22–23, 578, 609, 613, 617–18, 659, 661–62, 670, 672–73, 680, 682–83, 685, 689–90. Most of the influential Western Apache males under discussion here, including Eskiminzin, took their wives from the *i-ya-aiye* or *biszahe* clans; see Goodwin, *Social Organization*, 20, 117, 152, 670, 683, 685, 689–90. See also Davisson, "New Light," 428–30, and Collins, *Apache Nightmare*, 6–7. Major Green arrived at the selected sight of Fort Apache just after the appearance of miner Corydon Cooley, whose party had been escorted in by Diablo and Miguel. It is interesting to note that Cooley, who would become very influential, married two of Pedro's daughters, certainly a blow to the *ti-uk-a-di-gaidn*; see Davisson, "New Light," 431–32.

3. Davisson, "New Light," 428–29, is the best source for this material, in conjunction with Goodwin, *Social Organization*, 19–20, 95–96, 106, 578, 600–601, 619, 666–67.

4. Downey and Jacobsen, *Red/Bluecoats*, 9; Dunlay, *Wolves*, 111–12. See also Smits, "Fighting Fire."

5. For work on "men who run with Indians," see Smits, "'Squaw Men'"; Goodwin, *Social Organization*, 95–96, 106, 600–601, 610, 613, 654, 666–68, 668.

6. Calloway, *New Worlds*, 152. Yescas, Brillo, Severiano Gracias, and several others were liberated from their captors under terms of treaty with Major Green, hence their presence and involvement with, as well as testimony at, the Camp Grant Massacre trial in December 1871. A page from a quartermaster's ledger from Fort Whipple dated February 1870 and signed by Lt. Howard Cushing of the Third Cavalry clearly demonstrates that "Mickey Free" was an enlisted scout by that date; see Mickey Free file, Hayden Library, ASU, *Registers of Enlistments of Indian Scouts*, roll 70, vol. 150, August 23, 1871. For monograph on Indian scouts, see Dunlay, *Wolves*, and Smits, "Fighting Fire."

7. Faulk, *Destiny Road*, 163–65.

8. Colyer, "Peace," 32–33; Bourke, *Border*, 148–57; Crook,

Autobiography, 167–68. As Smits has noted, most scouts were not truly "free" to enlist, given the circumstances. Although some welcomed the opportunity for warrior-activity, or the chance to attack traditional enemies under any circumstances, others were coerced by means of intimidation, compulsion, bribes, and the manipulation of rations. Indians in the position of the Western Apaches "had virtually no choice but to perish or to assist the frontier army and hope that their service would win them government favors in return" ("Fighting Fire," 102–9).

9. Crook, *Autobiography*, 168; Thrapp, *Conquest*, 102–7, Bourke, *Border*, 166–67; Altshuler, *Chains*, 205–9, Debo, *Geronimo*, 84.

10. Thrapp, *Conquest*, 102–11; Altshuler, *Chains*, 224; Clum, *Apache Agent*, 94; Sweeney, *Making Peace*. Howard described Concepcion as "a queer-looking little man, half Mexican and half Indian" who "looked like a dark-skinned boy of twelve or thirteen, but had the husky voice of an old man, and was probably about twenty-five years old" (*Famous Indian Chiefs*, 77).

11. See Altshuler, *Chains*, for Delshe's early attempts to negotiate with Second Lt. Richard Dubois, 90–96.

12. Thrapp, *Conquest*, is the standard reference for the Tonto campaign. For the Yavapai perspective, see Braatz, *Surviving Conquest*.

13. Bourke, *Border*, 138, 183, 187, 188–201, 203, 210; Bourke, *Apache Campaign*, 40; *Diaries of John G. Bourke*, vol. 1, December 31, 1872, NARA Microfilm; Calloway, *New Worlds*, 123.

14. For Harris family, see *Douglas Dispatch*, November 11, 1935, AHS.

15. Crook, G. O. Number 13, April 8, 1873. Copy of official orders in Bourke, *Diaries*, 1: 88–89, ASU Microfilm.

16. *Third Calvalry Regimental Returns* indicate "John Daisy's" head brought to post on June 13, Chuntz's head on July 27; see also Thrapp, *Conquest*, 160–61; for primary accounts, see Merritt, "Three Indian Campaigns," and Johnson, "War Chief of the Tontos"; Walker and Bufkin, *Historical Atlas*, 40.

17. For the Western Apaches' introduction to barter, see "John Rope" in Basso, *Apache Raiding*, 99–100. For details on the early

interaction between Western Apaches and military, see *Social Organization*, 14, 600, 658, 672–76, 685; Meketa, *One Blanket*, 62–65; Altshuler, *Chains*, 37, 44–51; Scott, *War of the Rebellion*, 1:50:2, 1180; NARA RG 94, AGO, *Post Returns*, Fort Goodwin, March 1865, microfilm 617; *Santa Fe Gazette*, April 22, 1865. For Crook paying the scouts in horses, see Altshuler, *Chains*, 200; Thrapp, *Conquest*, 102–3; Bourke, *Border*, 128–29.

18. Crook, *Autobiography*, 164–65; Davisson, "New Light," 432–33; Thrapp, *Conquest*, 99; Bourke, *Apache Campaign*, 40; Altshuler, *Chains*, 187; Clum, *Apache Agent*, 76–77; "John Rope," in Basso, *Apache Raiding*, 101–2.

19. For the vacuum in leadership, see Sweeney, *Cochise*, 395–97; Davisson, "New Light," 434.

20. Bourke, *Diaries*, 2: 99, AHF Microfilm.

21. Karttunen, *Between Worlds*, xi, xii, 76, 79, 241.

22. Standard reference for the consolidation is Clum, *Apache Agent*, 126–32; Thrapp, *Conquest*; see also Davisson, "New Light."

23. L. Y. Loring, "Report on Coyotero Apaches," Camp Apache, January 11, 1875, cited in Davisson, "New Light," 436, 444n34; see also 437, 439; Clum, *Apache Agent*, 161–63; Debo, *Geronimo*, 96–97.

24. *Tombstone Epitaph*, April 29, 1926; *Douglas Dispatch*, November 11, 1935; this may or may not be the Harris referred to in *Apache Raid Statistics*, 1885–86, AHS [1869–71 raid statistics enclosed], on July 21, 1871; "Thrilling Rescue of Kate Harris and Mother," 28–33, in Barney, *Apache Warfare*.

25. Faery, *Cartographies*, 180–82, 188–89.

26. Clum, *Apache Agent*, 173–83; Debo, *Geronimo*, 101; the U.S. Indian Police Service was formed under the urging of Clum in 1875; Clum viewed the police as an "army" to counter the scouts and military; see Clum, *Annual Report*, 1875, cited in Mason, "Use of Indian Scouts," 113.

27. Hauzous, "Geronimo Forced Warm Springs Apache" (transcript of Hauzous 1956 tape recording at Fort Sill OK); Hitchcock, "Geronimo Was Captured," 194; Clum, *Apache Agent*, 204–5,

230–37; Thrapp, *Conquest*, 172; Debo, *Geronimo*, 105–7; "Rope," in Basso, *Apache Raiding*, 103.

28. Debo, *Geronimo*, 115; Thrapp, *Conquest*, 177.

29. Rope, "Experiences," 1: 42. According to *Registers of Enlistments of Indian Scouts*, vol. 154, Rope enlisted for the first time on April 1, 1882.

30. *Prescott Miner*, May 23, 1879; Rope, "Experiences," 2: 42, 58; Basso, "Rope," 103, 310n63; Gatewood, "Campaigning against Victorio," 101; Clum, *Apache Agent*, 204–5; Cruse, *Apache Days*, 30, 38, 41–42, 46–47, 51–59.

31. Rope, "Experiences," 1: 58; Cruse, *Apache Days*, 70–82; Thrapp, *Conquest*, 198–99; Thrapp, *Sieber*, 216–17; Kraft, *Gatewood*, 5–6; Webb, *Chronological List*, 88. Sergeant Dick is the scout Rope refers to as "Richard Bylas' uncle." Richard Bylas's father was Dja-la-ta-ha. Both brothers were from the *t'uagaidn*, the same clan as Nayudiie's father, to whom he was unusually close; see Goodwin, *Social Organization*, 97, 179, 579, 658, 673, 676; Rope, "Experiences," 2: 42, 44, 49, 58; and Basso, *Apache Raiding*, 103, 310n63; Gatewood, "Campaigning against Victorio," 101. The document trail later gets murky when some writers confused Clum's Police Sergeant Rip with the scout Sergeant Dick, who worked closely with Gatewood. Rip outlived Dick, to the best of my understanding; Rope sometimes confuses sequences, and may have done so here. There is no doubt that the Chiricahuas had killed an important clan leader and scout related to Richard Bylas. See also Clum, *Apache Agent*, 204–5, and Thrapp, *Sieber*, 322–40.

32. See "Letter of B. Tiernan, March 26, 1900; he encountered Victorio north of Silver City (UA SC MS 074); Rope, "Experiences," 1: 58; Webb, *Chronological List*, 89; Ball and Kaywaykla, *Days of Victorio*, 15, 58–60, 113; Debo, *Geronimo*, 123–25; Thrapp, *Sieber*, 217; Thrapp, *Conquest*, 202–3, 208–9; Bowen-Hatfield, *Chasing Shadows*, 39; Cruse, *Apache Days*, 83–84.

33. Rope, "Experiences," 2: 33–35; Davisson, "New Light," 423, 434, 440. Goodwin says Hacke-idasila was related to Diablo's brother Miguel: they were a type of brother-in-law because both

chose wives from the *iya-aiye* (as did Eskiminzin); therefore, Polone must have been killed by Pedro's *tca-tci-dn*. See Goodwin,
Social Organization, 578, 660, 609, 672.

34. Kessel, "Battle of Cibecue," 131–32; Bourke, *Apache Campaign*, 40; Bourke, *Border*, 178–19; Platten, *Ten Years*, 28; Horn,
Life, 76, 78; Wells, *Argonaut Tales*, 403–4; Cruse, *Apache Days*,
11, 91, 93–94, 105, 111, 118–19, 135; Barnes, *Apaches and Longhorns*, 53–56, 65–69; Webb, *Chronological List*, 92; Sweeney, *Grijalva*, 59–60; Davisson, "New Light," 440–41; Thrapp, *Conquest*,
217–21, 226, 231–35, 256; Thrapp, *Sieber*, 220–22; Collins, *Apache
Nightmare*, 67, 242. Noche-del-klinne was probably either of the
de-stci-dn or *tsect-ehe-sdjune*; Goodwin, *Social Organization*,
610, 619.

35. Platten, *Ten Years*, 28; Platten goes on to distinguish Kid
Indian from the better-known Apache Kid, explaining, "Variations
of that name 'Kid' seemed to be popular among Apaches." Garza,
Apache Kid, 172, adds another Kid into the mix: the "Carlysle
Kid."

36. The following passage regarding the raid on Ash Flats is com-
piled from Rope, "Experiences," 2: 2, 44; Basso, *Apache Raiding*,
"David Longstreet," 192, 310n62; Wells, *Argonaut Tales*, 148–49;
Clum, *Apache Agent*, 272; Goodwin, *Social Organization*, 579,
658, 676; Thrapp, *Sieber*, 224; Thrapp, *Conquest*, 235–38; Kathy P.
Pitts, "A Tale of Two Ranches: Cattle in Greenlee County, Arizona,
1870s–1970s," Arizona Historical Convention Papers, AHS, 1996.
Victoriano Mestas appears on 1870 census, age 34, farmer, born in
New Mexico, living at Camp Grant; George Stevens was born in
Massachusetts, married Francesca, daughter of Natash; Stevens
served as interpreter prior to Crook's arrival, and then guide and
interpreter, and later served on the territorial legislature; Manuel
Duran married Francesca's sister Dolores.

37. Rope, "Experiences," 2: 44.

38. Rope, "Experiences," 2: 44.

39. Rope, "Experiences," 2: 48–49.

40. Rope, "Experiences," 2: 48–49.

41. Western Apache males could count on their brothers-in-law

as allies; in this case, the *ti-sie-dtn-dn* would have been joined by the *bizahe* clan of Rope and his brothers, and the *t'uagaidn* of Nayundiie's father; see Goodwin, *Social Organization*, 20, 117, 152, 578, 660, 609, 670, 672, 683, 685.

42. Horn, *Life*, 48.

43. Debo, *Geronimo*, 149.

44. Debo, *Geronimo*, 151–52.

45. Debo, *Geronimo*, 152.

46. Debo, *Geronimo*, 156–57.

47. "The Life Story of Mrs. Andrew Stanley," Grenville Goodwin Papers, ASM.

48. "Life Story," 1.

49. "Life Story," 2.

50. "Life Story," 3–4.

51. "Life Story," 5.

52. "Life Story," 6.

53. "Life Story," 7.

54. "Life Story," 7.

55. "Life Story," 7, 689–90.

56. "Life Story," 8.

57. "Life Story," 9–12.

58. "Life Story," 13–16.

59. "Life Story," 17.

60. "Life Story," 17.

61. "Life Story," 18; Smits, "Fighting Fire," 97.

62. "Life Story," 19.

63. "Life Story," 22.

64. "Life Story," 20–21.

65. "Life Story," 22–26.

66. "Life Story," 26–30.

67. "Life Story," 31.

68. "Life Story," 31–33.

69. "Life Story," 33.

70. "Life Story," 35–36.

71. "Life Story," 36–38.

72. "Life Story," 39–47.

73. Horn, *Life*, 74–75, 80, 87, 93; Goodwin, *Social Organization*, 23; Davis, *Truth*, 10; Thrapp, *Conquest*, 254–55. Both Free and Rope enlisted at San Carlos on April 1, 1882; see *Registers of Enlistments*, vol. 153.

74. Horn, *Life*, 87.

5. 1883–1886

1. Lamar, *Far Southwest*, 403, 407; Faulk, *Destiny Road*, 171–74, 183–84; Walker and Bufkin, *Historical Atlas*, 41; Altshuler, *Starting with Defiance*, 54–58; Thorne, *White Eyes*, 30; Barnes, *Apache Days*, 43.

2. Hezekiah Brooks file, SH; *Yuma Sentinel*, June 2, 1877; *Arizona Enterprise*, April 10, 1878.

3. Edward G. Peck file, SH. Peck discovered a mine on War Eagle Creek while hunting deer; in three years it yielded $1.2 million. For complications, see *Arizona Weekly Citizen*, November 30, 1877, and May 9, 1879; also *Arizona Enterprise*, January 5 and April 10, 1878.

4. Thrapp, *Conquest*, 259, 263–64; Thrapp, *Sieber*, 259; Bourke, *Border*, 451; NARA RG 393, *Records of San Carlos*, "Naiche's Statement to Emmett Crawford at San Carlos, November 5, 1883." Archie McIntosh and his wife, Dominga, interpreted for Naiche and Crawford.

5. Bourke, *Border*, 435; Thrapp, *Conquest*, 260–61; Kraft, *Gatewood*, 21.

6. Thrapp, *Sieber*, 262; Kraft, *Gatewood*, 20–21; Rope, "Experiences," 2: 49.

7. Free claimed membership in Biulka's Tag Band A; Biulka, a *nadots-usn* clan leader, had succeeded the murdered Polone and the aging Hacke-idasila; it was probably Free's wife's clan; see Goodwin, *Social Organization*, 577. According to Basso, *Apache Raiding*, 305–6n15, Goodwin's informants used the same word, *salada*, an appropriation of the Spanish *soldado* (soldier), to refer to both military scouts and civilian Indian Service police. Except for difference in pay ($8 a month for police, $13 for scouts), the

Apaches made little of the difference between the two. The exchange between agent Willcox and Commissioner Price regarding Free's racial status is found in the Mickey Free file, AHS ; Mickey Free file, ASU Hayden.

8. Thrapp, *Sieber*, 262 and n. 7; Horn, *Life*, 17; Connell, "Apaches Past and Present," AHS.

9. Horn, *Life*, 17; Connell, "Apaches Past and Present," 3,18, 20; "Santiago Ward Memoir," John Ward file, AHS; Basso, "Rope," 135; Thrapp, *Sieber*, 185n28; Griffith, *Mickey Free*, 20; Kartunnen, *Between Worlds*, italics added for emphasis. The author subscribes to the bear theory. An early photograph of Free in SH seems to reveal tooth marks below Free's right knee and other scars (see illustrations).

10. Radbourne, "Salvador or Martinez?"; *Sonoran Census, 1831;* according to Woods, *Hispanic First Names,* "Abad" can be traced to Lebanese, while "Syriaca" means "belonging to God" in Syrian. Germans comprised a minority in Sonora by 1762, and by 1855, eight to nine thousand lived in Mexico. A list of settlers at Fronteras in the 1720s included two Indians with the surname "German." In 1769 Viceroy Galvez banned native surnames, ordering all Indians who still carried their traditional names to adopt European surnames. See F. Smith, *Phantom*, 98, 169n75, 170, 170n90, 99; McCarty, *Desert Documentary*, 20, 491; Froschle, *Die Deutschen;* Mallafe, "Importance of Migration," 303–13; see also Borah, "Mixing of Populations"; Browne, *Tour*, 171–72. The original Martinez in New Spain is thought to be one Enrio Martin of Hamburg. He went to Mexico with an appointment in the royal mint under the name Martinez; see Hoberman, *Mexico's Merchant Elite*, 332–33.

11. Thrapp, *Sieber*, 264; Rope, "Experiences," 2: 49; Thrapp, *Conquest*, 250. Additionally, Goodwin, *Social Organization*, 673, claims that the men belonging to the clan of a husband's wives were considered like brothers-in-law; they could be counted on for protection (176).

12. Horn, *Life*, 145.

13. Thrapp, *Conquest*, 265–66.

14. Hayes, "Quest"; see also Simmons, *Massacre*.

15. Orphaned, unattributed three-page document in author's file, probably from Sharlot Hall, bearing the file number 11, FF4, D519; see photographs of Jack Devine, prospector, at Sharlot Hall.

16. Davis, *Truth*, 58–59, 67; Debo, *Geronimo*, 174.

17. Bowen-Hatfield, *Chasing Shadows*, 53; Thrapp, *Conquest*, 273–78; Kraft, *Gatewood*, 25–26.

18. Bourke, *Apache Campaign*, 23–53.

19. Rope, "Experiences," 2: 50–51, 57; Bourke, *Apache Campaign*, 42, 58, 64; Thrapp, *Conquest*, 284.

20. Rope, "Experiences," 2: 50–51; there is some discrepancy in the identity of the photographer; Cattermole, *Famous Frontiersmen*, and Porter, *Paper Medicine Man*, both relying on Bourke, say it was Randall's equipment; however, Hatfield, *Chasing Shadows*, says it was Ben Wittick's. All agree that Randall captured the owl.

21. Rope, "Experiences," 2: 58–62; Webb, *Chronological List*, 93; Bourke, *Apache Campaign*, 70–79.

22. Rope, "Experiences," 2: 65–68; Thrapp, *Conquest*, 286–87; Hayes, "Quest," 20–22.

23. Thrapp, *Conquest*, 288–91; Bourke, *Apache Campaign*, 82–99; Bourke's *Diary*, vol. 67, ASU, contains this sequence.

24. Rope, "Experiences," 2: 71; Thrapp, *Sieber*, 283.

25. Thrapp, *Conquest*, 288–91; Thrapp, *Sieber*, 283.

26. Rope, "Experiences," 2: 68–69.

27. Rope, "Experiences," 2: 71; Goodwin, *Social Organization*, 538.

28. Rope, "Experiences," 2: 67. In conversation with the author, Ed Sweeney has indicated he has documents describing Dji-li-kinne as a Mexican known as Chino. This is possible, but Rope described him as a "'white' man"; he had a brother—Sergeant Sagotol, also known as Navajo Bill, an Indian policeman—at San Carlos; Dji-li-kinne means "pine-pitch house," a phenomenon not usually associated with Mexico; see also Sweeney, *Cochise*, 232, and C. Smith, "Unpublished History," 60; see also Rope, "Experiences," 1: 51–55 and 2: 44, and Thrapp, *Conquest*, 236–37.

29. "Santiago Ward Memoir," John Ward file, AHS.

30. "Santiago Ward Memoir."

31. "Santiago Ward Memoir." It is the author's guess that Pete Kitchen informed Ward of his brother's survival, because Kitchen conducted business at San Carlos at that time and because Kitchen would have been one of the very few people who could remember/ identify Feliz Tellez Ward from the Sonoita era; also, Kitchen's stepson, killed by Apaches on July 26, 1872, was a Martinez. See Kitchen MS, AHS and *Apache Raid Statistics, 1885–86*, AHS (contains copy of raid statistics, 1869–71). Ward says his mother and siblings lived with the Suastiquis in Magdalena, found on the 1852 Sonoran census, and said in Allison Family MS, series 4, file 30, AHS, to be Basque from Pyrenees. Suastiquis was also related to the Ronstadts; see Ronstadt, *Borderman*, and Wilbur-Cruz, *Beautiful, Cruel Country*.

32. G. O. Number 10, reprinted in *Arizona Daily Star*, June 20, 1883; Hayes, "Quest," 20–22.

33. NARA RG 393, LR, 1883.

34. NARA RG 393, LR, 1883.

35. NARA RG 393, LR, 1883.

36. NARA RG 393, LR, 1883; Davis, *Truth*, 68.

37. Hayes, "Quest," 20–22.

38. Davis, *Truth*, 106; NARA RG 391, *Registers of Enlistments*, June 1884; Horace Dunlap file, AHS; Basso, *Apache Raiding*, 173, 175; Dunlay, *Wolves*, 175.

39. Hayes, "Quest," 20–22.

40. These arguments are summarized in Hayes, "Quest."

41. Indian Rights Association, *Apaches*, 17; Davis, *Truth*, 82–101, 106; Ogle, *Federal Control*, 224–26.

42. "Santiago Ward Memoir."

43. Horn, *Life*, 149–50.

44. Horn, *Life*, 150.

45. Horn, *Life*, 150–55.

46. Ogle, *Federal Control*, 227–28; Davis, *Truth*, 138.

47. Free was enlisted as "Feliz" by Davis on March 10, 1885, at the Camp on Turkey Creek; see *Registers of Enlistments*, M233, roll 71, vol. 153; see also Davis, *Truth*, 138.

48. Davis, *Truth*, 145–46; alcohol on reservations was prohibited in 1881.

49. Davis, *Truth*, 146–49.

50. Davis, *Truth*, 149–95.

51. Aranda, "Santiago McKinn"; Martin is listed as killed on the 1885–86 *Raid Statistics*, AHS.

52. Aranda, "Santiago McKinn."

53. Aranda, "Santiago McKinn."

54. Ogle, *Federal Control*, 234; Arizona State Museum, Goodwin Collection, Testimony of Walter Hooke.

55. Davis, *Truth*, 197; Horn, *Life*, 175–76.

56. Horn, *Life*, 184–196.

57. Bourke, *Border*, 476; Davis, *Truth*, 200–18; Horn, *Life*, 201.

58. Simmons, "Captivity."

59. Simmons, "Captivity."

60. Bourke, *Border*, 477; Davis, *Truth*, 200–218; Horn, *Life*, 201.

61. Aranda, *Santiago McKinn*, 42–43, and Simmons, "Captivity."

62. Aranda, *Santiago McKinn*, 42–43; S. Lindauer bought Santiago his clothes; G. B. Hudson worked for Lindauer, and left a brief, rather inaccurate account of Santiago's return; see *Arizona Republican*, April 18, 1928. Zesch, *Captured*, offers a sensitive, comparative study of similar captives and their problematic reintegration in relation to Texas and the Comanches.

63. Aranda, *Santiago McKinn*, 42–43.

64. Bigelow, *Bloody Trail*, 183.

65. Trini was an orphan: "She only had an aunt . . . named Maria Cuen who brought her to the Peck ranch and left her there with her married cousin, Petra Cuen de Peck" (McCarty, "Trinidad Verdin," 157). See another relative in *Arizona Daily Star*, June 27, 1886. Trini is listed on the *Apache Raid Statistics*, 1885–86, AHS, mistakenly described as "taken prisoner and killed." Kieran McCarty, "Trinidad Verdin," has compared the three official versions of Trini's captivity; I have used them freely here.

66. This was an apparent nephew of the Ed Peck who had carried Bessie Brooks into captivity almost twenty years earlier; tradition in the Peck family holds that the Apache who saved his life warned Peck not to go near the house, but he did so anyway.

67. McCarty, "Trinidad Verdin," 154.

68. McCarty, "Trinidad Verdin," 156.

69. McCarty, "Trinidad Verdin," 158.

70. For Verdin's captivity, see *Arizona Daily Star*, April 28, 1886, and June 25, 1886; the *Star* of June 27, 1886, reports a slightly different version of Trini's rescue, although both it and the reports in McCarty's article might be intertwined.

71. Davis, *Truth*, 220; Tellez, "Reminiscences"; quotation from "The Reminiscences of Octaviano Gastelum," typescript found in Juan Tellez file, AHS, Tucson Biographical Files.

72. "Reminiscences of Octaviano Gastelum."

73. Davis, *Truth*, 222–24; Mazzonovich, *Trailing Geronimo*, 51–56; Debo, *Geronimo*, 291–301; the first Chiricahuas left Holbrook on September 13; for a treatise on the merits of removal, see *Arizona Daily Star*, May 2, 1886.

74. Slaughter file, AHS.

75. James Tevis file, ASU; *Tucson Daily Citizen*, April 25, 1953.

76. Allen Irwin MS, box 2, series 3, file 12, AHS.

77. Debo, *Geronimo*, 275.

78. Debo, *Geronimo*, 276–78.

79. J. Hayes, *Apache Vengeance*, undated article reprint, 185.

80. See, for example, Ball, *Indeh*, 110.

6. 1896–1900

1. Harriet Hankin, "True Story of Apache Girl Captured from Indians Wins First Prize in Essay Contest," in *Douglas Daily Dispatch*, clipping in A. Irwin MS, box 1, series 3, file 15, AHS, hereafter cited as Hankin, "True Story." Hankin was the wife of a Bisbee dentist; the essay was awarded the "best paper" prize by the "Bisbee Woman's Clubs," date unknown. The article prints the full text of the paper, probably 1920s or 1930s.

2. Wharfield, "Footnotes to History," 37–46, 38–39; Thrapp, *Sieber*, 323–25; Hubert Heywood, "The Terror of the Border," *Leslie's Weekly* 80 (April 25, 1895), in Goodman, *Arizona Odyssey*. The Arizona Historical Foundation has copies of every article in Goodman's *Arizona Odyssey* publication.

3. Schellie, *Vast Domain*, 251; Thrapp, *Sieber*, 325.

4. Thrapp, *Sieber*, 325–28.

5. Thrapp, *Sieber*, 328–29.

6. Thrapp, *Sieber*, 336–41.

7. Thrapp, *Sieber*, 344, 350; Debo, *Geronimo*, 300–301; Betzinez, *I Fought*, 144–45.

8. Thrapp, *Sieber*, 344; Garza, *Apache Kid*, 135–38; Schellie, *Vast Domain*, 251; Robinson, *Apache Voices*, 74.

9. From *Tombstone Epitaph*, July 23, 1892, quoted in Garza, *Apache Kid*, 139, see also 134; Heywood, "Terror of the Border," in Goodman, *Arizona Odyssey*, claims Kid captured a woman from San Carlos in September 1890, another in May 1892, and a third in October 1892. This source says the girl was the daughter of Indian scout Jack Long.

10. Garza, *Apache Kid*, 145–46.

11. Garza, *Apache Kid*, 146–49; the *Silver Belt* report is from this source.

12. Garza, *Apache Kid*, 151.

13. Thrapp, *Sieber*, 350.

14. Hancock, "Arizona Pioneer." Hancock was the postmaster at Paradise and a "widely known and popular pioneer."

15. Benton, *Cow by the Tail*, x; also in Garza, *Apache Kid*, 161–62.

16. Hancock, "Arizona Pioneer."

17. Irwin, *Southwest*, 299–300; Hankin, "True Story," and J. C. Hancock, "Judge Hancock: Squire of the Chiricahuas," *Brewery Gulch*, May 13, 1934, both in Apache May file, AHS.

18. Matilde Hampe MS, AHS, "A Trip with The Slaughters," file 11, hereafter cited as Hampe, "Trip with Slaughters"; see Chapel, "Camp Rucker."

19. Hankin, "True Story"; Irwin, *Southwest*, 303; the items are in the AHS collection today.

20. Hankin, "True Story"; Irwin, *Southwest*, 303; I have taken the liberty of placing the reference to gambling out of sequence from the original typescript.

21. Slaughter, "Reminiscences," Slaughter Family MS, AHS.

22. Many historians built the legend of John Slaughter, among them Irwin, *Southwest*; Sparks, *Apache Kid*; and Garza, *Apache Kid*. A thorough, updated study is in order; see also Slaughter, "Reminiscences." Hampe, in "Trip with Slaughters," says, "When I first met the Slaughters they were raising two young motherless children [in addition to Addie and Willie], a little Mexican girl and a small white boy. They were congenial, and played happily together."

23. Hancock, "Judge Hancock."

24. Clipping in A. Irwin MS, AHS, series 3, file 38.

25. Clipping in A. Irwin MS, AHS, series 3, file 38.

26. Forrest and Hill, *Lone War Trail*, 75.

27. Hankin, "True Story"; Margaret H. Canning, "Apache May," *Tradition: The Monthly Magazine of America's Picturesque Past* 2.1 (January 1959): 77–81, in Ephemera File, "Indians of North America—Apache People—Apache May," AHS, hereafter cited as Canning, "Apache May."

28. Hampe, "Trip with Slaughters."

29. Hampe, "Trip with Slaughters."

30. Hampe, "Trip with Slaughters."

31. Hankin, "True Story"; Canning, "Apache May," 79.

32. Hankin, "True Story"; Canning, "Apache May," 79.

33. Hankin, "True Story"; Canning, "Apache May," 79.

34. Hancock, "Arizona Pioneer" and "Judge Hancock."

35. Tom Vaughn, "Times Past: Apache May," *Arizona Capitol Times*, September 3, 1993, clipping in Ephemera File, "Indians of North America—Apache People—Apache May," AHS.

36. Hankin, "True Story."

37. Rachel Stevens interview, AHS.

38. Canning, "Apache May," 81.

39. Hankin, "True Story."

40. Hankin, "True Story."

41. Edwin Flint Williams, *Brewery Gulch Gazette*, April 30, 1936, in Apache May file, AHS.

42. Williams, *Brewery Gulch Gazette*.

43. Charles A. Nichols MS, AHS, file 2, "Dear Old Cochise," 154.

44. Lamar, *Far Southwest*, 410–11; Walker and Bufkin, *Historical Atlas*, 61.

45. Lamar, *Far Southwest*, 414.

46. *Tombstone Prospector*, July 22, 1889; Bourke, *Border*, 487.

47. Santiago Ward Memoir, John Ward file, AHS; C. Smith, *Tanque Verde*, 3, 22–23, 27, 32, 126, 237–38. According to Smith's sources, the Tellezes were rumored to be Portuguese or Italian.

48. Mickey Free file, AHS; Mickey Free file, ASU Hayden; Clendenin to AAG, September 29, 1890, RG 94, LR, Dept. AZ; see Feaver, "Indian Soldiers."

49. Wilson, "Arizona Days," June 7, 1959; Weber, *Foreigners*, 217; Lockwood, "Who Was Who."

50. Debo, *Geronimo*; 364; Britton Davis would have a serious falling out with the group, resulting in his classic *The Truth about Geronimo*.

51. Griffith, *Mickey Free*, 206–7; Garza, *Apache Kid*, 170–71; Wharfield, "Footnotes to History," 46; Peterson, "Automobile Comes to Territorial Arizona."

52. Walker and Bufkin, *Historical Atlas*, 61–62; Lamar, *Far Southwest*, 423–24.

53. Thrapp, "'Marriage' of Al Sieber." Thrapp's argument aginst Sieber's children is entirely self-referencing.

54. Thrapp, "'Marriage' of Al Sieber." The article is written around a letter from Clara Woody to Dan Thrapp, October 8, 1966.

55. Charles A. Anderson file, AHS.

56. Art Leibson, "Rancher Reveals 40-year Secret, Posse Killed Apache Kid," in Irwin Allen MS, box 1, series 3, file 12. It should

be noted that Garza, *Apache Kid*, strenuously disagrees with this account of Kid's demise.

57. Tomsho, "Geronimo's Skull."

58. Lamar, *Far Southwest*, 436; Faulk, *Destiny Road*, 198–99; Santiago Ward Memoir, AHS; Davis, *Truth about Geronimo*, 271; Edward G. Peck file, AHS.

59. AHS Microfilm AG-680.42.

60. Connell, *Tucson Citizen*, April 10, 1921, AHS.

61. Irwin Allen file, AHS, box 1, series 3, file 12.

62. Moreno Family Papers, AHS.

63. Bowden, "Apaches Honor the Memory."

64. Allen, "Kin Want Death Site Marked."

65. Betzinez, *I Fought*, 18.

66. Pascoe, "Miscegenation Law," 466.

67. Mike Burns MS, Hayden Library, ASU, 21.

BIBLIOGRAPHY

MANUSCRIPTS AND ARCHIVES

Most of the research used in the creation of *Captive Arizona* was conducted at the Arizona Historical Society (AHS), Southern Arizona Division, Tucson, an invaluable resource for anyone interested in learning more about the history of captivity during the state's territorial era. Other resources are located in the University of Arizona (UA) Library's Special Collections; the archives of the Arizona State Museum at the University of Arizona; the Arizona State University's Hayden Library, Arizona Collection, in the Luhrs Reading Room; the Arizona Historical Foundation, also located in ASU's Hayden Library; and the Sharlot Hall Museum (SH) in Prescott, Arizona.

A single document found in the file of Palatine Robinson (MS 691) at AHS testifies to the experience of nine-year-old Ramona, a Mexican child held by Robinson in 1858 and subsequently sold by him "at the Rio Grande." While most of the material on Olive Oatman is taken from Royal B. Stratton's well-known and widely distributed *Captivity of the Oatman Girls*, AHS holds a copy of the hard- to-find *Olive Ann Oatman's Lecture Notes* (970.1P511), edited by Edward Pettid in 1969. Jimmy Miller's childhood recollection of Olive shortly after her release from the Mojaves is located in the James H. Miller file (AHS MS 495). Another source for Olive Oatman is in the alphabetized AHS Clippings Files under the name Olive Oatman.

The Pennington Family files (AHS MS 936) contain genealogical information on Larcena Pennington Page's family of origin, while the Robert Humphrey Forbes file (AHS MS 261, box 3, file

2) contains Larcena's daughter Georgie Scott Forbes's version of her mother's captivity by Apaches. Further information relating to the life of Larcena is found in the biographical files of William Fisher Scott (AHS MS 720), J. C. Handy (AHS Tucson Biographical File), Elias Pennington (AHS Tucson Biographical Files), and Francis Heney (AHS MS 585). References to Larcena's family are also found in the AHS Ephemera Files entitled "Criminals—Sonoita Valley Murders."

Material for the life of Mercedes Saiz Shibell is scanty but can be found in the Charles Shibell Family Papers (AHS MS 728), which contain a copy of Robert Forbes's book *The Penningtons: Pioneers of Southern Arizona*; this file also contains George Hand's account of Mercedes's funeral. There is a brief account of Mercedes's life under the surname "Sais" in the AHS Clippings Files. The files of William Kirkland (MS 1102, box 1, file 7) contain Kirland's account of Mercedes's rescue from the Apaches. A list of purported victims of the Aravaipa Apache chief Eskiminzin is located in the Francis H. Goodwin file (AHS MS 297). Another list of presumed Anglo victims of the Apaches is found in *Apache Raid Statistics* (AHS MS 381).

Most material relative to the life of Mickey Free must be extracted from the National Archives and Records Administration (NARA). Fortunately, the Mickey Free file at AHS (Tucson Biographical Files) contains photocopies of Free's enlistments with the Indian scouts (NARA RG 92) and as a member of the Indian police force (NARA RG 75). The reminiscence of Free's half-brother, Santiago Ward, is found in the John Ward file at AHS (Tucson Biographical Files). The Allison Family file (AHS MS 13, series 4, file 30) claims that the Suastiqui family of Sonora, whom Mickey Free's mother fled to following the death of her husband John Ward, were of Basque descent. The file of Pete Kitchen, suspected of being responsible for informing Santiago Ward that his brother, Mickey Free, was alive and employed at San Carlos, is in AHS MS 408. The Mickey Free files at ASU's Hayden Library, Arizona Collection (HB HAY BIO FRE, MIC, and CM MSM-204/OV2), hold the singular copy of the quartermaster's records showing that Free was at Fort Whipple in

1870 with Lieutenant Howard Cushing, as well as records of Free's service with the Indian Police. The Horace Dunlop file (AHS MS 233) discusses Mickey Free and the Chiricahua Apache Chatto living together at the White Mountain reservation in a wooden house. The Arizona Historical Foundation houses a complete set of the John Gregory Bourke diaries (124 volumes) on microfilm, wherein Free is occasionally mentioned, as noted in the relevant endnotes in *Captive Arizona*. AHS also holds a carbon-copy typescript of John T. Connell's inflammatory description of Mickey Free from the *Tucson Citizen*, February 5–July 32, 1921 (970.3A639C7523, 1921).

Accounts of the captivity and life of the young Yavapai girl known as Bessie Brooks are extracted primarily from newspaper accounts, mostly the *Prescott Miner*, as indicated in the endnotes of the relevant chapter in *Captive Arizona*. However, supporting documents are also found in the Sharlot Hall Museum biographical files of Hezekiah Brooks, Mary Smith Leib Brooks, and Edward G. Peck. A preliminary work on the life of Bessie Brooks, written by Al Bates, is on file in the AHS Arizona History Convention Files.

A complete transcript of the Camp Grant massacre trial is located in the AHS Ephemera File "Indians of North America— Apaches—Camp Grant Massacre." This file also contains copies of official correspondence between army officers and Tucson officials regarding the massacre. Further information concerning the Camp Grant Massacre is held in the files of Sam Hughes (AHS MS 366, box 4, file 21) and Sidney DeLong (Tucson Biographical Files) and the Oury Family Papers at UA Special Collections (AZ 016). UA Special Collections also contains the Papers of Dr. Reuben Wilbur (AZ 565), who was instrumental in locating the captive Aravaipa children.

Regarding the Ash Flats Massacre at George Stevens's ranch in 1881, Kathy Pitts's paper "A Tale of Two Ranches" can be found in AHS Arizona History Convention Papers, as well as another entry in the AHS Clippings File under James S. Stevens, the son of George. The transcriptions of Rachel Stevens's oral history interview can be found at AHS AVO152. Further information regarding

Apaches and Apache scouts is in the AHS Arizona History Convention Files "Destroying Angels: The Evolution of Indian Scouting
in Territorial Arizona" and "Geronimo's Yodascin: The Role of
Captivity in the Chiricahua Wars, 1882–86," both authored by
Victoria Smith. The transcript of Grenville Goodwin's interview
of Mrs. Andrew Stanley, a White Mountain Apache woman taken
captive by the Chiricahuas, is at UA's Arizona State Museum archives, in the Grenville Goodwin Collection. Albert Peck's file at
AHS Tucson Biographical Files is relevant to the life of the captive
Trinidad Verdin. James Tevis (AHS 786) was the father of the Tevis
girl who had an encounter with Geronimo in 1886. A two-page
autobiographical account of Octaviano Gastelum's captivity by
Geronimo in 1886 is found in the Juan I. Tellez file, AHS, Tucson
Biographical Files.

Information on the life of Apache Kid is located in the files of
Charles Anderson (AHS 018) and Charles Morgan Wood (AHS 881)
and in the AHS Clippings Files under James B. Hancock. Accounts
of the "adoption" and death of Kid's daughter, Apache May, by
the Slaughter family of Cochise County, Arizona, are found in the
AHS Ephemera File "Indians of North America—Apache People—
Apache May," as well as in the files of Allen A. Irwin (AHS MS
249, box 1, series 3, file 12), Charles A. Nichols (AHS MS 586, file
2, unpublished manuscript "Dear Old Cochise"), and Slaughter
family friend Matilde Hampe (AHS MS 324, file 11). Finally, the
death certificate of the aged Yaqui deaf-mute taken captive by
Geronimo and later sold to the Watts family of Los Angeles is
found in the Moreno Family Papers file at AHS (MS 1111).

For other relevant information see NARA: RG 94, *Registers of Enlistments in the United States Army*, 1798–1914, microfilm 3748,
M233, reels 70, 71, *Enlistments of Indian Scouts*; RG 94, *Returns
from Regular Army Cavalry Regiments*, 1833–1916, microfilm
3336, M744; RG 94, *Returns from United States Military Posts*,
1800–1916, microfilm 1520, M617; and RG 393, *Headquarters Records of Fort Verde, Arizona Territory*, 1866–1891, LR, microfilm
3748, M1076.

Ackernecht, Erwin H. "White Indians." *Bulletin of the History of Medicine* 15 (1944): 18–35.

Ainsa, Joseph Y. *History of the Crabb Expedition into Northern Sonora.* Phoenix AZ: s.p., 1951.

Allen, Paul L. "Kin Want Death Site Marked." *Tucson Citizen,* April 3, 1995.

Altom, Mila Capes, ed. and transcriber. *Students at Haskell Institute from 1884 to 1889.* Lawrence KS: Haskell Indian Nations University, Dept. of Archives, 2000.

Altshuler, Constance Wynn. *Cavalry Yellow and Infantry Blue: Army Officers in Arizona between 1851 and 1886.* Tucson: Arizona Historical Society, 1991.

———. *Chains of Command: Arizona and the Army, 1856–1875.* With Maps by Don Bufkin. Tucson: Arizona Historical Society, 1981.

———. *Starting with Defiance: Nineteenth Century Arizona Military Posts.* Tucson: Arizona Historical Society, 1983.

Aranda, Daniel. "Santiago McKinn, Indian Captive." *Real West* (June 1981): 41–43.

"Arizona History from Newspaper Accounts: Tribal Atrocities Alleged in Divorce Suit against Wealthy Mohave Indian Outdoes Fiction." Reprinted from *Arizona Republican,* April 30, 1922, in *Arizoniana* (Spring 1961): 29–30.

Arnold, Elliott. *Blood Brother.* New York: Duell, Sloan & Pearce, 1947.

Axtell, James. *The Invasion Within: The Contest of Cultures in Colonial North America.* New York: Oxford University Press, 1985.

———. "The White Indians of Colonial America." *William and Mary Quarterly* 32 (January 1975): 55–88.

Ball, Eve. *Indeh: An Apache Odyssey.* With Nora Henn and Lynda A. Sanchez. Norman: University of Oklahoma, 1980.

———, and James Kaywaykla, narrator. *In the Days of Victorio: Recollections of a Warm Springs Apache.* Tucson: University of Nebraska Press, 1970; rpt. 2003.

Barnes, Will C. *Apaches and Longhorns: The Reminiscences of Will C. Barnes.* Edited by Frank C. Lockwood. Los Angeles: Ward Ritchie Press, 1941.

——. *Arizona Place Names.* Revised and enlarged by Byrd H. Granger. Tucson: University of Arizona Press, 1960; rpt. 1985.

Barney, James. *Tales of Apache Warfare.* S.p., 1933.

Bartlett, John Russell. *Personal Narrative of Explorations and Incidents in Texas, New Mexico, California, Sonora, and Chihuahua connected with the United States and Mexican Boundary Commission during the years 1850, '51, '52, and '53.* 2 vols. New York: D. Appleton & Company, 1854.

Basso, Keith, ed. *Apache Raiding and Warfare, from the Notes of Grenville Goodwin.* Tucson: University of Arizona Press, 1971.

——. *Wisdom Sits in Places: Landscape and Language among the Western Apache.* Albuquerque: University of New Mexico Press, 1996.

Begay, Alberta. "Massai-Broncho Apache." *True West* 6.6 (July–August 1959): 4–48.

Bell, William A. *New Tracks in North America.* 2 vols. London: Chapman & Hall, 1869.

Benton, Jesse James. *Cow by the Tail.* Introduction by Richard Summers. Boston: Houghton Mifflin Co., 1943.

Betzinez, Jason. *I Fought with Geronimo.* With William Sturtevant Nye. Lincoln: University of Nebraska Press, 1959.

Bigelow, Lt. John, Jr. *On the Bloody Trail of Geronimo.* Los Angeles: Western Lore Press, 1998.

Borah, Woodrow. "The Mixing of Populations." In *First Images of America*, ed. Fredi Chapelli, 2 vols. Berkeley: University of California Press, 1976, 2707–22.

Bourke, John G. *An Apache Campaign in the Sierra Madre.* New York: Charles Scribner's Sons, 1958.

——. Diaries of John G. Bourke.

——. *On the Border with Crook.* Lincoln: University of Nebraska Press, 1971.

Bowden, Charles. "Apaches Honor the Memory of Massacre Victims." *Tucson Citizen*, April 30, 1984.

Bowen-Hatfield, Shelly. *Chasing Shadows: Indians along the United States–Mexican Border, 1876–1911*. Albuquerque: University of New Mexico Press, 1998.

Braatz, Timothy. *Surviving Conquest: A History of the Yavapai Peoples*. Lincoln: University of Nebraska Press, 2003.

Brooks, James F. *Captives and Cousins: Slavery, Kinship, and Community in the Southwest Borderlands*. Chapel Hill: University of North Carolina Press, 2002.

Browne, J. Ross. *A Tour through Arizona, 1864*. Tucson: Arizona Silhouettes, 1950; 2nd ed., 1951.

Calloway, Colin G. *New Worlds for All: Indians, Europeans, and the Remaking of Early America*. Baltimore: Johns Hopkins University Press, 1997.

Cattermole, E. G. *Famous Frontiersmen*. Tarrytown: W. Abbatt, 1926.

Chapel, William L. "Camp Rucker: Outpost in Apacheria." *Journal of Arizona History* (Summer 1973): 95–112.

Chapelli, Fredi, ed. *First Images of America*. 2 vols. Berkeley: University of California Press, 1976.

Clum, Woodworth. *Apache Agent: The Story of John P. Clum*. Lincoln: University of Nebraska Press, 1978.

Collins, Charles. *Apache Nightmare: The Battle at Cibecue Creek*. Norman: University of Oklahoma Press, 1999.

Colwell-Chanthaphonh, Chip. *Massacre at Camp Grant: Forgetting and Remembering Apache History*. Tucson: University of Arizona Press, 2007.

Colyer, Vincent. "Peace with the Apaches." *Report to the Board of Indian Commissioners*. Washington DC, 1872.

Conklin, Enoch. *Picturesque Arizona*. New York: Mining Record Print, 1878.

Conner, Daniel Ellis. *Joseph Reddeford Walker and the Arizona Adventure*. Edited by Donald Berthrong and Odessa Davenport. Norman: University of Oklahoma Press, 1956.

Crook, George. *General George Crook, His Autobiography*. Edited and annotated by Martin F. Schmitt. Norman: University of Oklahoma, 1960.

Cruse, Thomas. *Apache Days and After*. Edited with an introduction by Eugene Cunningham. Lincoln: University of Nebraska Press, 1987.Davis, Britton. *The Truth about Geronimo*. Lincoln: University of Nebraska Press, 1976.

Davisson, Lori. "New Light on the Cibecue Fight: Untangling Apache Identities." *Journal of Arizona History* 20.4 (Winter 1978): 423–44.

Debo, Angie. *Geronimo: The Man, His Time, His Place*. Norman: University of Oklahoma Press, 1976.

Dillon, Richard. "Tragedy at Oatman Flat: Massacre, Captivity, Mystery." *American West* (March/April 1981): 46–59.

Downey, Fairfax, and Jacques Noel Jacobsen Jr. *The Red/Bluecoats*. Fort Collins CO: Old Army Press, 1973.

Duffen, William A. "Overland via the Jackass Mail in 1858: The Diary of Phocion Way." *Arizona and the West* 2 (Winter 1960): 353–75.

Dunlay, Thomas W. *Wolves for the Blue Soldiers: Indian Scouts and Auxiliaries with the United States Army, 1860–90*. Lincoln: University of Nebraska Press, 1982.

Faery, Rebecca Blevins. *Cartographies of Desire: Captivity, Race, and Sex in the Shaping of an American Nation*. Norman: University of Oklahoma Press, 1999.

Faulk, Odie B. *Destiny Road: The Gila Trail and the Opening of the Southwest*. New York: Oxford University Press, 1973.

Feaver, Eric. "Indian Soldiers, 1891–95: An Experiment on the Closing Frontier." *Journal of the National Archives* 7.2 (1975): 109–18.

Forbes, Robert H. *Crabb's Filibustering Expedition into Sonora*. Tucson AZ: Arizona Silhouettes, 1952.

———. *The Penningtons: Pioneers of Arizona*. Tucson AZ: Tucson Archeological and Historical Society, 1919.

Forrest, Earle Robert, and Edwin B. Hill. *Lone War Trail of Apache Kid*. Illustrations by Charles Russell. Pasadena: Trails' End Publication Co., 1947.

Fröschle, Hartmut. *Die Deutschen in Latinamerika.* Tübingen, Basel: Erdmann, 1979.

Furst, Jill Leslie. *Mojave Pottery, Mojave People: The Dillingham Collection of Mojave Ceramics.* Santa Fe NM: School of American Research, 2001.

Garza, Phyllis de la. *The Apache Kid.* Tucson AZ: Western Lore Press, 1995.

Gatewood, Charles B. "Campaigning against Victorio in 1879." *Great Divide* (April 1894): 102–4.

Goodman, David M., ed. *Arizona Odyssey: Bibliographic Adventures in Nineteenth-Century Magazines.* Tempe: Arizona Historical Foundation, 1969.

Goodwin, Grenville. *Social Organization of the Western Apaches.* Tucson: University of Arizona, 1942; rpt. 1969.

Griffith, A. Kinney. *Mickey Free: Manhunter.* Caldwell ID: Caxton Printers, 1969.

Hancock, J. C. "Arizona Pioneer Writes Interesting History of Early Galeyville." *Tombstone Epitaph*, April 29, 1926.

Harris, Benjamin Butler. *The Gila Trail: Texas Argonauts and the California Gold Rush.* Edited and annotated by Richard H. Dillon. Norman: University of Oklahoma Press, 1960.

Hauzous, Sam. "Geronimo Forced Warm Springs Apaches to Fight U.S., Mexico, and Other Indians." *Tel-Ectric Topics* (April 1978): 6–8.

Hayes, Jess G. *Apache Vengeance: The History of Apache Kid.* Albuquerque: University of New Mexico Press, 1954.

Hayes, Mick. "Quest for Charlie McComas." *Old West* (Spring 1989): 20–23.

Heard, J. Norman. *White into Red: A Study of the Assimilation of White Persons Captured by Indians.* Metuchen NJ: Scarecrow Press, 1973.

Hitchcock, J. R. W. "How Geronimo Was Captured." *Youth's Companion* 62(May 1884): 194.

Hoberman, Louisa Schell. *Mexico's Merchant Elite, 1590–1660.* Durham NC: Duke University Press, 1991.

Horn, Tom. *Life of Tom Horn: Government Scout and Interpreter.*

Introduction by Dean Krakel. Norman: University of Oklahoma Press, 1964; rpt. 1983.

Howard, O. O. *Famous Indian Chiefs I Have Known.* New York: Century Co., 1908.

Indian Rights Association. *The Apaches of the White Mountain Reservation, Arizona.* Philadelphia: Executive Committee of the Indian Rights Association, 1885.

Irwin, Allen A. *The Southwest of John Slaughter, 1841–1922.* Glendale CA: Arthur H. Clarke Co., 1965.

Iverson, Peter. *Carlos Montezuma and the Changing World of American Indians.* Albuquerque: University of New Mexico Press, 1982.

Jacobs, Margaret D. *Engendered Encounters: Feminism and Pueblo Cultures, 1879–1934.* Lincoln: University of Nebraska Press, 1999.

Johns, Elizabeth A. H. *Storms Brewed in Other Men's Worlds: The Confrontation of Indians, Spanish and French in the Southwest, 1540–1795.* Norman: University of Oklahoma Press, 1996.

Johnson, Carl P. "A War Chief of the Tontos: A Story of Arizona." *Overland Monthly* 28(November 1896): 528–32.

Karttunnen, Frances. *Between Worlds: Interpreters, Guides and Survivors.* New Brunswick NJ: Rutgers University Press, 1994.

Kessel, William B. "The Battle of Cibecue and Its Aftermath: A White Mountain Apache's Account." *Ethnohistory* 21–22 (Spring 1974): 123–34.

Kolodney, Annette. *The Land before Her: Fantasy and Experience of the American Frontiers, 1630–1860.* Chapel Hill: University of North Carolina Press, 1984.

Kraft, Louis. *Gatewood and Geronimo.* Albuquerque: University of New Mexico Press, 2000.

Kroeber, A. L. *Olive Oatman's Return.* Kroeber Anthropological Society Papers, no. 4. Berkeley CA: Kroeber Anthropological Society, 1951.

Lamar, Howard. *The Far Southwest, 1846–1912.* Albuquerque: University of New Mexico Press, 1966; rpt. 2000.

Lockwood, Frank C. "Who Was Who in Early Arizona: Hiram S. Stevens," *Arizona Daily Star*, December 1, 1940.

Mallofe, Rolondo. "The Importance of Migration in the Viceroy of Peru." In *Population and Economics: Proceedings of Section V of the Fourth Conference of the Economic History Association*. Edited by Paul DePrez. Winnipeg: University of Manitoba Press, 1970. 303–13.

Mason, Joyce Evelyn. "The Use of Indian Scouts in the Apache Wars." Master's thesis, Indiana State University, 1970.

Mazzonovich, Anton. *Trailing Geronimo*. Edited by E. A. Brininstool. Los Angeles: Gem Productions, 1926.

McCarty, Kieran. *Desert Documentary: The Spanish Years, 1767–1821*. Tucson: Arizona Historical Society, 1976.

———, ed. and trans. "Trinidad Verdin and the 'Truth' of History." *Journal of Arizona History* (Summer 1973): 149–64.

McGinty, Brian. *The Oatman Massacre: A Tale of Desert Captivity and Survival*. Norman: University of Oklahoma Press, 2005.

Meketa, Charles, and Jacqueline. *One Blanket and Seven Days Rations: 1st Infantry New Mexico Volunteers in Arizona, 1864–1866*. Globe AZ: Southwest Parks and Monuments Association, 1980.

Merritt, Wesley. "Three Indian Campaigns." *Harper's New Monthly Magazine* (April 1890): 720–37.

Namias, June. *White Captives: Gender and Ethnicity on the American Frontier*. Chapel Hill: University of North Carolina Press, 1993.

Nentvig, Juan. *Rudo Ensayo: A Description of Sonora and Arizona in 1764*. Tucson: University of Arizona, 1980.

Ogle, Ralph H. *Federal Control of the Western Apache*. Albuquerque: University of New Mexico Press, 1940.

Pascoe, Peggy. "Miscegenation Law, Court Cases, and Ideologies of 'Race' in Twentieth-Century America." In *Sex, Love, Race: Crossing Boundaries in North American History*, ed. Martha Hodes. New York: New York University Press, 1999.

Peterson, Thomas H. "The Automobile Comes to Territorial Arizona." *Journal of Arizona History* (Autumn 1974): 249–52.

Pettid, Edward J., ed. *Olive Ann Oatman's Lecture Notes and Oatman Bibliography*. Bloomington CA: San Bernardino County Museum Association, 1969.

Pfefferkorn, Ignaz. *Sonora: A Description of the Province*. Translated and annotated by Theodore Treutline. Albuquerque: University of New Mexico Press, 1949.

Platten, Fred. *Ten Years on the Trail of the Redskins*. Williams AZ: Williams New Press, 1959.

Porter, Joseph C. *Paper Medicine Man*. Norman: University of Oklahoma Press, 1986.

Radbourne, Allan. *Mickey Free: Apache Captive, Interpreter, and Indian Scout*. Tucson: Arizona Historical Society, 2005.

———. "Salvador or Martinez? The Parentage and Origins of Mickey Free." *English Westerners Brand Book* 14 (January 1972): 2–24.

Radding, Cynthia. *Wandering Peoples: Colonialism, Ethnic Spaces and Ecological Frontiers in Northwest New Spain*. Durham NC: Duke University Press, 1997.

Randall, Kenneth A. *Only the Echoes: The Life of Howard Bass Cushing*. Las Cruces NM: Yucca Tree Press, 1995.

Rice, William B. *The Los Angeles Star, 1851–1864: The Beginnings of Journalism in Southern California*. Berkeley: University of California Press, 1947.

Roberts, Virginia Cullen. *With Their Own Blood: A Saga of Southwestern Pioneers*. Fort Worth: Texas Christian University Press, 1992.

———. "Jack Penington in Early Arizona." *Arizona and the West* 23 (Winter 1981): 317–23.

Robinson, Sherry. *Apache Voices: Their Stories of Survival as Told to Eve Ball*. Albuquerque: University of New Mexico Press, 2000.

Rockwell, Susan L. "The Autobiography of Mike Burns, Yavapai Apache." Master's thesis, Arizona State University, 2001.

———, ed. *The Journey of a Yavapai Indian: A Nineteenth Century*

Odyssey by Robert Burns. Introduction by Susan L. Rockwell. Princeton NJ: Elizabeth House, 2002.

Ronstadt, Federico. *Borderman: Memoirs of Federico Jose Maria Ronstadt.* Albuquerque: University of New Mexico Press, 1993.

Rope, John, as told to Grenville Goodwin. "Experiences of an Indian Scout: Excerpts from the Life of John Rope, an 'Old-Timer' of the White Mountain Apaches." *Arizona Historical Review* 7.1 (January 1936): 31–68, and 7.2 (April 1936): 31–73.

Sacks, Benjamin. "New Evidence on the Bascom Affair." *Arizona and the West* 4 (Autumn 1962): 261–78.

Saxton, Dean, and Lucille. *O'Othham Hoho'ok A'agitha: Legends and Lore of the Papago and Pima Indians.* Tucson: University of Arizona Press, 1973.

Schellie, Don. *Vast Domain of Blood: The True Story of the Camp Grant Massacre.* Los Angeles: Western Lore Press, 1968.

Scott, Robert N. *The War of the Rebellion: A Compilation of the Official Records of the Union and Confederate Armies.* Pasadena CA: Historical Times, 1985.

Sherer, Lorraine M. *The Clan System of the Fort Mojave Indians.* Los Angeles: Historical Society of Southern California, 1965.

Sierras, Eugene L., transcriber. *Mexican Census: Arizona Pre-territorial.* Tucson: Arizona State Genealogical Society, 1986.

Simmons, Marc. "The Captivity of Jimmy McKinn." *New Mexico Magazine* (May 1983): 49–50.

———. *The Massacre on the Lordsburg Road: A Tragedy of the Apache Wars.* College Station: Texas A&M Press, 1997.

Smith, Cornelius C. "Some Unpublished History of the Southwest: An Old Diary Found in Mexico by Mrs. Granville Oury." *Arizona Historical Review* (January 1935): 45–65.

———. *Tanque Verde: The Story of a Frontier Ranch.* Tucson AZ: s.p., S. L., S. N., 1978.

———. *William Sanders Oury: History Maker of the Southwest.* S.p., 1967.

Smith, Fay Jackson. *Captain of the Phantom Presidio: A History of the Presidio of Fronteras, Sonora, New Spain, 1698–1735.* Spokane WA: A. H. Clark, 1993.

Smith, Victoria A. O. *White Eyes, Red Heart, Blue Coat: The Life and Times of Mickey Free.* Ann Arbor MI: UMI Microform, 2002.

Smits, David D. "Fighting Fire with Fire: The Frontier Army's Use of Indian Scouts and Allies in the Trans-Mississippi Campaign 1860–1890." *American Indian Culture and Research Journal* 22.1 (1998): 73–109.

———. "'Squaw Men,' 'Half-Breeds,' and Amalgamators: Late Nineteenth-Century Anglo-American Attitudes toward Indian-White Race-Mixing." *American Indian Culture and Research Journal* 15.3 (1991): 29–61.

Sparks, William. *The Apache Kid, A Bear Fight, and Other True Stories of the Old West.* Los Angeles: Skelton Pub. Co., 1926.

Spicer, Edward H. *Cycles of Conquest: The Impact of Spain, Mexico and the United States on the Indians of the Southwest.* Tucson: University of Arizona Press, 1962.

Spring, John A. *John Spring's Arizona.* Edited by A. M. Gustafson. Tucson: University of Arizona Press, 1966.

Stratton, Royal B. *Captivity of the Oatman Girls: A True Story of Emigration to the West.* Salem: Oregon Teacher's Monthly, 1909.

———. *Captivity of the Oatman Girls: Being an Interesting Narrative of Life among the Apache and Mohave Indians: Containing also an Interesting Account of the Massacre of the Oatman Family, by the Apache Indians in 1851. . . .* San Francisco: Whitton, Towne, and Co., 1857.

Sweeney, Edwin R. *Cochise: Chiricahua Apache Chief.* Norman: University of Oklahoma Press, 1991.

———. *Merejildo Grijalva: Apache Captive, Army Scout.* Southwestern Studies Series no. 96. El Paso: University of Texas, 1992.

———, ed. *Making Peace with Cochise: The 1872 Journal of Captain Joseph Alton Sladen.* Norman: University of Oklahoma Press, 1997.

Tellez, Juan. "Reminiscences of Juan Tellez." *Arizona Historical Review* 7.1 (1936): 85–89.

Thompson, Jerry D. *Desert Tiger: Captain Paddy Graydon and the Civil War in the Far Southwest.* El Paso: University of Texas, 1992.

Thorne, Dr. V. Keith. *White Eyes, Long Knives, and Renegade Indians.* Sedona AZ: Thorne Enterprises, 1993.

Thrapp, Dan L. *Al Sieber: Chief of Scouts.* Norman: University of Oklahoma Press, 1964.

———. *The Conquest of Apacheria.* Norman: University of Oklahoma, 1967.

———. *Encyclopedia of Frontier Biography.* Glendale CA: A. H. Clarke Co., 1988–94.

———. "The 'Marriage' of Al Sieber." *Journal of Arizona History* 11.3 (Autumn 1970): 175–78.

Tomsho, Robert. "Dig through Archives Reopens the Issue of Geronimo's Skull." *Wall Street Journal,* May 8, 2006.

Trimble, Stephen. *The People: Indians of the American Southwest.* Sante Fe: School of American Research Press, 1993.

Turner, Frederick Jackson. *The Frontier in American History.* New York: Henry Holt and Company, 1921.

Udell, John. *Journal.* Los Angeles: N. A. Kovich, 1946.

Underhill, Ruth M. "A Papago Calendar Record." *University of New Mexico Bulletin* 322, March 1, 1938: 29–30.

Vaughn, Alden T., and Edward W. Clark, eds. *Puritans among the Indians: Accounts of Captivity and Redemption, 1676–1724.* Cambridge: Harvard University Press, 1981.

Walker, Henry P., and Don Bufkin. *Historical Atlas of Arizona.* 2nd ed. Norman: University of Oklahoma Press, 1979.

Warren, Elizabeth von Till, and Ralph J. Roske. *Cultural Resources of the California Desert, 1776–1980: Historic Trails and Wagon Roads.* Spanish translation and interpretation by Elizabeth Nelson Patrick. Riverside CA: U.S. Department of the Interior, Bureau of Land Management, 1981.

Webb, George W. *Chronological List of Engagements between*

the Regular Army . . . and Various Tribes . . . New York: AMS Press, 1976.

Weber, David. *Foreigners in Their Native Land: Historical Roots of the Mexican Americans.* Albuquerque: University of New Mexico Press, 1973.

Wells, Edmund W. *Argonaut Tales: Stories of the Gold Seekers and the Indian Scouts of Early Arizona.* New York: F. H. Hitchcock, 1927.

Wharfield, H. B. "Footnotes to History: Apache Kid and the Record." *Journal of Arizona History* (Spring 1965): 37–46.

White, Ned. *Ballad of Tombstone's Yesteryears.* Bisbee AZ: Edward P. White, 1929.

Wilbur-Cruz, Eva Antonia. *A Beautiful Cruel Country.* Tucson: University of Arizona Press, 1990.

Woods, Richard D. *Hispanic First Names.* Westport CT: Greenwood Press, 1984.

Zesch, Scott. *The Captured: A True Story of Abduction by Indians on the Texas Frontier.* New York: St. Martin's Press, 2004.

INDEX

captivity (*cont.*)

69; and false accusations, xxx, 3, 4,
11–12, 22, 24, 34, 54, 58–60, 69, 149,
155–56, 162, 168; and guides, xxi, 77,
95, 184; and guilt and blame, 89–99,
103, 117, 119, 134, 144, 154, 164,
181–82, 189–90, 196; and heredity
and environment, xxxiii, 82–83,
100, 102, 157, 176, 178–80, 181, 182;
and intermarriage, xvi, 18, 21, 23,
29–33, 84–85, 105–6, 113–14, 118,
194, 195, 200, 221, 207n69, 207n76;
and marriage, xix, 28–29, 65, 66–67,
110, 133, 158, 169–70, 173–74, 200;
and orphans, xiv, 33–34, 57, 74, 81,
101–2, 113–14, 122, 126, 158, 160,
195, 227n65; and parenthood, 6, 32,
33, 67–68, 178; and place, xxv, 23,
127–28, 189–90; and racial constructions, xv–xvi, 1, 3, 77–78, 84–88,
102, 137–40, 153, 156, 164, 175–77,
178–79, 181–82, 188, 194–96; and
re-integration, xxxii, 22, 25, 52–54,
101–2, 129–33, 146, 149–50, 156–58,
198, 227n62; and rescue, xvi, 19–20,
41, 50–51, 53, 70, 73–74, 93–94,
98–102, 128, 141–44, 146, 147–48,
154, 156–57, 160–61, 163–64, 169–70,
179–80, 197; and scouts, 71, 75, 76,
78, 105–6, 119, 133–34, 142, 143,
147, 151, 212n21, 217n6; and sexual
violence, 1, 24–25, 130–33, 160–61,
192–93; and slavery, xxi–xxiii, 2–3,
12, 17, 39–41, 42, 78, 93, 94, 98–99,
102–3, 121; and U.S. Army, 74, 106;
and violence, 1, 2, 12, 16, 46–61, 63,
118–221, 153–54, 160–61, 176, 179
captivity narratives, 1, 22
captivity systems, xiii–xiv
captors, as males, xxi, xxviii, 13,
14–15, 198–99
Carillo, Leopoldo, 100, 101
Carlisle Indian School, 148, 163, 167
Carlota (Aravaipa captive), 102–3, 189
Carlton, Gen. James, 79
Carson, Kit, 73

Cassa, Jeanette (Western Apache), 190
Cassadore, Phillip (Western Apache),
190
Cibecue AZ, 116
Chatto (Chiricahua), xxxi, 121, 140,
141, 147, 148, 152, 153, 163, 164, 184
Chevlon's Fork, 133–34
Chicago Board of Trade, 186
Chihuahua (Chiricahua), 118, 143,
152, 156
Chino Valley, 81
Chiricahuas, and false accusations, 59
Chita (Aravaipa), 167, 169, 170
Chivarria, Juan (Maricopa), 77
Clark, Edward, xvi
Clendenin, Colonel, 184
Clum, John, 112, 114
Cochise, 38, 55, 58–59, 60, 73, 76,
107–8, 111, 114
Cocopah Indians, 17
Colyer, Vincent, 107
Connell, John, 138, 188
Conner, Daniel Ellis, xxix
Coro (Sobaipuri), 56
Crabb Expedition, 44
Crawford, Emmett, 139, 143, 151,
154–55
Crook, Gen. George, 57, 104, 107–8,
136, 143, 151–52, 154, 158, 163, 183
Cruse, Lt. Thomas, 115
Cushing, Lt. Howard, 77, 212–13n24,
217n6
Cutter, Francis, 190

Davis, Lt. Britton, 139, 141, 147, 148,
152, 153
Debo, Angie, 120–21
DeLong, Sidney R., 96, 103
Delshe (Yavapai), 108, 218n11
Devine, Jack, 140–41
Diablo (Western Apache), xxv, 105,
111, 116, 220–21n33
Dja-la-ta-ha (Ear Tips; Western
Apache), 118
Dji–li–kinne (captive, race undeter-
mined), xxxii, 145, 225n28
Dunn, Captain, 93

Index

Index

Index

Mowry, Sylvester, 38, 62, 72
Munguia, Jesus, 146
nadots-usn, xv, xxv, xxxi, 104, 122,
    123, 124, 127, 129, 223n7
Nah-thle-tla (Warm Springs), xxx, 36,
    39–41, 75
Naiche (Chiricahua), 114, 118, 126,
    143
Namias, June, xvi
Nana (Warm Springs), 144
Navajos, 73, 164
Navajo Springs AZ, 72, 79, 80
Nayudiie (Western Apache), xxv,
    70–71, 76, 113, 118–19
Needles CA, 14
New Mexico Territory, 78
"new western Adam," 78–79, 92, 98
"new western males," 78–79, 91
Noche-del-klinne (Western Apache),
    116, 133, 164
Nogales AZ, 161

Oatman, Estelle, 30–32
Oatman, John (Mojave), 30–32, 33
Oatman, Lorenzo, 7, 10–11, 18, 20–21,
    22
Oatman, Mary Ann (American cap-
    tive), 3, 4, 7–8, 11, 14, 17
Oatman, Olive: as "Aliutman," 16;
    as American captive, xxix–xxx; as
    captive of the Mohaves, 14, 16–20; as
    captive prototype, 33–34; as captive
    of the Yavapai, 8, 11–14; as mother
    of Mohave children, 29, 32–33, 34; as
    a Mormon, 3, 28; as public lecturer,
    26–28; and redemption negotiations,
    19–20; and reintegration, 23, 28–29;
    release of at Fort Yuma, 20–21; and
    Royal B. Stratton, 22–23; and tat-
    toos, 17–18, 22, 25; as wife of John
    Fairchild, 28–29; as wife of Mohave
    man, 18, 20, 21
Oatman, Royce, 3–4, 5, 6, 7–10
Order of Indian Wars, 184–85, 231n50
Otis, T. L., 85, 86
Oury, Grant, 96

Oury, William S., 90, 91, 92, 96, 103,
    183
Owits (Mojave clan), 14, 16

Page, John Hempstead, 45, 51, 61, 65
Page, Mary Anne (Handy), 62, 67–68
Peck, Albert, 158–60, 228n66
Peck, Edward G., 65, 81–82, 83, 87,
    94–95, 135–36, 187, 223n3
Pedro (Western Apache), 105, 111,
    113, 136
Pennington, Ann, 64
Pennington, Caroline, 45, 64
Pennington, Elias Green, 42, 43, 57, 61,
    62, 64–65
Pennington, Elijah, 42–43
Pennington, Ellen, 65
Pennington, Jack, 45, 62, 64, 65
Pennington, James, 44, 62, 64
Pennington, Larcena (American cap-
    tive), xxx, 3, 45, 46–50, 53–54, 61, 98,
    61, 62, 63, 65, 66, 187, 214n56
Peralta, Jose Luis, 164
Petone (Western Apache), 116
Phillips, John, 187
Phoenix AZ, 106, 188
Platten, Sgt. Fred, 117, 221n35
Polone (Western Apache), 111, 116
Prescott AZ, 72–73, 78, 79, 95, 187
Pinal Apaches, 50, 51, 54, 77
Poston, Charles, 61

Quechan (Yuma) Indians, 37
Quiroz, Mercedes Sais (Mexican cap-
    tive), xxx, 36, 45, 46, 50–53, 54, 59,
    66, 67

Radding, Cynthia, 139
Rafferty, Captain, 147
Ramona (Chiricahua), 148
Ramona (Mexican captive), xxiii
Randall, Frank, 142, 225n20
Reynolds, Glenn, 168
Rigg, Col. Edwin, 74
Rockwell, Susan, xvii
Robinson, Palatine, xxiii
Robinson, Sherry, xxix
Romero, Francisco, 100, 101

Index   253

Index   255